VIOLENCE AND ABUSE

Implications for Psychiatric Treatment

Edited by

Shirley A. Smoyak
and
D. Thomas Blair

SLACK Incorporated, 6900 Grove Road Thorofare, New Jersey 08086

Copyright ©1992 SLACK Incorporated

Printed in the United States of America

Published by: SLACK Incorporated 6900 Grove Road Thorofare, NJ 08086-9447

Last digit is print number: 10 9 8 7 6 5 4 3 2 1

Library of Congress Cataloging in Publication Data

Violence and Abuse

Includes bibliographies

1. Psychiatric nursing. I. Smoyak, Shirley A., and Blair, D. T.

[DNLM: 1. Mental Disorders—nursing. WY 160 C557] Library of Congress Catalog Card Number 92-85140

ISBN: 1-55642-224-5

VIOLENCE AND ABUSE

Implications for Psychiatric Treatment

Contents

Contributors

Bruce L. Bird, PhD, is Assistant Director of Operators for the Post Acute Division, New Medico Head Injury System, Center Ossippee, New Hampshire.

D. Thomas Blair, RN, C, MS, is Nurse Manager in Extended Care Psychiatry, Colmery-O'Neil Veterans Administration Medical Center, Topeka, Kansas.

Janis J. Bowers, RN, MSN, is Psychiatric Consultant/Liaison Nurse, CPC Redwoods Hospital, Santa Rosa, California.

Kathleen C. Buckwalter, RN, PhD, FAAN, is Professor, University of Iowa College of Nursing and Consultant, Abbe Center for Community Mental Health, Cedar Rapids, Iowa.

Ann Wolbert Burgess, RN, DNSc, FAAN, is van Ameringen Professor of Psychiatric Mental Health Nursing, University of Pennsylvania School of Nursing, Philadelphia, Pennsylvania.

William H. Burke, PhD, is Executive Director, Highwatch Rehabilitation Center, New Medico Head Injury System, Center Ossipee, New Hampshire.

Cathy L. Clover, MA, is Director, Extended Care Division, Human Services Center, New Castle, Pennsylvania.

Alana Dauner, RN, C, BSN, is Staff Nurse, Acute Adult Psychiatry, Stormont-Vail Regional Medical Center, Topeka, Kansas.

Dennis M. Gorman, PhD, is Director, Division of Prevention, Center for Alcohol Studies, Rutgers-The State University of New Jersey, New Brunswick, New Jersey.

Chris A. Grant, RN, PhD, is Assistant Professor of Psychiatric Nursing, Widener University, Chester, Pennsylvania.

Carol R. Hartman, RN, DNSc, is Professor of Psychiatric Mental Health Nursing, Boston College, Chestnut Hill, Massachusetts.

Judith Wood Howe, MS, ATR, is an Art Therapist, Therapeutic Arts Program, Department of Psychiatry, The Children's Hospital, Boston, Massachusetts.

Loretta A. King, BS, is Staff Therapist, Forensic Mental Health Services, Human Services Center, New Castle, Pennsylvania.

Gloria C. McFarland, MS, is Assistant Director of Classification and Movement, New York State Division for Youth, Albany, New York.

Eileen F. Morrison, RN, PhD, is Assistant Professor, Department of Nursing, University of New Hampshire, Durham, New Hampshire.

Sue Ann New, RN, C, MSN, is Clinical Nurse Specialist, Mental Hygiene Clinic, Colmery-O'Neil Veterans Administration Medical Center, Topeka, Kansas.

Patricia J. Neubauer, RN, PhD, is a psychologist in private practice, and is on staff at CenterPoint, Kansas City, Missouri.

Daniel J. Pesut, RN, PhD, CS, is Associate Professor, College of Nursing, University of South Carolina, Columbia, South Carolina.

Darcy Reeder, RN, MN, CS, is Nurse Manager, Inpatient Psychiatry, Harborview Medical Center, Seattle, Washington.

Edward R. Shaw, PhD, is Director of the Bureau of Mental Health Services, New York State Division for Youth, Albany, New York.

Marianne Smith, RN, MS, is a Geropsychiatric Clinical Nurse Specialist, Abbe Center for Community Health, Cedar Rapids, Iowa.

Shirley S. Smoyak, RN, PhD, FAAN, is Professor II, Institute for Health, Health Care Policy, and Aging Research, Rutgers-The State University of New Jersey, New Brunswick, New Jersey, and Editor, *Journal of Psychosocial Nursing and Mental Health Services.*

William Snyder is Program Director, Juvenile Sex Offender Program, Human Services Center, New Castle, Pennsylvania.

Introduction

By D. Thomas Blair, RN, C, MS

Violence and its aftermath in modern American culture is of concern to everyone. Society is constantly being bombarded by violence in the arts, the media, and in everyday life, and the trend is increasing. Each year, the US Justice Department releases statistics on violent crimes, and each year shows a frightening increase. The year 1991 was the bloodiest year in US history, with more than 25,000 murders as compared with 23,440 in 1990. The US has the highest homicide rate in the Western world with 10 killings per 100,000 population, compared with 5.5 in Great Britain and 1.3 per 100,000 in Japan (Ellis, 1992).

Clinical and administrative professionals in a wide variety of health-care settings are increasingly concerned about the violence occurring within their agencies and institutions. High rates of violence are reported in outpatient clinics, nursing homes, and emergency departments (Drummond, 1989), but by far, the highest incidence of assaults to staff occur in the psychiatric setting (Sheridan, 1990). Injury to psychiatric staff has been identified as a major occupational risk (Carmel, 1989). Violence presents the most critical challenge to modern psychiatric care, and the implications for psychiatric treatment are profound. Psychiatric patients certainly reflect cultural trends toward the increased use of violence as a perceived solution to personal problems and as a form of communication. Staff in psychiatric facilities are called on to treat an increasingly violent patient population and to deal with the psychological consequences of victims of violence.

Various political and economic circumstances influence the increasingly violent nature of psychiatric patients. The first is deinstitutionalization. This movement has resulted in a drastic reduction of psychiatric beds on a national level. For example, state hospital beds numbered 339 per 100,000 population in 1955. By 1990, this number had dropped to 41 beds per 100,000, with some states providing as few as 14 per 100,000 (Lamb, 1992). Consequently, a greater number of potentially more dangerous outpatients is not under direct care, and thus is more likely to become acute and violent prior to rehospitalization (Davis, 1988).

As the economy continues to suffer and adequate health insurance becomes an impossibility for a greater number of Americans, the availability of psychiatric care becomes more restricted. Acute episodes of violence related to mental illness occur in the community with greater frequency. Earlier intervention might be preventive. Some estimate that the homeless number more than 2 million in the US, and as many as half may be mentally ill (Bachrach, 1992).

The movement toward "least restrictive" treatment may create management difficulties for health-care providers (Felthous, 1987). Court decisions concerning the patient's right to refuse medications and issues of informed consent may curtail chemical management of violence (Adler, 1983). The growing number of successful lawsuits against treaters and consumer awareness of the potential for serious side effects from antipsychotic medications may also prevent medications from becoming a viable intervention (Blair, 1990).

The conventional rationale for hospitalization is dangerousness to self or others, and this has become a common legal criterion for commitment. Most states now set standards limiting civil commitment to severe mental impairment or dangerousness, resulting in a larger concentration of aggressive and violent patients in psychiatric facilities (Barber, 1988). Although these factors create a potentially more violent patient population, they also make psychiatric settings more dangerous to those who staff them.

The mission of psychiatric treatment is clear. Health-care providers must understand that violence is becoming commonplace and is more likely to concern treatment and management of a greater number of violent patients. Treatment of the combative, threatening, or abusive patient is difficult and complex, as is dealing with their victims. Although violence in the psychiatric setting has been extensively studied over the past 2 decades, the problem continues to grow worse. New, effective interventions must be sought, and the pitfalls of traditional thinking and outdated treatment approaches must be avoided.

On the clinical level, psychiatric staff must be capable of treating a variety of patients, both those who are victims of violence and abuse and those who commit violence against others. These patients may challenge professional and personal values. Care planning must accommodate cultural norms concerning violence and the various political and economic factors that influence treatment. Treatment must not be reactionary; rather, it must become progressive, understanding, and therapeutic.

The purpose of this book is to examine these most difficult and challenging problems. This work will explore state-of-the-art thinking on violence and psychiatric treatment from a variety of viewpoints. Personal and social dynamics that influence violence and assaultive behavior, and those factors that affect treatment of both victims and perpetrators will be explored. Each chapter discusses an area of study and focuses attention on current trends or issus important to this purpose.

Shirley Smoyak and Dennis Gorman explore the sociological contributions to understanding the relationships between mental illness and violent behavior. They offer a unique and thoughtful perspective from which to conceptualize violent behavior and how it relates to the treatment and management of the mentally ill.

Eileen Morrison examines the traditional organizational aspects of inpatient psychiatric settings and how these factors influence violent and aggressive acts. She identifies the "tradition of toughness" and provides valuable and exciting insight into these dynamics. D. Thomas Blair and Sue Ann New review the traditional identification of risk factors associated with violence and assaultive behavior, and then explore the more modern conceptualizations of violence as an interactive process. The dynamics of violent acts within psychiatric settings are discussed, and certain treatment characteristics are identified that may themselves be provocation for violence.

Another important patient population to consider is that of neurologically damaged or impaired individuals. Incidence of these pathologies is found in general psychiatric populations, in correctional or forensic settings, and in special head injury treatment settings. William Burke and Bruce Bird offer a review of the etiologies and examine the severe challenges these patients present to psychiatric and rehabilitative treatment and management.

The intractably violent patient can be encountered in any variety of treatment settings. Commonly, these patients are referred to a forensic psychiatric unit or to corrections, depending on legal outcomes and the results of psychiatric evaluations. Darcy Reeder discusses the implications and design of psychiatric care for this population and explores the management options for these most difficult patients.

In October 1991, the Surgeon General reported that the home is more dangerous to American women than are the streets. Domestic violence and abuse have become more fully recognized over the last few years, and the implications for psychiatric care are profound. Alana Dauner discusses the characteristics and treatment implications for the adult victims of domestic violence and explores social learning theory in an effort to make sense of the conflicting and confusing issues associated with violence and abuse in the home. Patricia Neubauer then examines the dynamics and characteristics of the perpetrators of family violence and discusses family interactions and treatment for these patients.

Kathleen Buckwalter and Marianne Smith speak to the crucial issue of the aggression and violence in the institutionalized elderly. This population accounts for an extremely high incidence of aggression in treatment settings. The treatment and management of this growing population is extremely important.

Daniel Pesut presents an important and intriguing discussion of the cognitive framing of violence and the therapeutic use of the positive intent behind violent and disruptive behavior. Reframing and understanding the message behind violence offers a valuable mechanism to enhance the treatment of violence for both patients and treaters.

Janis J. Bowers examines post-traumatic symptomatology as it relates to the victims of sexual abuse and explores the techniques of art therapy to facilitate the access of repressed traumatic memories and emotions. She offers a fascinating perspective from which to view intrapsychic processes as they relate to the aftermath of violence and abuse and how these dynamics direct treatment implications.

To more fully understand violence and to explore the motivational dynamics of those who are violent or abusive, Ann Wolbert Burgess, Carol R. Hartman, Judith Wood Howe, Edward Shaw, and Gloria C. McFarland offer a unique perspective on juvenile murderers. Burgess' other chapter, coauthored by Carol R. Hartman, Chris A. Grant, Cathy L. Clover, William Snyder, and Loretta A. King, concerns the information processing model and the unlinking of violent behaviors to the reinforced consequenses of repetition.

It is hoped that nursing staff in a variety of settings can benefit and grow from the contributions of this volume. Each chapter provides unique insight into the complex factors of violence and abuse and how treatment can be conceptualized and directed. The incidence of assaultive and violent episodes in psychiatric settings must begin to diminish, and this can be accomplished with an improvement in treatment effectiveness. The number of victims of violence or abuse who seek psychiatric treatment is also increasing, and treatment can be designed with a full understanding of the psychological impact of violent trauma.

REFERENCES

Adler, W., Kreeger, C., Ziegler, P. Patient violence in a private psychiatric hospital. In J. Reid (Ed.), *Assaults within psychiatric facilities.* New York: Grune & Stratton, 1983.

Bachrach, L.L. What we know about homelessness among the mentally ill: An analytical review and commentary. *Hosp Community Psychiatry* 1992; 43:453-464.

Barber, J., Hundley, P., Kellogg, E. Clinical and demographic characteristics of 15 patients with repetitive assaultive behavior. *Psychiatr Q* 1988; 59:213-224.

Blair, D.T. Risk management for extrapyramidal symptoms. *QRB* 1990; 16:116-124.

Carmel, H., Hunter, M. Staff injuries from inpatient violence. *Hosp Community Psychiatry* 1989; 40:41-45.

Davis, D., Boster, L. Multifaceted therapeutic interventions with the violent psychiatric inpatient. *Hosp Community Psychiatry* 1988; 39:867-869.

Drummond, D.J., Sparr, L.F., Gordon, G.H. Hospital violence reduction among high risk patients. *JAMA* 1989; 261:2531-2534.

Ellis, D. The deadliest year. *Time* 1992; 139(2):18.

Felthous, A.R. Liability of treaters for injuries to others: Erosion of three immunities.

Bull Am Acad Psychiatry Law 1987; 15:115-125.

Lamb, H.R. Is it time for a moratorium on deinstitutionalization? *Hosp Community Psychiatry* 1992; 43:669.

Sheridan, M., Henrion, R., Baxter, V. Precipitants of violence in a psychiatric inpatient setting. *Hosp Community Psychiatry* 1990; 41:776-780.

1 | A Sociological Perspective on Violence in Psychiatric Patients

By Shirley A. Smoyak, RN, PhD; and Dennis M. Gorman, PhD

The view that there is a definite association between aggressive or destructive behavior and psychiatric disorder is widespread within the US, being present not only in private beliefs, but also in such cultural products as jokes, cartoons, and television programs (Link, 1987; Scheff, 1966). In recent years, we have seen our politicians attribute the acts of aggression and hostility committed by other nations to the mental instability of their leaders and argue that the need to remove such persons from power (or at least contain their activities to within their own borders) represents sufficient justification for military intervention. In light of such pervasive presentations of what a "mentally ill" person might do or be, it is not surprising that for many people, the term conjures images of an unpredictable, volatile, and potentially dangerous person (Link, 1986; 1987).

In this chapter, we review the relationship between violence and psychiatric illness from a sociological perspective. The review is selective, given limitations of space, with the emphasis on the types of broad theoretical perspectives that exist within sociology and the specific influence of these positions on how clinical understanding emerges. We begin by briefly addressing issues of definition: What are aggressive and destructive behaviors (violence) and what is psychiatric illness? What is a sociological perspective?

What is Violence?

Both conceptually and operationally, many types of destructive and aggressive behaviors and many types of psychiatric illnesses are difficult to differentiate (Swanson, 1990). There is no generally accepted definition of violence, thus making valid comparisons across studies nearly impossible. Some reports include verbal abuse or threatening behavior; others include damage to property and self-harm. Some investigators are concerned with physical attacks on persons, whereas others limit their interest to attacks on staff. Each study defines a different population and reports findings on a different sample. An additional problem is that violent patients have largely been studied with no reference to nonviolent groups (James, 1990). It would not be surprising, of course, to find more people with schizophrenia among violent patients in a hospital where most patients have schizophrenia (Haller, 1984). Violence has been classified according to severity, but the use of outcome as a measure of severity ignores the role of chance in determining the degree of injury. For instance, when nursing staff are especially vigilant, they may deter or deflect serious injury when either blunt or sharp instruments are being used by patient assailants (Shah, 1991).

Just as assault has different meanings in different legal jurisdictions, investigators vary greatly in what they choose to include as criteria for aggression, assault, or violence. Some require simple physical contact, whereas others insist that injury be present; still others include credible threats and unsuccessful attempts to cause injury. Few take an interactionist perspective, including the role of staff as deterrents or escalators of violent events.

There is some evidence that substantially similar conclusions can be drawn for a range of definitions (Rice, 1989). The greatest difficulty with the literature is the lack of comparability across studies, often created by the fact that authors fail to report the details of their sample selection or fail to specify their belief systems that guide their work. Many studies, especially those conducted by researchers who are primarily clinicians, present "facts" with no attempt to offer the basis of the meaning that they report as flowing "naturally." In fact, the biases of researchers greatly influence both the process and form of their studies. Consider, for example, that there are far more studies about the characteristics of violent patients than staff who are present at the time, or the milieu in which the violence takes place. There are even researchers who believe that violence is an integral part of the clinical picture in psychopathology. For example, Krakowski, Volavka, and Brizer (1986) state: "Diagnosis, course of illness and various symptom clusters are important variables which help predict the incidence of violence in psychiatric populations." In their literature review, they go on to categorize four contexts for patient violence.

What is Psychiatric Disorder?

"What is psychiatric disorder?" is an even more difficult question to answer than that of defining aggressive and destructive behavior. The example of alcohol dependence will be used to illustrate the inclusion/exclusion controversy in illness definition.

Historically, excessive alcohol consumption was not considered a form of illness in the US. In Colonial times, for example, heavy drinking was widespread throughout the adult population and generally not considered problematic; "drunkards," those who were financially unable to support their drinking, were grouped with the poor and criminals (Levine, 1978). By the 19th century, the harmful consequences of drinking were beginning to be recognized, but the explanation of these did not focus on individual pathology (ie, illness) but on the inherently addictive and dangerous properties of alcohol (Levine, 1984). As a result of such views, expressed most vociferously by the Temperance Movement, prohibition of the distilling and sale of alcohol was introduced in 1919. It was only with the repeal of Prohibition in 1933 that the "disease model" of alcoholism became dominant. Thus, what is now considered by many to be a psychiatric illness was, until fairly recently, considered a form of problem behavior, the solution to which was to be found at the level of social policy rather than medical intervention. Moreover, in contemporary times, many highly plausible alternatives to the disease model of alcoholism have been set forth, each of which carries certain assumptions about etiology, course, treatment, and prevention. A number of these alternative models consider alcohol dependence (along with other abuse disorders) to be a form of self-destructive behavior, the causes of which reside not within the individual but within the societal and cultural norms and values that govern such behavior (Fingarette, 1989).

The argument that alcohol dependence is more appropriately considered a form of deviant or non-normative behavior rather than an illness is understandable when one considers the various diagnostic criteria proposed over the years by the American Psychiatric Association. From 1952, when the American Psychiatric Association's *DSM-I* was published, until now, alcoholism has been grouped as a sociopathic personality disturbance (drug addiction, antisocial behavior, and sexual deviation), as a substance abuse problem, and finally, as a problem with considerable physiological underpinning (tolerance and withdrawal being emphasized). Other behaviors, such as overeating, gambling, and hypersexuality, have been "medicalized." As Wakefield (1992) has recently observed, much of the difficulty arises from the fact that the concept of psychiatric disorder comprises both a judgment of dysfunction at a biological level and a judgment of what is harmful on social norms. With psychiatric disorders such as substance abuse, pathological gambling, and hyperactivity, the biological basis of the dysfunction is not clearly understood and the social norms determining what is considered harmful vary over time and place.

For many sociologists, the inclusion of such behaviors in psychiatric diagnostic nomenclature is a clear indicator of the dual trend towards the medicalization of deviant behavior and the increased use of medicine as an agent of social control in industrial societies (Conrad, 1981). However, even

if one does not entirely accept the medicalization thesis, careful consideration of the way in which we define and classify such behaviors remain
important, as they have clear implications for how society responds to such
problems (eg, treatment or punishment) and chooses to allocate its
resources in overcoming them. In addition, the way in which a problem is
defined (as an illness, as a deviant behavior, as a normal behavior) will also
influence the level of analysis at which we search for causal factors. As Wing
(1978) observes, the greater the social component in the definition of a
problem, the less useful a disease theory is likely to be in explaining it. Put
simply, we tend to explain illness in terms of biological phenomena and
deviant behavior in terms of social phenomena. As the above discussion of
alcohol dependence makes clear, a particular phenomenon can variously be
described in either social/behavioral or disease/etiological terminology.
The more the definition emphasizes the former, the more likely we are to see
sociological theories offered as an explanation.

Sociological Approaches to Violence and Psychiatric Disorder

In this chapter, we focus on the three broad sociological perspectives
which can be used to understand the relationship between violence and
psychopathology. The first attempts to explain phenomena in terms of
factors such as social disorganization, which can be studied at either macro
or micro levels of analysis. The second includes a number of studies
conducted by sociologists in clinical settings. The third approach attempts to
explain phenomena in terms of societal norms and sanctions that regulate
individual and group behavior.

The Sociostructural Perspective

The starting point for sociostructural research is the observation that
phenomena are not simply randomly distributed within a society, but vary
according to such factors as gender, age, ethnicity, geographical region, and
social class. For example, in the US both the perpetrators and victims of
violence are disproportionately male, young, black, urban-dwellers of low
socioeconomic status (Messner, 1988; Sampson, 1987). This suggests that
there might be something about the conditions under which specific groups
of individuals live, such as economic deprivation and family disruption,
that are important in the development of social problems such as violence.

It should be noted, however, that this broad body of research within
sociology varies considerably both in terms of the types of theoretical

concepts that are described (eg, social deprivation, alienation, overcrowding, anomie) and in the type of data used to test theories (eg, secondary analysis of official datasets or social surveys). It is beyond the scope of this chapter to discuss all of these theories, many of which would be of only minimal relevance to the study of aggressive and destructive behavior in psychiatric patients. However, this approach can be examined for the purposes of this discussion through Durkheim's (1897) study of suicide. Durkheim is one of a handful of individuals who established sociology as an academic discipline, and his analysis of suicide addresses both the issue of destructive behavior and mental illness.

DURKHEIM AND THE SOCIOLOGICAL STUDY OF SUICIDE

One of Durkheim's main concerns was to establish sociology as a scientific discipline. To accomplish this, it must have a subject matter distinct from that of other disciplines, such as psychology. For Durkheim, the distinctive subject matter of sociology as a scientific discipline was that of "social facts," which, he maintained, "must be studied as things, that is, as realities external to the individual" (1897). These external realities operated so as to exercise control over the behavior of individuals, and according to Durkheim could only be explained in terms of other social facts. The study of suicide was well-suited to Durkheim's task of establishing sociology as a discipline, because explaining such a seemingly individual and personal act in terms of purely social factors would represent something of a triumph.

The question arises as to why a phenomenon such as suicide should be considered a social as opposed to an individual fact, and hence as a subject appropriate to sociological analysis. Durkheim contended that the existence of suicide as a social phenomenon was evident from an examination of the rates of suicide displayed by contemporary European countries. These rates tended to remain stable within each country but showed consistent variation across countries. For Durkheim, this stability in the rates of specific societies indicated that one was dealing with "a new fact *sui generis*, with its own unity, individuality, and... nature" (1897), as clearly the individuals who contributed to the suicide rate from one year to the next were not the same. Something other than individual impulses or drives must explain this stability. Thus, the suicide rate of a given society constituted a collective total—that is, a social fact—beyond the mere sum of the independent deaths of which it was composed. Durkheim set about developing a purely sociological explanation of this social fact that is focused purely on social forces and influences.

Like most of the founders of sociology, Durkheim was concerned with the issue of social dissolution, particularly with the forms of moral obligation through which individuals were bound to society. Given this interest, Durkheim was especially concerned with the role of regulation and integration in determining the suicide rate. More specifically, he argued that where there was either excessive or insufficient regulation or excessive or insufficient integration, this led to a high rate of suicide (Hynes, 1975).

Under conditions where individuals were insufficiently integrated into society, there resulted a state of "excessive individualism," which Durkheim termed "egoism." He also argued that the rate of suicide varied inversely with the degree of integration into religious, domestic, and political groupings, and called the specific type of suicide resulting from such excessive individualism egoistic suicide. In contrast, altruistic suicide results "when social integration is too strong" (1897). Durkheim argued that this form of self-destructive behavior was most frequent in primitive societies (eg, wives killing themselves upon the death of their husbands), although he also explained the high rate of suicides in contemporary European military societies in terms of altruism. In such cases, it is the duty or obligation of individuals to sacrifice themselves for the perceived good of society.

In addition to its integrative functions, Durkheim considered society to be "a power controlling [individuals]" and argued that there was "a relation between the way this regulative action is performed and the social suicide rate" (1897). Durkheim considered people as having biological desires and needs that were potentially insatiable because there was nothing about their organic or psychological constitution that that would limit these needs. Upon this biological base, social man was superimposed, and it was this social dimension that kept the biological base in check. If no such external constraints exist, such insatiable needs become a source of torment. In discussing the regulatory functions of society, Durkheim was principally concerned with conditions in which these were insufficient, such as during economic crises. He argued that the suicide rate was high during such times and called this specific form of self-destruction anomic suicide. In contrast, when societal regulation was excessive, individuals would feel their "futures pitilessly blocked and passions violently choked by oppressive discipline" (1897), and this would result in fatalistic suicide.

In attempting to provide a uniquely sociological explanation of suicide, Durkheim was at pains to eliminate all individualistic explanations. This led him to reject the idea that suicide was related to psychiatric disorder or to alcoholism. The methods whereby he did this—namely the selective presentation of competing hypotheses, argument by elimination, and comparison of the geographical distribution of the conditions—have been subject to much criticism both from sociologists and those working within other disciplines. In addition, such a narrowly focused approach is unnecessary because the social structural interpretation is not at odds with the observation that psychiatric disorder and suicide are related. Factors such as lack of integration, cohesion, and social constraints are probably conducive to both types of problems (Mechanic, 1978). Mechanic also notes that such macro-level variables are, however, influential only through their effects on micro-level variables, such as interpersonal relationships and personal affect.

Ultimately, an explanation focused exclusively on sociostructural variables begs some psychological theory, the focus of which is why some
individuals are more vulnerable to their effects than others. This vulnerability may be sociopsychological (such as the effects of childhood loss and lack
of care on depression and suicide), or psychobiological (such as the
dysfunctions in arousal processes hypothesized to be important in the
etiology of schizophrenia and substance abuse disorders). Sociologists have
studied these types of factors in clinical settings.

Sociological Theory and Clinical Research

An excellent example of such sociological research is that of Brown and
his colleagues. They studied the role of social factors on the course of
schizophrenia, beginning in the late 1950s in Great Britain. This work led to
the development of the concept of expressed emotion (Brown, 1985). Here
the sociological variables studied do not pertain to broad macro-level
concepts, such as regulation and integration, but to family relationships.
Durkheim, of course, was also concerned with such factors; for example, he
noted that suicide rates were higher among divorced men than their
married counterparts. However, the interpretation of such relationships
was always in terms of some higher level "social fact," such as anomie, that
could provide a complete explanation of suicide (ie, one without recourse to
individual or personal variables). In contrast, the importance of family
relationships in schizophrenia is seen as a result of the stress that these
engender for individuals who are vulnerable at a psychobiological level to
such emotional arousal (Bebbington, 1988).

The first of this series of studies showed that men with schizophrenia
were more likely to relapse within 1 year of hospital discharge if they
returned to live with their parents or spouses than if they went to live in
lodgings or with siblings (Brown, 1959). In addition, those who returned to
different households from those in which they had been living prior to
hospitalization were less likely to relapse. Of particular interest was the
finding that a smaller proportion of those who had been violent before
admission but changed their living group relapsed, compared with those
who had been violent but returned to the same domestic situation (4 of 19
versus 21 of 44, $p<.05$). Outbursts of temper and violence occurred more
often among those living with parents and wives, whereas the incidence of
symptoms such as delusions was comparable in all living groups. As Brown
(1985) observes, such findings suggested influences emanating from
relationships within the home, particularly that patients might be reacting
adversely to close relationships. Alternatively, it could simply be that the
more disturbed patients were returning to live with spouses and parents,
and hence the relationship between living group and relapse was simply
spurious.

Subsequent studies were designed to address this issue and demonstrated that the relationship between family living group and relapse was not simply the result of differences in severity of disorder at the time of discharge (Brown, 1972). In addition, through the use of in-depth interviews (Brown, 1966), the research specified which aspects of family life were important, demonstrating that the level of "expressed emotion" (as measured by an index comprised of critical comments, hostility, and emotional overinvolvement) was a powerful predictor of relapse. The severity of behavioral disturbance (defined in terms of aggressive or delinquent acts) before admission was also predictive of relapse. Brown and his colleagues (1972) noted that although it was not possible to unequivocally specify the direction of cause and effect from their data, "the fact that a decrease in expressed emotion at follow-up accompanies an improvement in the patient's behavior strongly suggests that there is a two-way relationship, each depending on the other" (Brown 1972).

Although the basic findings concerning the predictive power of expressed emotion in schizophrenic relapse have been replicated in a number of cross-cultural studies (Bebbington, 1988), the role of the patient's level and type of behavioral disturbance in mediating this relationship has not been extensively investigated. In particular, the extent to which aggressive and violent behaviors in former psychiatric patients elicit marked expression of emotion from relatives or are themselves a response to family environment remains unclear. Most likely, some reciprocal process of the type suggested by Brown et al (1972) is involved, with factors such as the age, gender, and diagnostic profile of the patient (Hogarty, 1985) influencing the exact nature of the relationship.

In a related longitudinal study of three psychiatric hospitals, Wing and Brown examined the role of social factors on the course of institutionalized patients with schizophrenia (Wing, 1970). Here the variables of interest were not those pertaining to family relations and dynamics, but rather to the therapeutic conditions and organizational structure prevailing on the ward. The conclusion drawn from this research was "that a substantial proportion, though by no means all, of the morbidity shown by long-stay schizophrenic patients in mental hospitals is a product of their environment" (Wing, 1970). More specifically, it was found that "environmental poverty" (eg, being engaged in few activities and having few personal possessions) was highly correlated with a syndrome of "clinical poverty," or negative symptoms (eg, flatness of affect and poverty of speech) as well with a set of "secondary" impairments (eg, a disappearance of previous social identities and roles and indifference or fear at the prospect of discharge). Florid or positive symptoms, such as delusions and socially embarrassing behavior, were not associated with the level of environmental poverty found on the hospital wards. Subsequent increases in the level of activity on specific wards (particularly through provisional work and occupational therapy) and reduction in ward restrictiveness were found to be related to clinical improvements, whereas increases in contacts outside of the hospital and in the number of personal possessions reduced secondary impairments (Wing, 1970).

Thus, specific aspects of the social milieu of the hospitals, which could be broadly characterized as understimulating, were found to be related to a specific clinical profile of negative symptoms and specific secondary social impairments. In contrast, the overstimulation of living in a family that was high in terms of expressed emotion was usually found to be related to an exacerbation of positive symptoms (Wing, 1989). Because the exact manifestations of violence, at least among those with schizophrenia, appear to vary according to such differences in symptomatology (Volavka, 1989), the question is raised as to whether certain types of ward structure and organization might be conducive to the manifestation of specific forms of aggressive and destructive behaviors by patients.

A recent Swedish study by Palmstierna, Hiutfeldt, and Wistedt (1991) suggests that the level of restrictiveness of the ward (in terms of not granting patients' requests) and increased crowding might be two such factors influencing the level of aggressive behavior in psychiatric settings. The Staff Observation Aggression Scale was used to systematically record all incidents of aggressive behavior on the ward. Katz and Kirkland (1990) reported that violence was more frequent and less extreme in wards in which staff functions were unclear and in which events, such as meetings or staff-patient encounters, were unpredictable. Violence was less frequent and less extreme in wards characterized by strong psychiatric leadership, clearly structured staff roles, and events that were standardized and predictable. Other ward and staff variables that may be important include level and adequacy of training, staff-to-patient ratios, the type of therapeutic regimen that is in operation, and staff attitudes and morale, although in each of these areas the evidence remains inconclusive (Shah, 1991).

A sociological perspective suggests that understanding any event requires stepping back and taking a broader or systems approach. For instance, Straus (1973) suggests that escalation of violence is best understood within a model that emphasizes institutionalized rules of order and expectations for both expanding and diminishing behaviors. Although the Strauss model was originally designed to analyze violence within families, it has been used by clinicians in their efforts to change hospital ward environments typified by increasing rates of violent episodes.

When the composition of patients in psychiatric hospital units began to change because of deinstitutionalization, staff were confronted with increasing numbers of difficult-to-manage patients (Mechanic, 1989). The patients were younger, stronger, and sicker, and the staff, who had become accustomed to more chronic conditions, were fearful and at a loss regarding how to cope with this changing situation. Public sector psychiatric hospital staff are faced with more challenges because they are more likely to have proportionately more violent/dangerous patients on their units than staff in the private sector (Smoyak, 1991).

In the late 1970s and early 1980s, staff education programs and efforts took the shape of providing information and strategies for managing the problematic behaviors of individual patients. The assumption was that the focus should be on the patients themselves rather than on the staff. Content of these education programs included early recognition of escalating behaviors, steps to defuse potentially violent situations, and factors associated with the increased likelihood of violence. Clinical strategies included methods to contain or prevent violent episodes, such as verbal persuasion. Seclusion, restraints, and the use of medication were seen as necessary only if the verbal tactics failed.

The tide of interest now has shifted to training clinicians to be aware of interaction effects, rather than to focus on the patient in isolation from other factors. Both staff attitudes and behaviors and environmental conditions such as crowding, room temperature, cigarette smoke, and availability of recreational resources are included in education and procedural manuals. As noted above, research into such interactive effects is still at an early stage and there remains much controversy as to how these might operate. For example, Palmstierna et al (1991) suggest that staff restrictiveness and increased instances of violent episodes are positively correlated, whereas Rosenbaum (1990) has suggested that increased violence on psychiatric units can be understood as a consequence of "dismantling hierarchical structures and instituting democratic principles in the formulation of ward policies and decision making." Rosenbaum advocates reinstituting the medical model and returning the psychiatrist to a position of leadership. Future research, in addition to attempting to identify clinical and demographic characteristics of patients that predict aggressive and destructive behaviors, should also examine how these interact with features of the settings and environments (eg, hospital, community, family) in which those with psychiatric disorders receive treatment and care.

The Societal Reaction (Labeling) Perspective

The societal reaction or labeling approaches emerged within sociology in the 1960s as a reaction against both the sociostructural explanations of deviant behaviors and sociological research that took clinical descriptions, such as schizophrenia, as a "given" rather than as a socially constructed phenomenon. In the 1970s, a number of critiques of the perspective were published, and its influence within the discipline subsequently declined. Recently, societal reaction theorists have endeavored to specify more precisely the mechanisms and processes through which labeling occurs, and in this respect the public's perceptions of how "dangerous" the mentally ill are have been shown to be important.

Societal reaction or labeling theory emerged within sociology in large part as a critique of sociostructural explanations of deviant behavior. As in sociostructural theories, however, acts of criminality and delinquency (such as violence towards others and destructive behaviors) and psychiatric disorders were dealt with separately by labeling theories. The former is generally the domain of criminologists, and, given the nature of the societal reaction perspective, there is a rejection of the idea that any pathology, such as psychiatric illness, accounts for the manifestation of such behaviors. The latter has been most thoroughly discussed by Scheff (1966), who considers the violations of social norms that invoke the label of mental illness to represent a residual category of rule-breaking for which modern industrial society has no other name. In other cultures, such "residual rule-breaking" is labeled witchcraft or spiritual possession.

The central tenet of the labeling approach, and the way in which this differs from the sociostructural approach, was perhaps most clearly stated by Becker in 1963. Becker began by observing that many sociologists:

> . . . look at society, or some part of society, and ask whether there are processes going on in it that tend to reduce its stability, thus lessening its chance of survival. They label such processes deviant or identify them as symptoms of social disorganization. They discriminate between those features of society which promote stability (and thus are "functional") and those which disrupt stability (and thus are "dysfunctional") (Becker, 1963).

He goes on to state that the societal reaction perspective also starts with the premise that deviance "is created by society." But, Becker continues, this statement is not meant:

> . . . in the way it is ordinarily understood, in which the causes of deviance are located in the social situations of the deviant or in "social factors" which prompt his action. I mean, rather, that *social groups create deviance by making the rules whose infraction constitutes deviance*, and by applying those rules to particular people and labeling them as outsiders. From this point of view, deviance is *not* a quality of the act the person commits, but rather a consequence of the application of others of rules and sanctions to an "offender." The deviant is one to whom that label has successfully been applied; deviant behavior is behavior that people so label (Becker, 1963, emphases in original).

It is not difficult to find examples that lend support to the general contention stated by Becker that "social groups create deviance by making the rules whose infraction constitutes deviance." To take one example, Segal (1989) has observed how countries differ in terms of their civil commitment standards principally along two dimensions: the need for treatment and the degree of dangerousness. Depending on which of these dimensions is emphasized in the legal statutes, a different subgroup of the mentally ill population is institutionalized (and hence, from the societal reaction perspective, formally labeled). In England and Wales, the emphasis on need for treatment leads to more older women being committed, whereas in the

US the emphasis on dangerousness leads to more young men being committed. Thus, each country gets the deviants that its laws define. Aviram and Smoyak (1992) have reported on another interesting legal label for psychiatric patients, "discharged pending placement" (DPP). This designation lays between the commitment and the discharged categories, and is used by judges in New Jersey to label patients who are no longer dangerous to self or others, but for whom no reasonable community alternative is available. This designation has been both applauded and criticized; those evaluating it favorably see it as a humane alternative, whereas the critics see it as bureaucratic nonsense.

In addition to the differences in nations and states noted above, a single society can show marked variations in definitions of deviance even over relatively short periods. For example, use of opiates was commonplace and not illegal in the US prior to the Harrison Act of 1914 (Hoffman, 1990). Once sanctions prohibiting the use of these substances were introduced, a new form of deviance named "opiate addiction" was created. Such a new class of deviant is socially constructed through a number of processes, such as the development of a nomenclature to describe the behavior, "symptoms" associated with use of opiates (eg, the diagnostic criteria described by the American Psychiatric Association, 1987) and the establishment of institutions that enforce legal sanctions (eg, the Bureau of Narcotics and the Drug Enforcement Agency) and that serve to punish (eg, imprisonment, seizure of assets) or treat (eg, detoxification, methadone maintenance) the deviant.

Social norms and sanctions can create a particular deviant category. The question arises, however, as to the extent to which such processes create the individual deviant. Put another way, because the use of heroin would not be a deviant act (in the legal sense) were it not for the Harrison legislation of 1914, would the absence of such legislation mean that opiate addiction would no longer manifest itself as a clinical syndrome (in the sense that prolonged use increases most individuals' psychological and physiological tolerance for the drug and leads to the onset of a withdrawal syndrome should they abruptly abstain)?

The early labeling theorists were, in fact, primarily concerned with explaining how societal rules and sanctions affect the individual (that is, explaining the consequences of medical and legal practice), rather than in exploring the ways in which the concepts and categories of scientific knowledge are socially constructed, such that definitions of deviance change over time. Today, for instance, another area of study might be the expansion of illness in the adolescent age group, where school failure might be relabeled illness, if families are willing to go to the expense of private psychiatric hospitalization.

Both psychiatrists working from within a traditional disease framework and sociologists working from a more traditional social causation perspective criticized the above approaches. According to these critics, recurrence of the behaviors and actions that initially led to a diagnosis of psychiatric disorder and violence is explained principally in terms of the natural history of the pathology from which the individual is suffering or through the continued influence of the factors that first precipitated the disorder (eg, continued stress or social disorganization). Also, these critics maintain that the reaction of others to the disturbed individual can be explained primarily in terms of the individual's behavior rather than others' responses being the cause of continued manifestation of symptoms.

As Horwitz (1979) notes, the debate between the proponents and critics of labeling theory has taken the form of a series of rebuttal and counter-rebuttals centered principally on the question of whether the central hypothesis of labeling theory (namely that labeling is the most important cause of the subsequent behavior of ex-psychiatric patients) is supported by empirical evidence. This empirical evidence will not be reviewed here; a detailed review of the literature has shown that the weight of evidence from experimental and quasi-experimental studies supports the view that it is the behavior and symptoms manifested by psychiatrically ill persons that activate societal reaction, rather than vice versa (Link, 1987). The general consensus that existed concerning the societal reaction perspective (at least in its radical form) by the late 1980s has been summarized by Mechanic:

> Although the societal reaction approach is provocative and obviously identifies processes that occur to some extent in the definition and care of mental patients, the relative importance of such processes were very much exaggerated. No one would deny that social labels can have powerful effects on individuals, but little evidence supports the idea that such labeling processes are sufficiently powerful to be major influences in producing chronic mental illness (Mechanic, 1989).

Thus, its most extreme form (ie, that labeling is the most important factor influencing the course of psychiatric disorder), the societal reaction perspective was simply unsupported by empirical evidence. However, as the quote from Mechanic makes clear, this is not to say that labeling has no influence on the lives of individuals suffering from psychiatric disorders (and certainly the accounts of many former patients attest to the fact that stereotyping by others does affect their lives [Link, 1987]). As Mechanic further notes, one of the main problems with the early societal reaction approach was that it was extremely vague in specifying the conditions and processes under which labeling will have an effect and precisely what this effect might be. In short, the theory was poorly specified and therefore difficult to test empirically.

More recently, Link and colleagues have attempted to address such issues in a series of studies (Link, 1982; 1986; 1987; 1990). This research has introduced a greater level of refinement and sophistication to the societal reaction perspective and is of special interest as a number of the studies deal directly with the issue of dangerousness. Link observes several consequences of applying a label: to create a deviant behavior (ie, to affect its etiology); to stabilize a deviant behavior (ie, to affect its course); and to influence other areas of the person's life (ie, employment and social life).

As noted above, it is in the first and second of these domains that the early societal reaction perspective was found wanting. The focus of Link's (1982) study is the third of these domains, specifically, the influence of labeling on level of income and employment status. Link observes that to examine this relationship, it is necessary to control for the possible effects of residual illness on income and employment. The study therefore compares a group of treated cases (ie, persons with a psychiatric disorder who have received treatment and therefore have been formally labeled) with a group of untreated cases (ie, persons with a psychiatric disorder who have not received treatment and therefore have not been formally labeled). Three different sets of analyses are presented, all of which demonstrate a lower income among the treated cases than untreated cases, even when psychiatric condition is held constant. Thus, labeling does appear to affect important areas of ex-patients' lives, even if, as critics would argue, it does not directly affect the course of the disorder. Link maintains that labeling may in fact indirectly influence the course of a psychiatric disorder in that a negative label is likely to increase environmental stresses, such as job losses and financial hardships, that will undermine individuals' coping strategies and hence make them vulnerable to relapse. In this manner, he sees the societal reaction perspective as complementing, and not challenging, the type of clinical research discussed above.

In a later study, Link et al (1987) examined the relative importance of labeling and behavior as determimants of responses to the mentally ill. However, they went beyond previous research in attempting to understand the meaning that the label "mental patient" has to the general public, and in particular the extent to which beliefs about the dangerousness of such persons influenced social distancing. Data were collected using vignettes. These took one of six forms, according to which of three types of behavior were described (no objectionable behaviors, mildly objectionable behavior, or severely objectionable behavior) and of which two levels of labeling were applied to the vignette (hospitalized for a psychiatric problem or hospitalized for a back problem).

Subjects (n=152) were randomly assigned one of the six vignettes and asked to rate the individual depicted on seven social distance questions. In addition, subjects completed an eight-item questionnaire concerned with perceived dangerousness of the mentally ill in general. At one level, the results of the study were consistent with the research reported by critics of the labeling perspective, in that although an increase in the severity of behavior depicted in the vignette led to greater social distancing, the presence or absence of the label "hospitalized for a psychiatric problem" did not. However, there was a strong interaction effect between labeling and the perceived dangerousness of psychiatric patients (ie, with the unlabeled vignettes, the perceived level of dangerousness had no effect on social distancing; whereas with the labeled vignettes, the extent to which subjects felt that psychiatric patients were dangerous influenced the amount of social distancing they expressed).

This research suggests that what is important about the label "psychiatric patient" is the meaning that it has, in this case, that such a person is potentially dangerous. When the meaning of the label is specified in this manner, it becomes apparent that for a large number of persons, it is not simply the behavior of the mentally ill that will influence their response to them. Rather, the beliefs about mental illness that they bring with them to the interaction will influence their response, and this might explain why many former patients feel that they are unfairly stigmatized. Link et al (1987) estimate that 39% of the subjects in their study consider psychiatric patients to be dangerous to a sufficient degree that they will endeavor to distance themselves from persons so labeled.

One question that arises from such research is the manner in which interaction with former patients influences such beliefs. Link and Cullen (1986) examined the effects of two types of contact with the mentally ill (contact that the person chooses versus contact that is beyond their control) on perceptions of dangerousness. In line with previous work, it was found that the more contact individuals had with the mentally ill, the less dangerous they considered the mentally ill to be. This relationship held for both men and women and across groups of varying ages and education levels.

Link et al's most recent study took as its starting point the observation that ex-psychiatric patients appear to be more violent than the general population (Link, 1990). This association between status as a former psychiatric patient and violence has been established primarily on the basis of official statistics on arrest rates, and is, as Link and colleagues observe, subject to a number of interpretations other than that which posits a simple causal relationship.

Two of these competing interpretations are of special relevance because one explains the association between arrest rates and psychiatric status from a broadly societal reaction perspective, and the other does so in terms of sociostructural factors, such as socioeconomic status. In the first of these interpretations, higher arrest rates simply reflect differential reactions on the part of law enforcement officers to the psychiatrically ill; that is, they are more likely to be arrested than "normal" individuals even when the type of offense is the same (the so-called "criminalization" hypothesis). In the second interpretation, it is proposed that the high arrest rates of ex-psychiatric patients simply reflects the social environment in which they live, rather than their propensity to violence. In arrest rate studies, chronically ill ex-patients who typically reside in disadvantaged areas tend to be compared with the "general population," which in socioeconomic terms is extremely heterogeneous. Thus, in terms of the type of broad sociostructural factors that influence violent behavior and arrest rate, such studies are not comparing like with like.

In testing these and other explanations, Link and colleagues (1990) used data collected from 232 psychiatric inpatients and outpatients attending a large New York hospital and 521 community residents in a household survey conducted in the neighborhoods in which the patients lived. What is especially noteworthy about this study is that data from a number of diverse sources were used in testing the competing hypotheses. To overcome the problems inherent in arrest rate data (ie, bias introduced by possible differential responses of police officers to the psychiatrically ill), both official arrest statistics and self-reports of arrests and violent behavior were used. To assess the influence of sociostructural factors on the association between psychiatric illness and violence, macro-level data pertaining to socioeconomic status, ethnic heterogeneity, family disruption, residential mobility, and homicide rates were used to assess the "crime potential" of the communities in which subjects resided. Finally, data were collected concerning psychiatric symptoms to allow more detailed specification of the relationship (assuming any was found) between mental health and violent behavior.

The results of the study showed that ex-patients displayed higher rates of violent behavior than comunity residents who had never received psychiatric treatment, whether assessed by official arrest statistics or by self-reports obtained during the interviews. Thus, the correlation between violence and psychiatric status reported in previous research does not appear to be simply an artifact of the type of data used (as suggested by the criminalization hypothesis), because the association holds even when assessed in terms of self-reports of violent acts that involved no arrest and that are, therefore, uncontaminated by the types of bias found in official statistics. In addition, although the sociostructural variables were found to be significantly related to arrest rates and reports of violent behavior, they did not account for the elevated rate of these variables among patients.

Thus, the association between psychiatric status and violence could not be explained either in terms of the criminalization hypothesis nor the sociostructural hypothesis. This suggests that the frequently observed association between psychiatric disorder and violent behavior is "real," rather than an artifact created by inadequate measures or explicable in terms of some third variable. However, the analysis presented by Link et al also indicates that the risk of violence posed by ex-psychiatric patients is extremely limited in both scope and magnitude. Compared with variables such as age, gender, and level of education, the magnitude of effect associated with status as a former psychiatric patient was modest. The authors note that were one to use the higher rate of arrests and violent behavior as a rationale for avoiding former psychiatric patients, then one might equally set about avoiding men in preference to women and high school graduates in preference to college graduates. In addition, the association between violent behavior and psychiatric disorder was limited to those patients exhibiting current psychotic symptoms, and such symptoms were relatively rare. The risk among all other ex-patients was no greater than that for the comparison group of nonpatients. In addition, the authors point out that even among currently psychotic individuals, one cannot assume a simple cause-and-effect relationship between symptoms and expressions of violence, because an association may well be mediated by the fearful or coercive reactions to such symptoms by those within the patient's social milieu. As noted above, a similar interactive model has been proposed by researchers in the field of expressed emotions.

Conclusion

Understanding aggressive and destructive behavior in psychiatric patients from a sociological perspective requires a willingness to use lenses in an uncommon way. Far more has been written, in both scholarly and popular literature, from perspectives that are intrapsychic, behavioral, or simply demographic. Belief systems, rather than science, permeate what is published. What we have done is to suggest how sociological theory can be applied to lend an understanding of this important topic, and then to present what is known from the standpoint of two broadly defined perspectives.

Although most sociologists look at variables and concepts at levels beyond human systems, what they choose to hold as operating premises for their theory development and design of studies produces significantly different outcomes. Some approach the phenomena associated with psychiatric patients as if they were objective data, withstanding the demands for stability across time and culture; these sociologists accept as a "given" the diagnoses, treatment language, and assumptions found in clinical areas. Others see, instead, that reality is what one makes it and see diagnosis and treatment as variable as social class or categories of deviance.

The societal reaction perspective was initially developed as a critique of sociostructural explanations of social problems. In addition, it was hostile to those sociologists who accepted as "givens" psychiatric diagnostic categories. They argued that behaviors such as those associated with schizophrenia were entirely understandable as products of a social, negotiated order, rather than as caused by any psychobiological vulnerability, which might react to social factors such as family stress.

However, the work of Link and colleagues, as well as that of Brown and associates, suggest that these approaches need not be seen as necessarily contradictory, but instead are parts of a much more complex interactive model. Sociostructural factors, such as social deprivation and anomie, will influence the overall levels of violence in a society. In addition, individuals will be vulnerable to the differential effects of such structural factors at both a psychobiological and a sociopsychological level. Finally, once an individual is suffering from a psychiatric disorder, social factors such as the response of family and treatment personnel will influence its course and outcome, both directly in terms of risk of relapse and indirectly in terms of secondary impairments.

References

American Psychiatric Association. *Diagnostic and statistical manual of mental disorders,* 3rd ed, rev. Washington, DC: Author, 1987.

Aviram, U., Smoyak, S. *Discharged pending placement: How courts created a new intermediate legal status for confining mentally ill persons.* New Brunswick, NJ: The Rutgers Institute for Health, Health Care Policy and Aging Research, 1992.

Bebbington, P., Kuipers, L. Social influences on schizophrenia. In P. Bebbington, P. McGuffin (Eds.), *Schizophrenia: The major issues.* Oxford: Heinemann, 1988, pp. 201-225.

Becker, H.S. *Outsiders: Studies in the sociology of deviance.* New York: Free Press, 1963.

Brown, G.W. Experiences of discharged chronic schizophrenic patients in various types of living group. *Milbank Mem Fund Q* 1958; 17:105-131.

Brown, G.W. The discovery of expressed emotion: Induction or deduction? In J. Leff, C. Vaughn (Eds.), *Expressed emotions in families: Its significance for mental illness.* New York: Guilford Press, 1985, pp. 7-25.

Brown, G.W., Rutter, M. The measurement of family activities and relationships: A methodological study. *Human Relations* 1966; 19:241-263.

Brown, G.W., Birley, J.L.T., Wing, K.K. Influence of family life on the course of schizophrenia disorder: A replication. *Br J Psychiatry* 1972; 121:241-258.

Conrad, P. On the medicalization of deviance and social control. In D. Ingleby (Ed.), *Critical psychiatry: The politics of mental health.* New York: Penguin, 1981, pp. 103-119.

Durkheim, E. *La suicide: Etude de sociologie.* Paris: Alcan, 1897. Translated by J.A. Spaulding, G. Simpson. *Suicide: A study in sociology.* London: Routledge & Keegan Paul, 1952.

Fingarette, H. *Heavy drinking: The myth of alcoholism as a disease.* Berkeley, CA: University of California Press, 1989.

Haller, R., Deluty, J. Assaults on staff by psychiatric in-patients: A critical review. *Br J Psychiatry* 1984; 152:174-179.

Hogarty, G.E. Expressed emotion and schizophrenic relapse: Implications from the Pittsburgh study. In M. Alpert (Ed.), *Controversies in schizophrenia: Changes and constancies.* New York: Guilford Press, 1985, pp. 354-365.

Hoffman, J.P. The historical shift in the perception of opiates: From medicine to social menace. *Journal of Psychoactive Drugs* 1990; 22:53-62.

Hynes, E. Suicide and *homo duplex:* An interpretation of Durkheim's typology of suicide. *Sociological Quarterly* 1975; 16:87-104.

Horwitz, A.V. Model, muddles, and mental illness labeling. *J Health Soc Behav* 1979; 20:296-300.

James, D., Fineberg, N., Shah, A., Priest, R. An increase in violence on an acute psychiatric ward: A study of associated factors. *Br J Psychiatry* 1990; 156:846-852.

Katz, P., Kirkland, F. Violence and social structure on mental hospital wards. *Psychiatry* 1990; 53:262-277.

Krakowski, M., Volavka, J., Brizer, D. Psychopathology and violence: A review of the literature. *Compr Psychiatry* 1986; 27:131-148.

Levine, H.G. The discovery of addiction: Changing conceptions of habitual drunkenness in America. *J Stud Alcohol* 1978; 39:143-174.

Levine, H.G. The alcohol problem in America: From temperance to alcoholism. *Br J Addict* 1984; 79:109-119.

Link, B.G. Mental patient status, work, and income: An examination of the effects of a psychiatric label. *Am Sociol Rev* 1982; 47:202-215.

Link, B.G., Cullen, F.T. Contact with the mentally ill and perceptions of how dangerous they are. *J Health Soc Behav* 1986; 27:289-303.

Link, B.G., Cullen, F.T., Frank, J., Wozniak, J.F. The social rejection of former mental patients: Understanding why labels matter. *Am J Sociol* 1987; 92:1461-1500.

Link, B.G., Andrews, H., Cullen, F.T. *Reconsidering the dangerousness of mental patients: Violent and illegal behavior of current and former patients compared to controls.* Presented at the Society for the Study of Social Problems Conference, Washington, DC, 1990.

Mechanic, D. *Medical sociology,* 2nd ed. New York: Free Press, 1978.

Mechanic, D. *Mental health and social policy,* 3rd ed. Englewood Cliffs, NJ: Prentice Hall, 1989.

Messner, S.F. Research on cultural and socioeconomic factors in criminal violence. *Psychiatr Clin North Am* 1988; 11:511-525.

Palmstierna, T., Hiutfeldt, B., Wistedt, B. The relationship of crowding and aggressive behavior on a psychiatric intensive care unit. *Hosp Community Psychiatry* 1991; 42:1237-1240.

Rice, M, Harris, G., Varney, G., Quinsey, V. *Violence in institutions: Understanding, prevention and control.* Toronto, Ontario: Hans Huber Publishers, Inc, 1989.

Rosenbaum, M. Violence and the unstructured patient milieu. *Hosp Community Psychiatry* 1990; 41:721.

Sampson, R.J. Urban black violence: The effect of male joblessness and family disruption. *Am J Sociology* 1987; 93:348-382.

Scheff, T.J. *Being mentally ill: A sociological theory.* Chicago: Aldine, 1966.

Segal, S.P. Civil commitment standards and patient mix in England/Wales, Italy, and the United States. *Am J Psychiatry* 1989; 146:187-193.

Shah, A.K., Fineberg, N.A., James, D.V. Violence among psychiatric inpatients. *Acta Psychiatr Scand* 1991; 84:305-309.

Smoyak, S.A. Psychosocial nursing in public versus private sectors: An introduction. *J Psychosoc Nurs Ment Health Serv* 1991; 29(8):6-12.

Straus, M.A. A general systems theory approach to a theory of violence between family members. *Social Science Information* 1973; 12:105-125.

Swanson, J.W., Holzer, C.E., Ganju, V.K., Jono, R.T. Violence and psychiatric disorder in the community: Evidence from the Epidemiologic Catchment Area Surveys. *Hosp Community Psychiatry* 1990; 41:761-770.

Volavka, J., Krakowski, M. Schizophrenia and violence (editorial). *Psychological Medicine* 1989; 19:559-562.

Wakefield, J.C. The concept of mental disorder: On the boundary between biological facts and social values. *American Psychologist* 1992; 47:373-388.

Wing, J.K. *Reasoning about madness.* New York: Oxford University Press, 1978.

Wing, J.K. The concepts of negative symptoms. *Br J Psychiatry* 1989; 155(suppl 7):10-14.

Wing, J.K., Brown, G.W. *Institutionalism and schizophrenia: A comparative study of three mental hospitals, 1960-1968.* Cambridge: Cambridge University Press, 1970.

2 | The Tradition of Toughness: A Study of Nursing Care in Psychiatric Settings

By Eileen F. Morrison, PhD, RN

Violence in inpatient psychiatric settings is a clinically significant and relevant problem requiring attention by the psychiatric community. Research has been conducted exploring the frequency of violence on inpatient psychiatric wards (Craig, 1982; Tardiff, 1980; 1983), the frequency of violence directed at staff in psychiatric settings (Adler, 1983; Lanza, 1983; Madden, 1976; Ruben, 1980), and patient characteristics related to violence (American Psychiatric Association, 1974). Despite the prevalence of research on violent behavior, however, only a few studies have explored aspects of the organization that influence patient behavior (Fairbanks, 1977; Goffman, 1961; Hall, 1975; Moos, 1974; Morrison, 1989, 1990; Sanson-Fisher, 1979; Strauss, 1975; Strauss, 1981). This study was conducted in response to the need for recent studies exploring the relationship of organizational factors and violence. Violence was defined as any verbal, nonverbal, or physical behavior that is threatening (to self, others, or property), or physical behavior that actually did harm (self, others, or property) (APA, 1974).

Method

DESIGN

An exploratory (or inductive) study was conducted using participant observation (Spradley, 1980) and in-depth interviews to collect data that were analyzed using the grounded theory approach (Glaser, 1967; 1978).

The investigator conducted other studies in the setting, but was not otherwise associated with the units for study.

DESCRIPTION OF THE SETTING

Formal access was obtained through review by the academic institution's Human Subjects Committee and the hospital Institutional Review Board. Three psychiatric units of an urban, general, public hospital in the Southwestern United States were used for data collection. The hospital had a crisis emergency room, outpatient psychiatric department, and three 20-bed inpatient psychiatric units. The units included psychogeriatric, treatment and admission, and evaluation units. About one third of all admissions were involuntary. All types of psychiatric patients were treated in the facility, but most had diagnoses of schizophrenia, manic depression, personality disorder, or substance abuse.

Psychiatric treatment is based on the medical model. The registered nurses perform routine administrative functions, while licensed practical nurses dispense medications and conduct medical treatments. RNs are responsible for completing assessments and care plans; however, the plans are rarely individualized. Only one RN attends the multidisciplinary team meeting, resulting in inconsistent communication with the remaining staff and problems with implementation of the treatment plan. The nonprofessional staffs, which include psychiatric technicians (PT), nurses' aides (NA), orderlies, and LPNs are responsible for the operational activities of the ward. Each staff member receives a daily assignment that is task-oriented, resulting in work that is highly routinized for both patients and staff members. For example, patients are awakened at 7 AM, eat, and are in the dayroom by 8 AM and all bedrooms are locked. By 9 AM, nursing staff attend to discharging, transferring, or escorting patients for medical tests (x-ray or laboratory). The nonprofessional staff members are assigned to patients; however, interaction is minimal.

The types of violence observed on the unit included verbal outbursts that were sarcastic, hostile, or argumentative, as well as physical outbursts such as throwing things, hitting, pushing, or shoving others. Two serious violent incidents occurred during the study time frame: a suicide and a stabbing (with a pencil). When patients appeared to be getting out of control, interventions included medications, "time out" (voluntary periods of isolation in unlocked seclusion room), restraints, and locked seclusion. Seclusion and time out were used on a daily basis and it was not unusual for several patients to be in seclusion at the same time.

It is important to note that an inservice education program existed for nursing staff for dealing with aggressive/out of control behavior. The program included a 2-day seminar that focused on the theoretical perspectives of aggression, the process of escalation, the therapeutic verbal techniques for "talking down" a potentially violent patient, and the physical management techniques necessary for restraining violent patients. Unfortunately, the program was primarily attended by the professional staff, rather than the nonprofessional staff, who were the ones most often involved in intervening with potentially violent situations.

SUBJECTS

Standard procedures for informed consent were used, eg, verbal consent from both staff and patient subjects. Subjects were obtained for audiotaped interviews from the informal network of the nursing staffs and included 14 nursing staff members and one registered nurse (from outside the system) who was involved in training psychiatric staffs to manage violent patients. Interviews with staff members were conducted that were open-ended, becoming more specific as concepts were identified and hypotheses generated (Glaser, 1967). Staff were asked to describe a "good day," a "bad day," what she/he liked or disliked about the job, and to describe any violent incidents she/he had been involved in or had observed. Patients were interviewed informally (without audiotaping) as part of the participant observation period of the study. The researcher conversed with patients about their hospital experience, their view of nursing care, and their view of violent behavior. Audiotaped interviews with patients could not be conducted as planned due to practical and legal considerations. Patients were suspicious and uncooperative when a tape recorder was used and the researcher could have been subpoenaed to testify against a violent patient for involuntary treatment.

PARTICIPANT OBSERVATION

Nursing staff and patients were observed in both formal and informal groups and during individual interactions, primarily in the dayroom and the nursing station. The researcher sat unobtrusively to conduct observations. Field notes were written, tape recorded and later transcribed for analysis. All nursing staff were the object of observation; however, since the registered nurses were engaged in the administrative functions of the unit, very few opportunities existed for their interaction with patients and nonprofessional staff were the primary focus of observation.

When a violent incident occurred during observation, the researcher asked several patients and nursing staff members in the vicinity to describe what had happened and why it happened. Patient charts and nursing notes were reviewed to corroborate information. The richest source of data, however, was the difference between data collected from different sources, ie, patients/staff/chart. Data collection took place over a 9-month period, approximately 8 hours/week. The admission unit was the primary site of observation; however, 3 weeks of observation occurred on the psychogeriatric unit, 4 weeks on the treatment unit, and 1 week in a private hospital. Two experts, a nurse and a sociologist, both engaged in long-term research programs (elder abuse and juvenile delinquency), were consulted frequently.

DATA ANALYSIS

Participant observation provided information regarding how nursing staffs interacted with patients, while interview data provided information about how nursing staffs thought they interacted with patients. The data were analyzed using open coding in which data bits were repeatedly sorted into categories (Glaser, 1967; Strauss, 1978). Criteria to evaluate the research findings were: credibility, transferability, dependability, and confirmability (Guba, 1981). Since many extreme stories of abuse were obtained from patients, credibility, or the truthfulness of the data, was an important criterion for evaluation. Several procedural strategies were used to determine credibility. First, and most important, all data were cross-checked for accuracy through observations and interviews with nursing staffs and patients. Data were not used if verification could not be obtained from a second source. Second, a subject was used to obtain information regarding the researcher's effect on the setting that might influence the data. For example, a patient had accused the staff of stealing his radio. The staff did a thorough job of determining the radio's whereabouts, while keeping the researcher informed. It was later determined that the staff believed the researcher was the "patient advocate," which explains why she was kept abreast of the progress. This situation occurred despite the formal introduction of the investigator through conferences with staff regarding the study purposes. The third procedure was to spread the visits over a prolonged period of time.

Transferability was determined by evaluating the emerging theoretical results in all three clinical sites and in the private hospital, as well as including all types of nonprofessional nursing staffs and patients in the analysis. Dependability of the analysis, or the stability and trackability of analysis, was determined by using overlap methods and by having two consultants conduct external audits by which the processes of data collection were reviewed. However, these experts did not function independently as data collectors, which is a limitation of the study. Confirmability of the analysis was ensured through three strategies. First, the researcher tested emerging hypotheses in the clinical setting. Second, the emerging theoretical formulations were presented to the nursing administration and alternative explanations explored. Third, an ongoing critique of the theoretical process by two consultants was conducted, allowing for early changes in the emerging theoretical formulations.

Findings

The results are a compilation of the researcher's own observations, stories from patients that include previous as well as current hospitalizations, and stories from nursing staff members that include both past and current work experiences. As such, the results do not solely reflect the clinical setting in

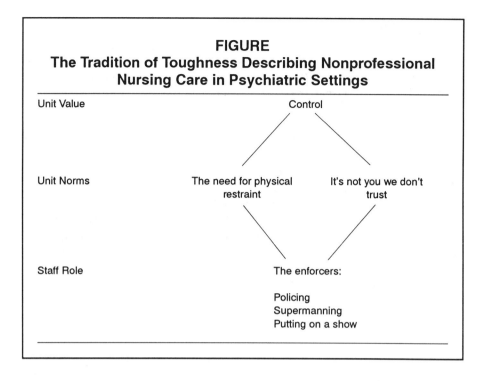

FIGURE
The Tradition of Toughness Describing Nonprofessional Nursing Care in Psychiatric Settings

Unit Value	Control
Unit Norms	The need for physical restraint It's not you we don't trust
Staff Role	The enforcers: Policing Supermanning Putting on a show

which observations were conducted. The key concept that emerged from the data was "the tradition of toughness." Glaser's cultural family, which includes social norms, values, beliefs, and sentiments, and the mainline family that includes social control, recruitment, socialization, and social order, were used for analysis (Glaser, 1978). An emphasis on the value of control and safety leads to the formation of two norms labeled "the need for physical restraints" and "It's not you we don't trust." The values and norms result in a defined role for nonprofessional nursing staff which is labeled "enforcing" and includes the strategies of "policing," "supermanning" and "putting on a show." The word "staff member," as used in this chapter, refers to the nonprofessional nursing staffs who deliver nursing care to patients on a daily basis (Figure).

Value Component

The hospital structure is characterized by a pragmatic value system designed to provide service to clientele in which functional outcomes are emphasized. The organizational ideology is based on the medical model, and patients are viewed as sick and must be treated as such. Therefore, patient behaviors are viewed as symptoms of their mental illness. Violent behavior, in particular, is viewed as a symptom of an illness. When asked why a patient was acting out, the subjects most frequently answered "the patient has low impulse control," the "patient is out of control," or "the voices tell him to do it." These answers contrast with the patients' most frequent response, ie, "to get these people off my back" (Morrison, 1990).

The belief in the medical ideology results in an emphasis on the values of control and safety within the setting. Since proponents of the medical ideology interpret violent behavior as a result of poor impulse control, the belief that patients must be controlled is prominent. If a family or staff member wants a report on a patient's condition, a nursing staff member will almost always say "the patient is quiet and in good control." Several observations of how staff members try to control patient symptomatology were made. A female patient sat at a table in the dayroom, pounded her fist on the table, and said, "I want to go home." The orderly responded by saying that if she cried she would go to seclusion. The patient started to cry and the orderly put her in seclusion. When questioned, the orderly's reason for using seclusion was "she needs time out," ie, she needs to regain control.

Norm Component

Two staff norms were identified: "the need for physical restraint" and "it's not you we don't trust." For these nursing staff members, doing a good job means "keeping patients under control" and the socialization of new staff members and patients to the norms of the system is conducted partially through the two identified norms.

THE NEED FOR PHYSICAL RESTRAINT

This category is defined as the process of how new staff members are socialized into the use of physical methods to control patients, as opposed to using verbal therapeutic interventions. Reciprocity is used as the primary mechanism for forcing compliance by new staff members. For example, if a target staff calls his/her colleagues for assistance with a potentially difficult situation and the target staff wants to talk with the patient until she/he is calm, then the enforcers retaliate in future situations by not responding and leaving the target staff vulnerable to assault.

One subject (RN) described how the norms of reciprocity and socialization work in the tradition of toughness. The subject referred to a potentially assaultive situation in which the target staff member wanted to verbally intervene with a patient, but the remaining staff members wanted to physically restrain the patient. Many subjects told similar stories about how peer pressure is used to socialize others into the tradition of toughness.

If you call them in (staff to help in a violent situation) and don't use them, what will happen is this: a couple of comments will occur like, "It's the last time I'm coming over here. . . next time they need help we'll see if we'll be there to back them up. It is said subtly, not to their face, behind their back, but where they can hear it. The message is you're not one of us. You can do it your way, but you won't get our help, and even to the point that if he needs help, they'll let him get beat up by the patient. So there is a strong message that he better conform to this (tradition of toughness) or we'll leave you out on a limb. If you try to buck the system, then you'll be left on your own.

IT'S NOT YOU WE DON'T TRUST

This norm is defined as a process of socializing patients into the hospital system through a tradition of rules that aim to control behavior for safety reasons. When talking with patients, the staff blame the system for the existence of these rules yet accept the need for the rules. For example, no patients are allowed to have matches and all cigarettes are lit by a wall electric lighter. When a patient asked an aide why no matches were allowed, she said: "it's not you we don't trust, but we once had a girl who set herself on fire." Patients have not been allowed to have matches since that incident.

The result is the development of and adherence to a rigid rule structure. For example, a ward rule that results in a great deal of violence has to do with cigarettes. Patients are encouraged to leave their cigarettes in the nursing station to prevent others from stealing them. However, each time a patient wants a cigarette, she/he must ask a staff member. The procedure increases the number of stressful interactions between staff members and patients and increases the opportunities for a violent situation to occur.

Other controlling unit procedures have been instituted to protect the safety of the staff from potentially dangerous patients. An aide reported the following to a patient after the patient expressed her fear of being in the hospital: "it's scary to have you here." The same NA talked about her fear of new patients.

> We don't know what they got under their clothes. They might have a gun or something. When you're in the dayroom working with prn (temporary) staff who don't know the patients, they (temporary staff) make it dangerous for us.

In response to the fear of violence during the admission procedure, nursing administration has instituted a procedure in which all new patients are taken to seclusion to be searched before entry to the ward. Other procedures previously described, such as removing personal articles, were developed in response to the fear that patients brought weapons or sharp objects to harm themselves or others.

Role Component

The primary role for the nonprofessional staff members is labelled "enforcing" and includes the strategies of "policing," "supermanning," and "putting on a show" and describes the process of how staff members operationalize the value of control within the organizational setting.

POLICING

Policing is defined as the process of effectively carrying out the rules aimed to control patient behavior. One subject described the process:

> The enforcers, or the police force (staff), are the ones who see themselves as expert crisis managers. The culture of toughness is based on the ideal of machismo, then, what you have is an increase in confrontation. When the value is placed on being tough, then you handle situations when things get out of hand. You go in and *handle* them. When the confrontation increases, then you have an increase in violence. When a unit operates from the culture of toughness, then staff are valued for their ability to physically manage assaultive patients.
>
> These guys are really good at handling themselves physically. So a take-down occurs (physically restraining a patient) and they call for backup (other male staff). The enforcers show up. The way they handle the crisis is that when it happens it happens quick. We don't talk. We move in and take control. We put him down (physically immobilize), we deal with it as quickly as possible.

Policies and enforcing the rules aimed to control patients inevitably leads to violence through the process of confrontation and escalation of the violent situation.

SUPERMANNING

Supermanning, the second category of the enforcers, is defined as how a leader emerges from among the enforcers. The leader is the toughest of the enforcers and is the principal person who sanctions the physical behaviors necessary for controlling patients. A story was told by a subject describing an orderly from a different setting, whom he identified as the "superman."

> A staff (superman) was teaching him (patient) karate. We had staff going to the hospital because of this guy (the patient). It took 10 people to take him down (restrain). And he would take three or fourth staff out (injure) during the procedure, knock him out. This one staff member was teaching him karate and I put a stop to it. The staff was hoping that by teaching this guy karate they would become karate buddies and he wouldn't attack him. The second thing was that he was hoping the patient would see him as tough and wouldn't attack him. It did work when the guy (staff) was around. But when he wasn't

there, then problems occurred. When you have a culture of toughness you usually have a superman. The problem is that when the superman is not there everyone else's anxiety goes up.

An additional aspect of the superman's job is to protect the remaining staff by taking the lead in managing potentially dangerous situations. The superman receives a great deal of positive reinforcement for his behavior from staff and usually achieves high status within the organization for his "expert" physical skills.

PUTTING ON A SHOW

Putting on a show is defined as the process of how the enforcers protect themselves from outside influences and negative sanctions for behavior not officially condoned by the system. During interviews, the enforcers reported a textbook approach to the delivery of nursing care. These staff members were shrewd enough to tell the researcher what they thought she wanted to hear. Instead, the enforcers focused the interviews on the importance of the therapeutic relationship and the patient's need for "unconditional positive regard."

The extent of the enforcers' abusive behavior could not be determined from observations on the ward. However, early in the study, the enforcers were observed to be rough, mildly aggressive, and provocative with patients. Later in the study, the enforcers became suspicious of the researcher, which resulted in a noticeable change in their behavior. The enforcers attempted to "charm" the researcher and "act good" with patients in the presence of the researcher, but their aggressive manner could not be totally hidden. For example, a patient fell on the floor in the dayroom and appeared to be experiencing side effects from the psychotropic medication. A staff member, who was later identified as the superman, looked at the researcher and said to the patient in a rough manner, "get up." The patient remained on the floor. Five minutes later, the superman approached the patient a second time and asked if he was all right. Without waiting for an answer, he roughly lifted the patient onto the couch and walked away. The patient was afraid and attempted to walk to the nursing station and fell a second time. The superman made a third approach, more forceful this time, to tell the patient to get up. But the staff left the situation without waiting for a response. Finally, a male LPN, who was not an enforcer, approached the patient and managed the situation in a thoughtful and therapeutic manner. Within seconds, the staff physically assisted the patient to lie down on the couch, correctly assessed the patient's condition as an extrapyramidal reaction to phenothiazines, explained this to the patient, and quickly administered medication to counter the reaction. Despite the superman's attempts "to act good" in this situation, evidence existed that he was rough with patients. The patients corroborated this information by identifying this particular staff member as one who uses "hands on" prematurely in potentially violent situations.

Putting on a show implies that the enforcers are capable of hiding behavior that would result in administrative action. To obtain "behind the scenes" information and to verify "hunches" about specific staff members, the researcher directly asked patients and nursing staff to identify the enforcers and to describe their behavior with patients. Many patients identified the same staff members as abusive and substantiated their reports with stories. All the nursing staff members refused to identify the enforcers and the superman until the study was over, when one subject verified the researcher's hunch about the identity of the superman. However, the following stories were told by staff about enforcers from other clinical settings.

> We had a guy here (staff member) everyone loved him on the unit. He was big, lifted weights, could control anybody. The most common thing he said to patients when they got out of line was, "try me" (hands gesturing in an aggressive come-on manner). He was smart enough not to do it in front of the unit chief. There was a lot of violence on the unit when he was there and it fed into the image that he was the one who could control it, because there was hardly anyone he couldn't control (physically).
>
> A patient was carrying around a belt. The staff were trying to figure out what to do about it. So the staff were waiting outside and the staff leader walked into the room. He and the patient were alone. He told the patient that if he didn't put the belt down that he would make sure that both his arms would be broken during the take-down and that no one would know how it happened. And he told the patient he better not tell anyone or it would happen another way.

The reports suggest that enforcers used physical management skills to excess and were aware that their behaviors would not be sanctioned by authority figures in the system. The result is an informal organization that emphasized loyalty to the group and confidentiality among the members of the group. In addition, several registered nurses suggested that nursing staff were both afraid of and protected the enforcers. An RN reported:

> The staff are family, blood is thicker than water. If you ever say anything negative about one of them, they will band together against you.

Another characteristic of the enforcers is their reluctance to intervene in patient situations when alone. An LPN reported the following story about an enforcer (PT) who had provoked a patient through repeated aggressive verbal exchanges. The enforcer asked the LPN to give the patient a dose of medication for agitation. When the LPN and enforcer approached the patient with medication, the patient swung and hit the LPN, without saying a word. While the enforcer stood there watching, another patient jumped over the table and successfully restrained the assaultive patient. The incident had a tremendous psychological impact on the LPN, who had just returned to work from a previous work-related injury.

Most of the "enforcers" were male nonprofessional staff; however, several notable exceptions were found. One male and female RN were enforcers and one female aide, one male LPN, and several female LPNs and RNs were not enforcers. The staff members who were not identified as enforcers rarely acted in a physically aggressive manner with patients and examples of high quality care were observed. For example, the aide often talked with patients and assisted them with basic tasks in a caring and thoughtful manner. Most of the patients identified her as a helpful staff member. In addition, one part-time female RN sat in the dayroom on a Monday morning and spontaneously talked with patients about her weekend. The result was a 15-minute therapeutic discussion, involving staff and patients, about skiing and problems of living associated with snow. However, the male nonprofessional staff did not often engage in any relaxed social or therapeutic activities with patients requiring verbal skills. Most nonprofessional staff either ignored patients or responded in an irritable manner when approached. When not occupied with tasks, these staff socialized with other staff but rarely with patients, except to play cards or pool with male patients who had similar interests. This result has been found in similar studies (Fairbanks, 1977; Hodges, 1986; Sanson-Fisher, 1979).

The data suggest that a relationship existed between the tradition of toughness and violence. When control and safety are highly valued, then procedures and standardized behaviors result that seem to promote violence. For example, many incidents of aggressive exchanges were observed to occur between patients and staff members when patients were not able to have their cigarettes, their clothes, or personal belongings. More serious violent incidents were observed when the enforcers overreacted to situations that could have been handled by verbal therapeutic interventions. In addition, the extent of stories from previous employment indicated that aspects of the tradition of toughness are present in many psychiatric settings.

The tradition of toughness was observed to be maintained by three strengths. First, the leader of the enforcers is rewarded with high status and prestige. Second, staff members develop a feeling of belonging to the group when they comply with the tradition of toughness. Third, the staff members promote the tradition of toughness to justify an organizational need to hire male staff members to manage violent patients. The same three sources of strength have been identified by Katz and Kahn (1966) as important to maintaining organizations. How much the formal system contributes to the tradition of toughness is unclear, since this study did not evaluate formal organizational factors such as hiring and firing procedures, evaluation of personnel, and procedures for disciplining and rewarding staff. However, the results suggest that the informal organizational system has a strong influence on promoting and maintaining the tradition of toughness through the informal mechanisms for training and socializing new staff members.

Discussion

The organization has an impact on the behaviors of persons within the setting. The tradition of toughness is partially a result of the preferred ideology within the setting and is based on an authority model of care. Second, the resulting norms, ie, the need for physical restraint and "it's not you we don't trust," emphasize the socialization of both staff and patients into the model of care. Third, the norms result in an organizational role that emphasizes controlling patient behavior that may be only partially related to the overall aims or goal of patient care, ie, treatment of the mentally ill. Last, the emphasis on control can promote violent behavior in patients through a rigid rule structure and strict adherence to a role that defines staff behaviors.

The model in this study was compared with the organizational and psychiatric literature to determine its consistency with available knowledge. The study is an analysis of a psychiatric institution and, as such, is consistent with the view of institutions as coercive, regimented organizations (Goffman, 1961). Edwards and Reid (1983) support this view of institutions as overstructured, authoritarian, and inflexible with too much emphasis on security at the expense of therapy. Authoritarianism in nursing staff members was well-documented in the psychiatric literature in the '60s and early '70s, and a higher level of authoritarianism has been found in nonprofessional nursing staff than in professional staff (Canter, 1963; Cohen, 1962; 1963; Rabkin, 1972). However, only a few researchers continued the study of authoritarianism to show that clinical effectiveness (Canter, 1963) and excessive dependence on physical intervention strategies were influenced by the level of authoritarianism (Scott, 1985). In a study of 55 psychiatric nurses, Milne (1985) found no relationship of personality variables with job performance and concluded that institutional variables may exert more control over job performance than personality correlates. These findings suggest that the degree of authoritarianism may be primarily determined by the setting, not by individual personalities.

Strauss (1975) and Strauss et al (1981) explored psychiatric ideologies, careers, negotiation, and coordination of work within psychiatric hospitals. Two issues were identified by Strauss (1975) as central to nursing: nurses must balance both administrative functions and therapeutic functions, and nurses must define "therapeutic action" in order to clarify our professional identify. Both issues continue to be of primary concern to psychiatric nursing. The results of this study and others (Milne, 1985; Strauss, 1975) suggest that nursing care is dependent on the hospital's prevailing ideology and less on personal attributes of nursing staff.

One issue frequently asked regarding violent behavior is that of staff-patient ratios. A common belief is that a higher staff/patient ratio is related to less violence. The present study would suggest the reverse: a higher ratio is related to a higher degree of violence, since increased opportunities for stressful interactions occur resulting in increased violence

(Morrison, 1990). Other studies support this finding by reporting that violence occurs more frequently at the change of shift when staffing is high (Depp, 1983).

The study has two limitations. First, the study is not generalizable to all psychiatric settings, particularly to settings that use different ideologies. However, the data and literature suggest that psychiatric institutions are surprisingly similar, since most utilize the medical model emphasizing a disease approach (Kavanaugh, 1988; Marler, 1971; Strauss, 1981; 1975). In addition, the extent of subjects' stories from previous settings and personal clinical experience suggest that aspects of the tradition of toughness exist in other psychiatric settings. Observations were conducted in the private hospital for comparison and less violence was observed. Two variables are most likely responsible for the difference. The primary reason was the difference in the type of patient treated in the private hospital, ie, patients were less likely to be indigent, involuntary, substance abusers, involved with the criminal justice system, or come from a subculture of violence (Morrison, 1990). Second, the private hospital had a higher ratio of professional/nonprofessional staff. The second limitation is that other interpretations of the data are possible. For example, a traditional psychological interpretation of authoritarianism would emphasize denial of fear that results in an over-reaction to the situation.

Although a qualitative study is only an initial exploration into a topic area, some implications for nursing administrators and professional psychiatric nurses working in psychiatric inpatient settings can be drawn. The first issue is that nursing care in many psychiatric units is based on the concept of authority implicit in the medical model, which results in maintaining the tradition of toughness, and not on the concept of cooperation and persuasion that is implicit in a nursing model. The degree of authoritarianism currently observed in institutions is likely a result of the mandate that nurses have received to "maintain order" on the wards (Strauss, 1975) and their ambiguous commitment to a radical model ideology (Strauss, 1981). One useful approach to changing the norms and roles within an institution is to change the value system. The adoption of a cooperation model of care would result in decreasing the tradition of toughness and violence. Kavanaugh (1988) conducted a study in a comparable setting and conclusions were similar, ie, differentiation of the curing aspect of the role (medical model) from the caring aspect of the role (nursing model).

The second issue is related to the use of nonprofessionals/professionals to provide care in psychiatric institutions. Some nursing administrators have made progress towards the increased utilization of professional nurses, and this trend is encouraging. However, many psychiatric hospitals continue to hire nonprofessional nursing staff members to provide the majority of nursing care (Marler, 1971; Kavanaugh, 1988) despite the abundance of literature that documents high authoritarianism within this group. The current health-care atmosphere of financial restraint in conjunction with the nursing shortage emphasizes the importance of continuing our efforts to explore options for the use of both professional and nonprofessional nursing staff and the use of nurses with during levels of education and experience (Kavanaugh, 1988).

However, other options are available for reducing the tradition of toughness. Nursing administrators need to be cognizant of policies and procedures that directly or indirectly positively reward "the enforcers" for controlling patients. Rewards for nursing staff members who successfully manage patients with "therapeutic techniques" should be developed and implemented as part of yearly evaluations. Third, routine unit rules can be reviewed to determine the usefulness and appropriateness of each rule and many can be eliminated or re-negotiated. Fourth, administrators can develop new orientation programs for new nursing staff members that emphasize therapeutic techniques, as well as physical techniques, for managing violent situations. Fifth, systems for the close supervision of nonprofessional nursing staff members should be developed and implemented.

Clinicians can do several things to reduce the tradition of toughness. First, nurses can report any unethical or unusually physically tough behavior by staff members to their supervisors. Second, nurses can learn to question unusually harsh rules. Nursing care needs to be planned that is individualized and less dependent on strict adherence to the rules in order to facilitate appropriate socialization of patients.

The results of the current study indicate that this area is a fruitful one for continuing nursing research. The results from this study have been used to develop a theoretical model of violence that takes into account both the individual patient variables and organizational variables that have an impact on violence by patients. Authoritarian ideology in nursing staff is an important variable within the new model, and the impact of staff variables such as stress and burnout on the degree of authoritarian ideology will be tested in future research. In addition, other variables such as the staffs' perspective of the organizational milieu will be explored to determine the degree of authoritarianism among varying psychiatric hospitals.

References

Adler, W.N., Kreeger, M.A., Zigler, P. Patient violence in a private psychiatric hospital. In J.R. Lion, W.H. Reid (Eds.), *Assaults in psychiatric facilities*. New York: Grune & Stratton, 1983, pp. 81-90.

American Psychiatric Association. *Task force on clinical aspects of the violent individual*. Washington, DC: Author, 1974.

Cantor, F.M. The relationship between authoritarian attitudes, attitudes toward mental patients and effectiveness of clinical work with mental patients. *J Clin Psychiatry* 1963; 19:124-127.

Cohen, J., Streuning, E.L. Opinions about mental illness in the personnel of two large mental hospitals. *Journal of Abnormal Social Psychology* 1962; 64:349-360.

Cohen, J., Streuning, E.L. Opinions about mental illness: Mental hospital occupational profiles and profile clusters. *Psychol Rep* 1963; 12:111-124.

Craig, T.J. An epidemiological study of problems associated with violence among psychiatric inpatients. *Am J Psychiatry* 1982; 139:1262-1266.

Depp, F. Assaults in a public mental hospital. In J. Lion, W. Reid (Eds.), *Assaults within psychiatric facilities.* New York: Grune & Stratton, 1983, pp. 21-45.

Edwards, J.G., Reid, W.H. Violence in psychiatric facilities in Europe and the United States. In J. Lion, W. Reid (Eds.), *Assaults within psychiatric facilities.* New York: Grune & Stratton, 1983, pp. 131-142.

Fairbanks, L.A., McGuire, M.T., Cole, S.R., Sbordone, R., Silvers, F.M., Richards, M., et al. The ethological study of four psychiatric wards: Patient, staff and system behaviors. *J Psychiatr Res* 1977; 13:193-209.

Glaser, B., Strauss, A.L. *Discovery of grounded theory: Strategies for qualitative research.* Chicago: Aldine Publishing, 1967.

Glaser, B.G. *Theoretical sensitivity.* Mill Valley, CA: Sociology Press, 1978.

Goffman, E. *Asylums.* Chicago: Aldine Publishing, 1961.

Guba, E.G. Criteria for assessing the trustworthiness of naturalistic inquiries. *Education and Communication Teaching Journal* 1981; 29:78.

Hall, B.A. Socializing hospitalized patients into the psychiatric sick role. *Perspect Psychiatr Care* 1975; 13(3):18-23.

Hodges, V., Sanford, D., Elzinga, R. The role of ward structure on nursing staff behaviors: An observational study of three psychiatric wards. *Acta Psychiatr Scand* 1988; 73:6-11.

Katz, D., Kahn, R.L. *The social psychology of organizations.* New York: John Wiley & Sons, 1966.

Kavanaugh, K.H. The cost of caring: Nursing on a psychiatric intensive care unit. *Human Organization* 1988; 47:242-251.

Lanza, M.L. The reactions of nursing staff to physical assault by a patient. *Hosp Community Psychiatry* 1983; 34:44-47.

Madden, D.J., Lion, J.R., Penna, M.W. Assaults on psychiatrists by patients. *Am J Psychiatry* 1976; 133:422-425.

Marler, D.C. The nonprofessionalization of the war on mental illness. *Mental Hygiene* 1971; 55:291-295.

Milne, D. The more things change the more they stay the same: Factors affecting the implementation of the nursing process. *J Adv Nurs* 1985; 10:39-45.

Moos, R.H. *Evaluating treatment environments: A social ecological approach.* New York: John Wiley & Sons, 1974.

Morrison, E.F. Theoretical modeling predicting violence in hospitalized psychiatric patients. *Res Nurs Health* 1989; 12:31-40.

Morrison, E.F. A typology of violent psychiatric patients in a public hospital. *Scholarly Inquiry for Nursing Practice* 1990; 4(1):65-82.

Rabkin, J.G. Opinions about mental illness: A review of the literature. *Psychol Bull* 1972; 77:153-171.

Ruben, I., Wolkon, G, Yamamoto, S. Physical attacks on psychiatric residents by patients. *J Nerv Ment Dis* 1980; 168:243-245.

Sanson-Fisher, R.W., Poole, D., Thompson, V. Behavior patterns within a general hospital psychiatric unit: An observational study. *Behav Res Ther* 1979; 17:317-332.

Scott, D.J., Philip, A.E. Attitudes of psychiatric nurses to treatment and patients. *Br J Med Psychol* 1985; 58:169.

Spradley, J.P. *Participant observation.* New York: Holt, Rinehart & Winston, 1980.

Strauss, A., Schatzman, L., Bucher, R., Ehrlich, Danuta Sabshin, M. *Psychiatric ideologies and institutions.* New Brunswick, NJ: Transaction Books, 1981.

Strauss, A.L. *Professions, work and careers.* New Brunswick, NJ: Transaction Books, 1975.

Tardiff, K., Sweillam, A. Assault, suicide, and mental illness. *Arch Gen Psychiatry* 1980; 37:164-169.

Tardiff, K.A. Survey of assault by chronic patients in a state hospital system. In J.R. Lion, W.H. Reid (Eds.), *Assaults in psychiatric facilities.* New York: Grune & Stratton, 1983, pp. 3-19.

Reprinted with permission from Image *1990; 22(1):32-38.*

3 | Patient Violence in Psychiatric Settings: Risk Identification and Treatment as Provocation

By D. Thomas Blair, RN, C, MS; and Sue Ann New, RN, C, MSN

Violent and assaultive behavior of patients is a critical problem for everyone in the health professions. Prediction, prevention, and intervention have been extensively examined to decrease the frequency and severity of assaults. The traditional focus of study has been on the recognition of factors associated with assaultive incidents and the identification of degrees of risk. More modern conceptualizations of violence view the interactive nature of assaultive behavior and consider factors that might provoke abusive episodes. Many characteristics of psychiatry treatment may act as provocation for violence, and it is vital that professionals be able to recognize these. Psychiatric settings and treatments can then be designed in ways which minimize these factors.

However, there is some violence that is unpredictable, no matter how well the treatment environment is designed and managed. In these cases, traditional risk factor identification can play an important role in the initiation of appropriate, preventive intervention. Therefore, an examination and integration of both these approaches is necessary for a complete understanding of this problem.

In the discussion of violence and assaultive behavior, conceptual confusion concerning definitions is common. Researchers have little consensus on criteria from which to define various behaviors for the purposes of operationalizing them for scientific research. Straus and Gelles (1990), propose the following definitions. Violence is any action carried out with the intention or perceived intention of causing physical injury of another, and is synonymous with the term "physical aggression." Although "assault" is a legal concept, the use of the term "assault" (or assaultive behavior) is interchangeable with violence in this discussion. Assault in the health-care setting is unlawful despite mitigation due to insanity or mental incompetence.

The Impact of Violence in the Health-Care Setting

Assaultive behavior is encountered in a wide variety of settings: the general hospital, clinics, psychiatric units, emergency rooms, and care homes. Violence is a threat to the welfare of the patient as well as other patients and staff. Assaults toward staff involve injury, lost work time, high stress, job dissatisfaction, and subsequent psychological consequences that can be as serious as physical injury.

The cost to delivery systems is high. Patient assaults generate costs in lost productivity, insurance and medical fees, administrative time, and monetary loses from litigation. Consequently, management of disruptive behavior is a vital task for health-care organizations and is generally identified as a major topic in curriculum planning for psychiatric nurses. Violence in health care is probably the single most important topic in health care today.

Yet despite a growing national concern and an increase in training and policy interventions, the health professions have failed to deal adequately with this problem. Reid and others (1985a) report that data from a sample of facilities show 2.54 assaults per bed per year. Kay (1988) demonstrated that 7% to 10% of patients in psychiatric facilities are involved in assaultive episodes. Nationally, this represents an enormous number of violent patients.

Assaults not only continue to occur, but a review of the literature quickly reveals that rates of violence are sharply increasing over time (Harris, 1986), and they are higher in the US than in other nations (Edwards, 1983). Adler and others (1983) described a sixfold increase in assaults over a 5-year period, and Noble and Roger (1989) report a 400% increase over an 8-year period. Rosenbaum (1990) reviewed the literature on violence in *Index Medicus* and found no references to violence until 1968. From four articles that year, there was an increase to 32 in 1988. Today, the literature is voluminous.

Data concerning staff injuries also indicate the increasing magnitude of this problem. Some have observed that the number of staff injured by patients increased by more than five times over a 5-year period and that this rate continues to increase (Drummond, 1989). Dubin (1988) reports that half of all health-care professionals will be assaulted during their careers. The National Safety Council has reported that assaults have been the leading cause of injury for staff in psychiatric settings, and injury to staff as a result of violence has been identified as a major occupational risk (Carmel, 1989).

Worse, there is agreement on the frequency of under-reporting. In a classic study by Lion and others (1981), it was found that underreporting occurs at a rate of five times that of reported assaults. Later studies have confirmed the magnitude of under-reporting (Jones, 1985). Convit (1988) discovered that assaults are 50% higher than those reported and involve 34.5% more patients than are reported.

In response to the scope of the problems concerning violence in treatment settings, the examination of risk factors for assaultive behavior became the focus of extensive research and study. Although these trends were becoming the focus of attention, several other factors came to light and influenced the direction of analysis and study.

The first is the concept of dangerousness. Since the landmark Tarasoff case in 1973 in California, psychiatric professionals have been held liable for harm sustained by third parties injured by psychiatric patients (Beck, 1985), and the issue of dangerousness has become an important concept. The case established the responsibility of treaters to make the distinction of dangerousness with respect to giving information and warning to third parties as well as to protect staff. Civil commitment in most states now requires that dangerousness to self and others must be established as a legal criterion for forced hospitalization.

Risk factor analysis has since been given priority in the courts and in the public eye despite strong objections by the psychiatric community. Ability to predict violent behavior in patients has been seriously questioned (Mullen, 1984), and Rossi (1986) questions the propriety of clinical professionals using the future probability of violence as a basis for forcing treatment. It is believed that the literature is inadequate to delineate such risk factors (Mills, 1988), and there is a paucity of empirical data and lack of consensus among professionals concerning what constitutes dangerousness (Swanson, 1990). Monahan (1984) found that prediction of dangerousness is twice as likely to be wrong as right.

It may be a common assumption by health professionals and the public that the most important predictor of dangerousness is violent behavior prior to admission, but this has yielded a high proportion of false negatives (Janofsky, 1988). The difficulty is the vagueness in definitions concerning violence, reliance on measures that are not predictors, and a disregard for environmental and situational influences for violence (Edwards, 1988; Reid, 1988). Therefore, it is imperative for professionals to examine critically the literature concerning risk factors and the dynamics that influence risk for violence.

The second factor is that of risk management. Facilities and individual professionals face serious liability for injuries sustained by others within the treatment setting. Nurses may be personally liable, and hospitals, clinics and care homes also assume liability under the legal principle of "vicarious liability" (Northrop, 1986). The legal repercussions can be substantial, and court decisions have favored victims of assault by patients (Felthouse, 1987; Sales, 1983). Although the motivation for risk factor analysis should be compliance with professional standards of practice, it has been observed that the purpose of risk management is the protection of corporate assets (Monagle, 1985). Nonetheless, this process is vital toward reducing injury. It is hoped that this is motivation enough and not simply a defensive response to financial and legal pressures and consumer demands.

For these reasons, risk factors and provocation must be examined. It may be useful to identify patients most at risk for violence, but the issue of false positives must also be considered (Cocozza, 1984). Risk factors that are patient-specific are fixed and not easily avoided by treatment design. However, awareness of these is important. Incidence of assault is high, and under-reporting is considerable, yet as many as half of reported incidents of assault are thought to be avoidable by victims (Aiken, 1984). It is clear, then, that understanding this most complex problem of violence is crucial.

Traditional Risk Factor Identification

For more than 20 years, researchers have been correlating various factors with incidence of assault. Attempts to predict violence based on identified risk factors usually produce only low levels of accuracy, and many lack cross-validation in independent samples from various settings (Convit, 1988). One conclusion is that assaultive behavior is precipitated by a combination of personal risk factors, situational factors, and treatment characteristics. The combination of various risk factors and their interaction with the patient's pathology also contributes to the dynamics of assault. The sum of these factors is complicated at best, and the usefulness of quantifying specific factors is questionable.

Nevertheless, the determination and examination of these factors can raise awareness. Many health-care workers, managers, and administrators may hold older, traditional beliefs concerning violence. Many believe that certain factors associated with the incidence of violence are causative, and therefore base interventions on the reduction of these characteristics. Many of these beliefs are unsupported by the literature, yet continue to influence treatment (Blair, 1991b). Therefore, these practices must be examined to dispel these notions and to allow for more meaningful and informed interventions.

By far, the most commonly associated risk factor for assault is a history of previous assault in a treatment setting, and such a positive history is the single best indicator of subsequent violent behavior (Blomhoff, 1990; Davis, 1988). Many studies attempt to correlate violence in the community with risk for assault in a hospital setting. McNeil and others (1988) observe that assaultiveness in the community and its relationship to assaults in the hospital is unclear. The Veterans Administration (Rofman, 1980) examined assaultiveness in regard to civilly committed patients, and Steadman (1981) looked at assaults by criminally committed patients. Both studies conclude that different dynamics are related to assault in the community and assault in the hospital. This suggests that violence in the hospital may be more related to the treatment setting itself, rather than any individual risk factor.

It has been demonstrated that approximately 45% of all psychiatric patients exhibit fear-inducing behaviors, and patients with a history of assault in treatment settings are much more likely to be readmitted (Rossi, 1985). Barber and others (1988) found that a small percentage (3.3%) of the patient population accounted for nearly half of all assaults. Rossi (1985) found that readmissions are over-represented by assaultive patients and that patients admitted on an involuntary basis were 82% more assaultive than voluntary patients.

The second most common factor to be correlated with assaultive behavior is the diagnosis. The most common are psychiatric diagnoses. Drummond and others (1989) found that 65.9% of assaults were by patients with a psychiatric diagnosis, 25% for substance abuse or alcohol intoxication, and the remainder were various medical diagnoses. Jones (1985) found that 85% of all diagnoses associated with assault were psychotic conditions or substance abuse. Palmstierna and Wistedt (1987) found the lowest incidence in nonpsychotic patients.

The highest rate of assault involves organic brain disorders or dementia (Jones, 1985), and Donat (1986) has described a stable overall prevalence of aggressive behavior in geropsychiatric patients. These patients are commonly assaultive, but injuries are more likely to be less severe or minor in nature, and more often go unreported (Palmstierna, 1987). This high incidence is presumably due to the fact that these disorders involve recurrent loss of impulse control (Rossi, 1986). A common characteristic of the violent elderly is cognitive impairment and a dependency on others for care. These patients may attempt to regain loss of control through complaining, demanding, resistant, and noncompliant behavior (Meddaugh, 1986).

With organic or demented patients, staff-patient interaction is a major triggering event for aggression (Colenda 1991). High incidence of assault is associated with performing or assisting with activities of daily living; that is, toileting, bathing, and dressing (Lanza, 1988; Palmstierna, 1987). It is presumed that any activity that involves the invasion of personal space increases risk for assault in these patients (Jones, 1985). Donat (1986) studied assaultiveness in a psychogeriatric setting and found that invasion of personal space is an important contributor. Negley and Manley (1990) agree and designed interventions to reduce the invasion of personal space of patients by environmental changes.

The second diagnosis that is highly associated with assault is schizophrenia (Blomhoff, 1990; Swanson, 1990), and in particular, paranoid schizophrenia or other psychotic disorders involving paranoid delusions (Aiken, 1984; Bradford, 1983). Delusions, hallucinations, and poor reality testing are assumed to be causes of violence in this population. There is also evidence that the more acute or disorganized the patient is, the more he or she is at risk for violent behavior (Tardiff, 1984).

Acute intoxication from drugs or alcohol is also highly associated with risks for violence. Drummond and others (1989) report that 72.7% of assaultive patients have substance abuse as a primary or secondary diagnosis. These patients are twice as likely as those with schizophrenia to exhibit violent behavior (Swanson, 1990). On inpatient units, use of intoxicating substances is curtailed and assaults by this group are more likely in outpatient settings and emergency rooms.

Other diagnoses have been identified with high rates of violence. Neurological disorders, head injuries, various forms of epilepsy, and temporal lobe abnormalities have high association with assaultive behaviors (Convit, 1988; Krakowski, 1989). High rates have also been identified for mental retardation, acute mania, personality disorders, and post-traumatic stress disorder.

Diagnosis may be useful in attempts to assign risk values, but Rossi and others (1986) point out that diagnosis in and of itself is not definitive. Rather, it is the severity of the pathology that is the predisposition to violence, making diagnosis only suggestive at best. Patients with the same diagnosis do not follow similar clinical courses over time, and so the use of diagnosis can be unreliable (Lee, 1989). Acuity of pathology and situational factors are more clearly an influence for risk (Durivage, 1989).

Demographic and epidemiological factors have been studied, but data have been mixed and contradictory. Rossi and others (1986) concluded that these variables are not useful in assigning risk, and others agree (Blomhoff, 1990). However, much effort has been made to examine these factors, and a brief review may be useful.

There is some evidence that lower socioeconomic standing is associated with violence (Edwards, 1988). Noble and Rodger (1989) found that blacks were more predisposed to violence; Lawson and others (1984) found that whites were. Some have determined that younger patients are more prone to violence (Pearson, 1986), and others have found that adolescents are most violent (Reid, 1989). But there is also the strong evidence concerning the violent nature of the institutionalized elderly (Donat, 1986).

Men have been identified in some studies as being most prone to violence, as have women in others; however, many studies have demonstrated that there is little or no relationship between violence and gender (Durivage, 1989; Kay, 1988). Tardiff (1983) suggests a blurring of sex roles and expectations when a person becomes an inpatient. Depp (1983) found that mixed-sex units have greater rates of assault than same-sex units. Social learning and family roles, marital status, level of education, and cultural values that are placed on violence have also been studied. In all these cases, the identification of these variables has not proven to be useful because results have been contradictory (Blomhoff, 1990).

Various environmental factors have produced similar outcomes. Day of the week, time of day, hospital shift, staff numbers, the sexual makeup of staff, type of unit, unit census, lack of privacy, and audience at the time of assault have all been examined, with the results being inconclusive (Durivage, 1989). This seems to dispel the belief that decreasing census, increasing the number of staff, or increasing male staff can generally reduce violence on inpatient units.

Modern Conceptualizations of Patient Violence

It is apparent that risk factors do not provide clear direction or prediction for treatment. Today, emphasis has shifted away from a patient-centered focus to a process-centered focus. Violence is the result of interactive and multifactorial variables and encompasses the patient-specific factors with various situational and treatment characteristics. These include medication, degree of interpersonal contact, staff patient interaction, unit structure, and routine.

It is well-established that medication compliance is a major issue in psychiatry. It is estimated that fully 75% of patients receiving antipsychotic medications experience extrapyramidal symptoms (EPS) as side effects (Schmidt, 1985). Fear of these side effects may account for the high rate of noncompliance among the mentally ill (McEvoy, 1989). Traditional interventions for noncompliance have focused on patient education, yet the problems continue. Many violent episodes are precipitated in treatment over the forced medication of resistive patients (Blair, 1990). Worse, some EPS, such as akathisia, can lead to suicide, self-mutilation, combativeness, and assaultive behaviors (Dauner, 1990).

Medications are considered invasive, and forcing patients to take them despite poorly tolerated side effects can be provocation for violence. Treatment involving as-needed medications must also incorporate adequate assessment of EPS and the consideration of the potential for serious discomfort or disability induced by these agents. If antipsychotic agents are a major component of treatment, EPS must be recognized and adequately managed.

Many have acknowledged the interactive nature of violent behavior between patient and staff (Roper, 1991), and Blair (1991a) has identified that certain characteristics of treatment itself may be provocation for violence. The examination of these factors is difficult and uncertain. Professionals must be able to critically examine treatment and not become defensive. Evaluation of treatment as provocation is a necessary process because treatment characteristics are factors that may be changed. This certainly does not exclude acknowledgment of patient responsibility for violent acts, nor does it ignore the fact that some assaults are unpredictable and are not provoked. Important factors include denial, staff attitude, personal bias, countertransference, and control issues.

Denial plays an important role in the process of violence and is, perhaps, the basis for all the difficulties involving treatment of violent patients. Lion (1987) speaks of psychiatry's reluctance to recognize violence as a critical treatment factor and he has stated that violence is "the dark side" of psychiatry. In fact, it was not until 1984 that the American Psychiatric Association published its task force report on psychiatric uses of restraint and seclusion, and even then it was in response to a court decision (Lion, 1987). Denial is used to avoid acknowledging the unpleasant reality of violence. Denial may also be used as a defense by staff to feelings of counteraggression or other countertransference (Lion, 1973). In one study, identification of past aggression or potential for violence was found in treatment plans for only 22% of violent patients, even though staff acknowledged that 66% of these patients were known to be violent (Sheridan, 1990).

Staff may also deny the possibility of assaults against themselves, and thus place themselves at risk (Lion, 1973). Madden and others (1976) reported that more than half of psychiatric staff who were assaulted conceded that they could have anticipated the assault had it not been for their denial. The issue of denial on an institutional level may account for the lack of motivation or innovation in the development of adequate interventions for violent and aggressive behaviors.

The idea that the nature of treatment itself may be a risk factor for violence, or that certain treatment characteristics become provocative, has become a focus of some attention (Blair, 1991a; Garrison, 1984). Because violent episodes are interactive, situational factors in the immediate environment or interaction with staff may in some way contribute to or provoke assaultive acting out (Durivage, 1989). Of all assaults in health-care facilities, 65% were found to be against staff, whereas only 32% involved other patients or property (Jones, 1985). Fottrell (1990) noted that staff are more than twice as likely to be victims as other patients. Considering the much higher number of patients, random violence would produce many more patients as victims. This implies that patient-staff interaction may be an important determinant for violent behavior. The most frequent victims are nurses and nursing assistants (Convey, 1986; Lanza, 1988), and nursing staff are considered most at risk for attack and injury. Of staff assaulted, 88% are nursing assistants or student nurses (Rada, 1981).

Carmel and Hunter (1989) found that recently hired staff were assaulted at a consistently higher rate than were the more experienced staff members. Because these groups are more frequently assaulted, clinical experience, educational level, and the provision of hands-on care are implicated as important factors when assessing provocative treatment characteristics.

Treatment as provocation can be understood from a number of viewpoints. From the patient's perspective, displacement of aggression from primary objects onto symbolic representations or substitutes for those objects can account for increased hostility toward treaters (Apter, 1989). Furthermore, patients are more likely to view events leading to restraint or seclusion as conflict with staff (Sheridan, 1990). Morrison (1990a) states that patients view violent episodes in terms of response to intrusive limits and structure and "to get staff off my back." Patients often claim that teasing or other provocation by staff causes assault, whereas staff report that there was not apparent reason for the assault (Soloff, 1983). Surprisingly, staff often seem unaware of provocative interactions and situations. Evidence of this is that some staff are consistently assaulted at higher rates than others, suggesting that staff attitude toward patients is an important factor (Fottrell, 1990).

Engle and Marsh (1986) suggest that the projection of staff expectations about violent patients may contribute to violence. Assaulted staff generally report that they "didn't like" the patient, and this animosity may be projected to the patient (Madden, 1976). Dubin (1989) found that aggressiveness on the part of the treater is more likely to provoke assault. Rubin and others (1980) discovered that 83% of staff who said they would "fight back" were assaulted, whereas only 38% of assaults were against those staff members who said they would not fight. Convey (1986) identifies a "macho" attitude, Dubin (1989) describes an adversarial stance, and Morrison (1990b) a "tradition of toughness" as provocative attitudes.

It has been suggested (Dubin, 1989) that some staff either consciously or unconsciously encourage patient violence. Madden (1976) found that 48% of psychiatric residents had been assaulted during training. When he evaluated the residents on an irritability scale, he found that a significantly higher proportion of those with a score above the mean were victims of violence. Researchers in corrections have long identified the "violence-generating" guard and have identified the characteristics of style and attitude as provocation (Toch, 1977). Soloff (1983) suggests that a staff's pathology can be acted out by violent patients.

Fear, anger, and hate are common countertransference reactions that are aroused in staff who work with violent patients (Colson, 1986). Fear and anger are principal long-term occupational hazards of such work (Lanza, 1985). When these feelings are left unattended, they become the driving force behind every decision made regarding patients and color every interaction. A common response is to deny these feelings, and recognizing them is often very difficult.

On an immediate level, certain behavioral cues are associated with assault: the "pre-assaultive tension state," or a period of acute excitement. This state is described as changes in posture, motor activity, verbal content, and pressured speech (Aiken, 1984). These cues have good predictive value and may seem obvious. But researchers have discovered that these cues may often go unheeded (Kay, 1988; Lee, 1989).

Sometimes behavioral cues are apparent to staff, but denial or fear prevent early interventions to de-escalate patients. Allowing a patient to remain in a pre-assaultive tension state only worsens the patient's fears concerning loss of control (Morton, 1986), and this can have serious consequences for other patients in the milieu. Other patients may fear for their own survival, or fear that they, too, may lose control (Dubin, 1989).

Munjas (1980) has identified various ways in which staff may inadvertently potentiate violence. Society tends to associate violent behavior with mental illness, and a certain amount of violence in the psychiatric setting is inevitable. However, stigmatizing images and beliefs concerning the mentally ill may create expectations for staff that violence is expected or is part of the job. The "norm of violence" on psychiatric units may, in fact, perpetuate the violence (Durivage, 1989). Staff may maintain patients as mentally ill through inadvertent rewarding of deviant behavior through everyday interactions with them. Violent behavior may play a role in getting staff attention, or it may lead to a tangible reward.

Locked units and severe structure may also imply that abnormal or disturbed behavior is acceptable and assaults may become an expected occurrence (Weaver, 1978). Such settings may change the nature of potentially violent situations or alter the expectations of violent acts (Reid, 1985b). Brailsford (1973a) emphasizes the role of frequent contact and interaction between patients and staff and suggests that a seclusive, isolated staff is the most profound factor of provocation for assault.

Another important factor is that of limit setting, which Lanza (1988) identifies as having an extreme level of provocation. She studied the types of limits and their association with assault. Physical limits involving the moving of a patient to another area, placing limits on eating or drinking certain foods, and limitations on cigarettes were the most risky, particularly with organic or demented patients. A greater number of assaults occurred where staff used only verbal limit setting. This would implicate the skill level, the style, and the educational preparation of those involved. Dubin and others (1989) state that failure to set effective limits may lead to escalation and assault.

Madden (1977) demonstrated increased risks of assault when limit setting was inconsistent. Kahneman and Tversky (1984) suggest that losses are much more important and have greater impact on people than possible gains. Viewed within this framework, taking something away from a patient would increase risk for assault. Donat (1986) identifies that taking objects away from demented elderly patients often precipitates combativeness. Reframing structure and limits in ways that avoid losses may circumvent unintended provocative interactions with patients.

Too often, treatment environments are structured according to the needs of the staff, who assume some amount of control over patients. Control is often the pervasive theme of many patient-staff interactions. Patients must accept treatment under the terms set by staff. Staff have this control and are rarely challenged about its use, and there often is not examination of the role of control issues in violent episodes. Mental illness and the limits of an inpatient setting impede the patient's ability to react suitably to difficult circumstances and limit the patient's ability to respond appropriately to conflict. The milieu may limit the options to only disruptive, desperate, or violent acts. A severely restrictive or controlled milieu may provoke the assaultiveness it is intended to control. Harrington (1984) believes that violence in a hospital setting is seldom a symptom of illness, but rather a reaction to a situation in which patients find themselves.

Conflict between patient and staff is an important factor, and a high number of assaults involve the enforcement of unit rules by staff (Sheridan, 1990). Lion and Pasternak (1973) state that common staff responses to violence are social avoidance and over-reaction, with increases in medication or excessive limit setting. Rigid, intolerant, and authoritarian styles are well-known to be provocative (Durivage, 1989; McNeil, 1987). Another important consideration is that psychiatric facilities tend to use nonprofessional personnel for most patient-care duties. Kavanaugh (1988) points out that this group of workers has a much higher incidence of authoritarian and inflexible styles in working with the mentally ill, and thus increases the likelihood of provocation due to style or personality.

Since Stanton and Schwartz published their classic studies of milieu and patient dynamics in *The Mental Hospital* (Stanton, 1954), it has been understood that staff conflict as well as institutional problems can have an impact on patient behaviors. These ideas have been refined, and various factors have been specifically associated with incidence of assault. Conflict between staff, low morale, and lack of staff cohesion have been identified as important factors for violence (Greenstein, 1990).

Others identify administrative responsibility for these conditions (Blair, 1991a; Snyder, 1983). If assaultive behavior is commonly viewed as a symptom of mental illness rather than a product of treatment, the structure of the treatment setting becomes one of controlling behavior by restrictive and intrusive interventions. If poor leadership, inept treatment practices, and staff conflict are seldom viewed as being related to assaultive behavior, then little reflective examination is ever conducted. If disharmony between the hospital administration and nursing staff exists, staff may become either over- or under-controlling. Tardiff and Sweillam (1982) note that reaction to these circumstances may be an authoritarian, nonflexible stance. All too often, adequate job performance is defined as keeping patients under control and the number of assaultive incidents low. Frequent heavy use of medications, restrictions, seclusion, and restraint are used to maintain this control—all of which are intrusive and provocative.

Economic factors in a facility also have an impact on this dynamic. Understaffing, overwork, a poor physical environment, or poorly educated staff lead to treaters who have a limited knowledge base and no confidence in themselves or their fellow workers for their own safety. They may then attempt to assume control by authoritarian means. Strict, inflexible structure and inappropriate consequences for behavioral problems set the stage for violence. If political or economic factors have a negative impact on nursing staff, they are left feeling powerless and with high stress and anxiety levels. This leads to the adoption of constricted, controlling, and negativistic behavior by staff, which is characteristic of an authoritarian approach. This also leads to isolation of staff from patients. Hodges and others (1986) demonstrated that authoritarian, overcontrolling staff rarely socialize with patients and have little person-to-person contact unless the interaction involves limit setting or confrontation.

Furthermore, this type of situation impedes the therapeutic milieu and creates an environment that is incapable of responding with sufficient sensitivity or empathy to distress or behavioral cues that precede violence. Little social interaction between patients and staff severely limits the options left to patients when they experience impulsive urges, anger, fears, doubts, or frustrations that treatment brings about. These conditions would seem, then, to provoke violent episodes. Coffey (1976) feels that treatment itself may be the single most important risk factor for assaultive behavior, particularly if treatment is perceived as coercive, controlling, or threatening.

Implications for Intervention

Ultimate responsibility for meaningful intervention begins with administration. Administration has the duty to assess the milieu, to support staff, and has the responsibility for the education and skills of the staff who manage the milieu. Interventions must be designed to minimize issues of provocation and to eliminate those that can be prevented.

Policy and procedure interventions by themselves are not supported by the literature in reducing violence. In fact, such interventions are contributory to violence in that policy changes without intervention at the unit level reflect denial and avoid the arduous task of self-examination of personal and organizational traditions. Inservice programs that teach self-defense techniques and how to place patients in restraints seem to have little influence on the incidence of assaultive behavior, but rather influence outcomes once assaultive episodes begin.

Staff education and awareness of potential risks and factors of provocation are crucial. The development of skills and the understanding of structure, limit setting, and the issues of provocation are extremely important. Infantino and Musingo (1985) demonstrated that staff who are trained in limit setting and other techniques had a significantly lower assault rate than did a group that was not trained.

More importantly, factors of provocation must be examined. Provocation by various elements of treatment or by staff, both knowingly or unknowingly, must be assessed. Issues of bias, control, and countertransference must be examined. Routine rules and structure on units must be reviewed; regulations that have been in place for years may have outlived their appropriateness. Many can be eliminated or modified to create a more flexible and responsive treatment setting and can allow for more individualized treatment.

Organizational and institutional factors must also be examined. Supervision of nonprofessional workers should be implemented and refined. Strict or harsh consequences for patients' behaviors should be assessed in terms of treatment goals for the patient or staff needs for control. Treatment approaches that do not focus on strict obedience of unit rules and regulations can minimize these types of provocation. Structure can be viewed as a vehicle by which assessment is made with regard to the patient's degree of independence and ability to conform to basic social functioning. Treatment can then become more individually directed, and can provide a measure by which resistance or treatment gains occur.

The design of specific interventions must begin with the assessment of assaultive episodes as well as the subsequent actions of staff and patient. Jones (1985) discovered that interventions occur after only 40% of assaults and usually involved seclusion, medication, or both. Rada (1981) makes the point that assessment must continue both during and after the assault. Information gained from observation and assessment of the assault and post-assault phases are invaluable. It would be important to note, for example, if the assault was generalized or focused, if delusions were an important factor, or if the assault was in some way provoked. After the episode, the patient must be assessed as to mental status, orientation, presence of a postictal (seizure) state, confusion, the ability to express regret, or continued hostility. This enables the assaultive behavior to be classified etiologically as situational or functional and would dictate future treatment interventions.

Every assault should be assessed with all involved staff, including responsible managers. Assessment should include review of known risk factors and a critical examination of the antecedents to the episode for factors of provocation. A formalized assessment can be implemented that would serve to raise awareness, evaluate treatment, and identify staff attitudes that may have an impact on the dynamics of the violent behavior. This type of assessment can be difficult or threatening and can present a challenge to unit administrators. But the potential gains in insight and understanding can be invaluable and may result in decreasing the frequency and severity of such incidents.

An example of such an assessment process is the use of an Assaultive Incident Assessment Guide (Figure), which can facilitate the evaluation of pertinent factors and characteristics that may have influenced the assaultive incident. Such a guide can help direct discussion and consideration of factors that may not have been apparent at the time of the incident. Use of the guide can also serve as an educational tool for raising awareness of risks and the identification of possible inappropriate responses by staff.

Conclusion

Violence in the treatment setting is a difficult and complicated problem. Assaults will undoubtedly continue to occur, incidence may continue to increase, and the literature will continue to attempt to identify specific

---

FIGURE
Assaultive Incident Assessment Guide—Staff Process and Evaluation

1. Is the diagnosis dementia or other organic pathology?
   If "yes," go to 2; if "no," go to 7.
2. Was crowding/personal space a factor?
3. Were activities of daily living being assisted or performed?
4. Was something being taken away from the patient?
5. Was the patient being physically moved or were physical limits being set?
6. Implications for future management (note staff consensus on future interventions).
7. Did the patient have a history of assault?
8. Was the patient intoxicated with alcohol or drugs?
9. Was a pre-assaultive tension state identified prior to assault?
10. Were delusions or hallucinations a factor?
11. Were medications assessed or use of as-needed medications reviewed?
12. Were extrapyramidal symptoms assessed?
13. What is the prevalent staff attitude toward the patient?
14. Were limits being set or structure enforced?
15. Are limits and structure appropriate for this patient?
16. Were behavioral consequences a factor and are these appropriate?
17. Are control issues or conflict between the staff and patient identified?
18. Was the patient able to interact with staff prior to incident?
19. Implications for future management (note staff consensus on future interventions).

---

factors or interventions aimed at reducing such episodes. Tragically, staff and patients alike may continue to suffer. Until delivery systems are able to examine and incorporate known risk associations and the various issues of provocation caused by certain treatment characteristics, or by the attitudes and style of staff, then the problems of violence will continue to be confusing and poorly managed. It is hoped that the integration of risk associations and the more modern conceptualizations of violence and interactional dynamics can begin to reduce the consequences of violence and assault in the psychiatric setting.

References

Aiken, G.J.M. Assaults on staff in a locked ward—Predictions and consequences. *Med Sci Law* 1984; 24:199-207.

Alder, W., Kreeger, C., Ziegler, P. Patient violence in a private psychiatric hospital. In J.R. Lion, W.H. Reid (Eds.), *Assault within psychiatric facilities*. New York: Grune & Stratton, 1983.

Apter, A., Plutchik, R., Sevy, S. Defense mechanisms in risk for violence. *Am J Psychiatry* 1989; 146:1027-1031.

Barber, J., Hundley, P., Kellogg, E. Clinical and demographic characteristics of fifteen patients with repetitively assaultive behavior. *Psychiatr Q* 1988; 59:213-224.

Beck, J.C. *The potentially violent patient and the Tarasoff decision in psychiatric practice.* Washington, DC: American Psychiatric Press, 1985.

Blair, D.T. Risk management for extrapyramidal symptoms. *QRB* 1990; 16:116-124.

Blair, D.T. Assaultive behavior: Does provocation begin in the front office? *J Psychosoc Nurs Ment Health Serv* 1991a; 29(5):21-26.

Blair, D.T., New, S.A. Assaultive behavior: Know the risks. *J Psychosoc Nurs Ment Health Serv* 1991b; 29(11):25-30.

Blomhoff, S., Seim, S., Friis, S. Can prediction of violence among psychiatric inpatients be improved? *Hosp Community Psychiatry* 1990; 41:771-775.

Bradford, J. The forensic psychiatric aspects of schizophrenia. *Psychiatr J Univ Ottawa* 1983; 8:96-103.

Brailsford, D.S. Psychiatric hospitals—A further viewpoint. *Nursing Times* 1973a; 69(31):1001-1003.

Brailsford, D.S., Stevenson, J. Factors related to violent and unpredictable behavior in psychiatric hospitals. *Nursing Times* 1973b; 69(3):9-11.

Carmel, H., Hunter, M. Staff injuries from inpatient violence. *Hosp Community Psychiatry* 1989; 40:41-45.

Cocozza, J.J., Steadman, H.J. The failure of psychiatric prediction of dangerousness: Clear and convincing evidence. *Rutgers Law Review* 1984; 29:1048-1101.

Coffey, M.P. The violent patient. *J Adv Nurs* 1976; 1:341-350.

Colenda, C.C., Hamer, R.M. Antecedents and interventions for aggressive behavior of patients at a geropsychiatric state hospital. *Hosp Community Psychiatry* 1991; 42:287-292.

Colson, R.B., Allen, J.G., Coyne, L. An anatomy of countertransference: Staff reactions to difficult psychiatric hospital patients. *Hosp Community Psychiatry* 1986; 37:720-724.

Convey, J. A record of violence. *Nursing Times* 1986; 82(46):36-38.

Convit, A., Jaeger, J., Lin, S.P., Meisner, M., Volavka, J. Predicting assaultiveness in psychiatric inpatients: A pilot study. *Hosp Community Psychiatry* 1988; 39:429-434.

Dauner, A., Blair, D.T. Akathisia: When treatment creates a problem. *J Psychosoc Nurs Ment Health Serv* 1990; 28(10):13-18.

Davis, D., Boster, L. Multifaceted therapeutic interventions with the violent inpatient. *Hosp Community Psychiatry* 1988; 39:867-869.

Depp, F.C. Assaults in a public mental hospital. In J.R. Lion, W.H. Reid (Eds.), *Assaults in psychiatric facilities.* New York: Grune & Stratton, 1983.

Donat, D.C. Altercations among institutionalized psychogeriatric patients. *Gerontologist* 1986; 26(3):22-27.

Drummond, D.J., Sparr, L.F., Gordon, G.H. Hospital violence reduction among high risk patients. *JAMA* 1989; 261:2531-2534.

Dubin, R.W., Wilson, S.J., Mercer, C. Assaults against psychiatrists. *J Clin Psychiatry* 1988; 49:334-338.

Dubin, W. The role of fantasies, countertransference and psychological defenses in violence. *Hosp Comm Psychiatry* 1989; 40:1280-1283.

Durivage, A. Assaultive behavior: Before it happens. *Can J Psychiatry* 1989; 34:393-397.

Edwards, J., Jones, D., Reid, W. Physical assaults in a psychiatric unit. *Am J Psychiatry* 1988; 145:1568-1571.

Edwards, J., Reid, W. Violence in psychiatric facilities in Europe and the United

States. In J. Lion, W. Reid (Eds.) *Assaults in psychiatric facilities.* New York: Grune & Stratton, 1983.

Engle, F., Marsh, S. Helping the employee victim of violence in hospitals. *Hosp Community Psychiatry* 1986; 37:159-162.

Felthous, A.R. Liability of treaters for injuries to others. *Bull Am Acad Psychiatry Law* 1987; 15:115-125.

Fottrell, E. A study of violent behavior among patients in psychiatric hospitals. *Br J Psychiatry* 1990; 136:216-221.

Garrison, W. Predicting violent behavior in psychiatrically hospitalized boys. *Journal of Youth and Adolescence* 1984; 13:225-238.

Greenstein, R.A., Gariti, K.O., Garite, P., Ciccone, P.E. Violence prediction in the psychiatric clinic: An organizational approach. *VA Practitioners* 1990; 39:47-54.

Harrington, A.J. Hospital violence. *Nursing Mirror* 1984; 135(3):12-15.

Harris, G., Varney, G. A ten-year study of assaults and assaulters on a maximum security psychiatric unit. *Journal of Interpersonal Violence* 1986; 1:173-191.

Hodges, V., Sanford, D., Elzingers, D. The role of ward structure on nursing staff behaviors: An observational study of three psychiatric wards. *Acta Psychiatr Scand* 1986; 73:6-11.

Infantino, A.J., Musingo, S. Assaults and injuries among staff with and without training in aggression control techniques. *Hosp Community Psychiatry* 1985; 36:1312-1314.

Janofsky, J.S., Spears, S., Neubauer, D.N. Psychiatrists' accuracy in predicting violent behavior on an inpatient unit. *Hosp Community Psychiatry* 1988; 39:1090-1094.

Jones, M.K. Patient violence. *J Psychosoc Nurs Ment Health Serv* 1985; 23(6):12-17.

Kahneman, D., Tversky, A. Choices, values and frames. *Am Psychol* 1984; 39:341-350.

Kavanaugh, K.H. The cost of caring: Nursing on a psychiatric intensive care unit. *Human Organization* 1988; 47:242-251.

Kay, S., Wolkenfeld, F., Mirrill, L. Profiles of aggression among psychiatric patients: Nature and prevalence. *J Nerv Ment Dis* 1988; 176:539-546.

Krakowski, M., Convit, A., Jaeger, J. Neurological impairment in violent schizophrenic inpatients. *Am J Psychiatry* 1989; 146:849-853.

Lanza, M.L. How nurses react to patient assault. *J Psychosoc Nurs Ment Health Serv* 1985; 23(6):6-11.

Lanza, M.L. Factors relevant to patient assault. *Issues in Mental Health Nursing* 1988; 9:239-257.

Lawson, W., Yesavage, J., Werner, P. Race, violence and psychopathology. *J Clin Psychiatry* 1984; 45:294-297.

Lee, H., Villar, O., Juthani, N. Characteristics and behavior of patients involved in psychiatric ward incidents. *Hosp Community Psychiatry* 1989; 40:1295-1297.

Lion, J.R., Pasternak, S.A. Countertransference reactions to violent patients. *Am J Psych* 1973; 130:207-210.

Lion, J.R. Training for battle: Thoughts on managing aggressive patients. *Hosp Comm Psychiatry* 1987; 38:882-884.

Lion, J.R., Snyder, W., Merrill, G.L. Underreporting of assaults in a state hospital. *Hosp Community Psychiatry* 1981; 32:497-498.

Madden, D.J. Voluntary and involuntary treatment of aggressive patients. *Am J Psychiatry* 1977; 134:553-555.

Madden, D.J., Lion, J.R., Penna, M.W. Assault on psychiatrists by patients. *Am J Psych* 1976; 133:422-425.

McEvoy, G.K. Central nervous system agents. In G.K. McEvoy (Ed.), *American*

Hospital Formularly Service, drug information. Bethesda, MD: American Society of Hospital Pharmacists, 1989.

McNeil, D.E., Binder, R.L., Greenfield, T.K. Predictors of violence in civilly committed acute psychiatric patients. *Am J Psychiatry* 1988; 145:965-970.

Meddaugh, D.I. Staff abuse by the nursing home patient. *Clinical Gerontologist* 1986; 6(2):45-57.

Mills, M.J. Civil commitment: The relationship between perceived dangerousness and mental illness. *Arch Gen Psychiatry* 1988; 45:770-772.

Monagle, J.F. *Risk management: A guide for health care professionals.* Rockville, MD: Aspen Publications, 1985.

Morrison, E.F. A typology of violent psychiatric patients in a public hospital. *Scholarly Inquiry for Nursing Practice* 1990a; 4(1):65-82.

Morrison, E.F. The tradition of toughness: A study of nonprofessional nursing care in psychiatric settings. *Image* 1990b; 22(1):32-37.

Morton, P.C. Managing assault. *Am J Nurs* 1986; 10:1114-1116.

Mullen, P.E. Mental disorders and dangerousness. *Aust N Z J Psychiatry* 1984; 18:8-17.

Munjas, B.N. Clinicity and mental health illness: Does "nursing care" maintain it? *Issues in Mental Health Nursing* 1980; 3:1-13.

Negley, E.N., Manley, J.T. Environmental interventions in assaultive behavior. *Journal of Gerontological Nursing* 1990; 16(3):29-33.

Noble, P., Rodger, S. Violence by psychiatric patients. *Br J Psychiatry* 1989; 155:384-390.

Northrop, C. Nursing actions in litigation. In G. Chapman-Cliburn (Ed.), *Risk management and quality assurance.* Chicago: Joint Commission, 1986.

Palmstierna, T., Wistedt, B. Staff observation aggression scale: Presentation and evaluation. *Acta Psychiatr Scand* 1987; 76:657-663.

Pearson, M., Wilmot, E., Padi, M. A study of violent behavior among inpatients in a psychiatric hospital. *Br J Psychiatry* 1986; 149:232-235.

Rada, R.T. The violent patient: Rapid assessment and management. *J Psychosom* 1981; 22:101-109.

Reid, W.H. Clinical evaluation of violent patients. *Psychiatr Clin North Am* 1988; 11(4):527-535.

Reid, W.H., Bollinger, M.F., Edwards, G. Assaults in hospitals. *Bull Am Acad Psychiatry Law* 1985a; 13:1-4.

Reid, W.H., Bollinger, M., Edwards, J. Serious injury by inpatients. *Psychosomatics* 1989; 30:54-56.

Reid, W.H., Edwards, G., Bollinger, M.F. Assaults by inpatients: Frequency and liability. *Psychiatr Med* 1985b; 2:315-319.

Rofman, E.S., Askinazi, C., Fant, E. The prediction of dangerous behavior in emergency civil commitment. *Am J Psychiatry* 1980; 137:1061-1064.

Roper, J.M., Anderson, L.R. The interactional dynamics of violence: Part 1. An acute psychiatric ward. *Arch Psychiatr Nurs* 1991; 5:209-215.

Rosenbaum, M. Violence and the unstructured psychiatric milieu. *Hosp Community Psychiatry* 1990; 41:721-724.

Rossi, A., Jacobs, M., Monteleone, M. Violence or fear inducing behavior. *Hosp Community Psychiatry* 1985; 36:643-647.

Rossi, A.M., Jacobs, M., Monteleone, M., Olsen, R., Surber, R., Winkler, E., et al. Characteristics of psychiatric patients who engage in assaultive or other fear-inducing behaviors. *J Nerv Ment Dis* 1986; 174:154-160.

Rubin, I., Wolkon, G., Yamamoto, S. Physical attacks on psychiatric residents by patients. *J Nerv Ment Dis* 1980; 168:243-245.

Sales, B.D., Overcast, J.D., Merrikan, K.J. Workers compensation protection for assault and batteries on mental health professionals. In J.R. Lion and W.H. Reid (Eds.), *Assaults within psychiatric facilities*. New York: Grune & Stratton, 1983.

Schmidt, L.G., Grohman, R., Heimehen, H. Adverse drug reactions. *Acta Psychiatr Scand* 1985; 70:77-89.

Sheridan, M., Henrion, R., Baxter, V. Precipitants of violence in a psychiatric inpatient setting. *Hosp Community Psychiatry* 1990; 41:776-780.

Soloff, P. Seclusion and restraint. In J. Lion, W. Reid (Eds.), *Assaults within psychiatric hospitals*. New York: Grune & Stratton, 1983.

Stanton, A.H. *The mental hospital*. New York: Basic Books, 1954.

Steadman, H.J. Special problems in the prediction of violence among the mentally ill. In T.K. Hays, T.K. Roberts, K.S. Olway (Eds.), *Violence and the violent individual*. New York: Spectrum, 1981.

Straus, M.A., Gelles, R.J. *Physical violence in American families*. New Brunswick: Transaction Publishers, 1990.

Swanson, J.W., Holzer, C.E., Ganju, V.K., Jono, R.T. Violence and psychiatric disorder in the community. *Hosp Community Psychiatry* 1990; 41:761-770.

Synder, W. Administrative monitoring of assaultive patients and staff. In J.R. Lion, W.H. Reid (Eds.), *Assaults within psychiatric facilities*. New York: Grune & Stratton, 1983.

Tardiff, K. A survey of assault by chronic patients in a state hospital. In J. Lion W. Reid (Eds.), *Assaults within psychiatric facilities*. New York: Grune & Stratton, 1983.

Tardiff, K. Characteristics of assaultive patients in private hospitals. *Am J Psychiatry* 1984; 141:1232-1235.

Tardiff, K., Sweillam, A. Assaultive behavior among chronic patients. *Am J Psychiatry* 1982; 139:212-215.

Toch, H. *Police, prisons and the problem of violence*. Rockville, MD: National Institute of Mental Health, 1977.

Weaver, S.M., Broome, A.K., Kat, B.J.B. Some patterns of disturbed behavior. *J Adv Nurs* 1978; 3:251-263.

Winkler, E.L., Wommack, A. Characteristics of psychiatric patients who engage in assaultive or other fear-inducing behaviors. *J Nerv Ment Dis* 1986; 174:154-160.

4

Violence and the Brain-Injured Patient

By William Burke, PhD; and Bruce Bird, PhD

Violent individuals in inpatient or residential psychiatric or rehabilitation programs are major challenges for the treatment team. Patients with aggressive or violent behavior resulting from neurological damage exhibit differences in symptoms and pathophysiology and respond differently to treatment compared with patients who have psychiatric disorders. Unfortunately, differential diagnosis and treatment does not always occur, and neurologically impaired patients frequently find their way into traditional psychiatric units or the criminal justice system. This chapter will review treatment approaches to managing and treating aggressive and violent patients who have neurological damage. Issues of etiology, diagnosis, and treatment are reviewed, and practical examples, with strategies for successful intervention, are provided for therapists and caregivers. Pharmacological and behavioral approaches are more extensively reviewed, as they have received more attention in the literature.

There are certain philosophical assumptions held throughout this review. One is that treating violent patients requires a learning/teaching approach that involves the gradual removal of external restrictions and controls, and, therefore, implies some level of risk. Managing these risks will be discussed in some detail. A second assumption is that successful intervention usually requires a transdisciplinary approach, where treatment technologies of more than one discipline are integrated into a cohesive approach that addresses the physical, cognitive, emotional/behavioral, and neuropharmacological needs of the patient. Finally, violence and aggression are behaviors that greatly limit a person's acceptability in society and produce severe penalties on individual freedom. Treating violence and aggression requires teaching the patient not only to reduce undesired behavioral excess, but also to increase positive, pro-social behaviors to better engage those with whom they interact in society. Pro-social behaviors are the opposite of antisocial behaviors. They are behaviors appropriate to the social environment in which the actions are taking place. Strategies and examples illustrating the importance of this approach will be reviewed.

Prevalence and Etiology

The developing literature on the persistent effects of head injury and neurological disorders indicates that the behavioral, social, and cognitive problems are often the most disabling for patients and families (Brooks, 1984; Burke, 1988a). The prevalence of violence or significant aggression has often not been separated from global rating categories such as "anger control" or "losing temper," which have been estimated to be prevalent in relatively high percentages of patients years after brain injury. Klonoff and Prigatano (1987), in a review of family member reactions to brain injury, report high frequencies of behavioral disorders and aggression. Thomsen (1984) reported that physical and cognitive disorders were much less critical factors in persons with brain injury resuming normal lifestyles than psychosocial or personality disturbances. Lewis and her colleagues (1986) have found that an alarmingly high percentage of adult criminal offenders who have records noting significantly high instances of assaults and murders have neurological disorders usually secondary to closed head injuries.

The etiology of violent behavior in people with neurological damage is conceptualized as an interaction of premorbid learning history or personality, neurological damage, and the person's present environment (Howard, 1988). Dunlop et al (1991), in a review of case records of traumatically brain-injured patients, found a potential relationship between premorbid alcohol abuse and violent assaults with deterioration in behavior after an initial period of recovery from injuries. Pelco et al (1992) found no support for the behavioral problems in children with head injuries versus other children in the general community. However, results of other studies have supported the general conclusion that in adults, premorbid personality characteristics (aggression and impulsivity, among others) are predictive of higher incidences of postneurologic insult aggression (Wesolowski, 1988b). An understanding of the neurology of aggression has been developing through both basic and clinical research and is producing a picture of hierarchically organized control of aggression. A brief review is in order, as the neuropathology has significant implications for treatment approaches.

Focal lesions, tumors, or focal neurochemical abnormalities in hypothalmic centers have been associated with unplanned stereotypic, repetitive, generalized (not specifically directed to select stimuli) aggression (Baer, 1991). These attacks are characterized as primitive, without use of weapons, plans, or special targets. Two excellent case reviews of episodic dyscontrol with violence in patients with craniopharyngiomas may be found in Tonkonogy and Geller (1992). Differential diagnosis requires careful behavioral observations for such clinical indicators as the specificity or stereotype of aggressive responses, clinical histories for possible chemical agents or traumatic events, and the use of diagnostic imaging to identify structural neuropathological changes. Hypothalmic lesions also may alter sleep patterns, appetite, regulation of hormones, and other autonomic functions (Baer, 1991).

The amygdala and temporal regions are proposed to modulate hypothalmic aggression based on sensory information received from primary areas of the cortex. As reported initially by Kluver and Bucy (1939), lesions of the amygdala-temporal lobe complex produce docile, apathetic behavior. The Kluver-Bucy syndrome can result from encephalitis, head injury, or degenerative diseases. In contrast, temporal lobe epilepsy (TLE) produces severely aggressive responses to stimuli, presumably as epileptic activity drives the hypothalmic aggression centers. Baer et al (1981) have proposed that individuals suffering from TLE demonstrate an exacerbated emotional response to stimuli, showing increased autonomic responses and random and interictal rage during seizures. Interictal behavior begins at the start of the electrical activity, continues through the seizure, and into the postictal phase. Specific interictal behavior patterns are evident, and include quick provocation to anger but with strong expressions of morality, paranoia, religious zeal, intense guilt, and sustained and intense affect of anger or indignation.

Lesions of the dorsolateral convexity, which sever reciprocal connections to the rest of the neocortex, produce apathy and lack of activity (Baer, 1991). Lesions of the orbitofrontal cortex produce impulsivity, lack of self-criticism, poor planning, disregard for consequences, and aggression. The aggression is characterized by provocation by slight or insignificant stimuli, little or no regret, and poorly sustained anger. Fornazzari et al (1992) have recently reported on three patients with deep orbitofrontal cortical epileptic foci, who also suffered from violent visual hallucinations and aggression. These cases were particularly interesting in regard to the intense hallucinatory fear produced during seizures. Damage to both orbitofrontal and dorsolateral frontal cortical areas may produce a patient with swings from apathy to aggression. It is also important to note that diffuse axonal injury, which occurs in a significant proportion of severe head injuries, is likely to produce significant frontal lobe damage and resulting behavioral disturbances (Burke, 1988a; Namerow, 1987; Wesolowski, 1988a).

Overview of Intervention Strategies

Interventions for aggressive behavior in patients with neurological disorders may be grouped into four basic categories: neurosurgery to remove damaged or malfunctioning tissue; drugs to normalize abnormal neuropharmacology; traditional psychotherapy for adjustment; and behavior therapy to teach needed social skills and self-control. This review will focus on pharmacological and behavioral treatments because they have generally been viewed as the treatments of choice in producing effective outcomes, and the psychiatric nurse is involved in direct monitoring and implementation of drug or behavioral treatment programs.

Of these interventions, the administration of medication and monitoring therapeutic levels, effects, and side effects require considerable skill on the part of the psychiatric nurse. However, the day-to-day social, caregiving, and teaching strategies used by nurses (and nurses' aides) and aggressive patients present far greater challenges and opportunities for patient learning and behavior change. Therefore, the section on behavioral therapy will receive more attention in this review. Interested readers are referred to more extensive reviews of neurosurgical (Jennett, 1981) and traditional psychotherapy (Prigatano, 1991) for neurological disorders.

PHARMACOLOGICAL INTERVENTION

Pharmacological treatments have been aimed at a variety of central nervous system mechanisms, differentially acting to reduce general arousal through sedation, to reduce emotional reactions of anxiety or anger, or to increase inhibition of impulsive behavior, all having the final benefit of reducing aggression (De Konig, 1991). Obviously, in patients with neurological damage who are experiencing cognitive and emotional dysfunctions, the sometimes unwanted side effects of decreased arousal or specific cognitive/attentional deficits may be especially debilitating. The selection of pharmacological agents and their therapeutic levels is therefore very complicated in these patients. The reader is directed to more detailed reviews regarding the use of pharmacological treatment following brain injury (Cope, 1987; Zasler, 1992).

Antipsychotic drugs are proposed to block dopamine receptors in limbic and striatal areas producing psychomotor slowing and emotional quieting, and they are frequently prescribed to alter behavioral problems associated with brain injury. Despite their reported success in normalizing cognitive and behavioral functions in psychiatric populations and patients with neurological disorders, they have generally had mixed results in those with head injuries, often producing unwanted sedation (Cardenas, 1987). In the clinical experience of the authors, neuroleptics such as haloperidol that act to reduce psychotic thinking and agitation in psychiatric patients have an unfortunate opposite effect in individuals with brain injuries, often exacerbating these symptoms. This opposite effect has been found particularly in patients suffering from temporal lobe epilepsy. Tardive dyskenesia, sedation, and a host of other autonomic side effects require careful monitoring when these agents are used (Haas, 1987).

Catecholamine agonists include L-dopa (now often used with carbidopa or a monoamine oxidase type B inhibitor to reduce unwanted side effects), amantadine hydrochloride, bromocryptine, and the psychostimulants (methylphenidate, dextroamphetamine, and pemoline). Dopaminergic and noradrenergic systems are proposed to be involved in arousal, attention, motor control, sleep-wake cycles, learning and memory, affective disturbances, and control of aggression. Special attention is given in this review to two types of drugs that have an impact in adrenergic systems. One additional drug with the potential for reducing aggression is clonidine (Horn, 1987).

Gabaminergic agonists, including the antispasmodics baclofen and diazepam (valium), and the anticonvulsants (valporate sodium), the barbiturates, and the benzodiazepines are not generally used in managing aggression as their sedative effects impair other aspects of cognitive, affective, and motor function (Zasler, 1992). Anticonvulsants, such as phenobarbital, phenytoin, and carbamazepine, are often used as seizure prophylactics following head injuries. Valproic acid has recently gained favor as the drug of choice for multifocal and generalized seizures, whereas carbamazepine remains the choice to treat complex partial seizures (Zasler, 1992). Carbamazepine has also been reported to reduce behavioral disturbances and aggression in a variety of patients with neurological injuries (Horn, 1987).

As noted earlier, two types of drugs that have an impact on adrenergic systems deserve special mention for their utility in controlling aggressive behavior in neurological disorders. One class is the beta-blockers, or antihypertensives, particularly propranolol. The exact mechanisms of propranolol are as yet uncertain and may include beta-blockade, serotonergic agonist, or membrane stabilization action (Horn, 1987). Whatever its mechanism, propranolol has been found to be effective in reducing hyperirritability and severe aggression with a variety of neurological disorders, ranging from Korsakoff's syndrome (Yudofsky, 1984) to traumatic brain injury (Elliott, 1977).

The tricyclic antidepressants, commonly used for treating depression, have been reported to be effective in reducing the nondirected agitation and aggression found in the early stages of recovery from brain injury; however, they are not effective in the later stages of recovery (Mysiw, 1987). Finally, lithium, best known for its effective treatment of bipolar affective disorders, has been reported to reduce aggressive symptoms as well as other symptoms related to agitation, restlessness, and hypomania in a variety of neurological patients (Glenn, 1987).

Most reviews of the benefits and risks of pharmacological treatment of aggression and related behavioral disturbances due to neurological disorders have stressed the ethical issues involved in such treatments (Cope, 1987; Haas, 1987; Zasler, 1992), many of which involve the direct care staff:

- The primacy of a behavioral, environmental approach (pharmacological treatment may correct the neuropathophysiology problem and set up the patient to learn, but will not teach the patient what to do);
- The importance of unwanted restrictions in arousal, attention, cognition, etc;
- The need to rely on empirical evidence in carefully monitored trials;
- The danger in selecting less expensive drugs versus more expensive teaching/learning treatments;
- The importance of informed consents (benefits, risks, alternatives);
- The importance of evaluating and periodically re-evaluating competency for consent.

When used judiciously, pharmacological treatment dramatically enhances the learning ability of the person with neurological damage. Applying teaching strategies along with appropriate pharmacological intervention follows.

BEHAVIOR THERAPY

In this review, behavior therapy refers to those procedures and associated research that is sometimes termed applied behavior analysis or behavior modification, but that all have the distinguishing features of a focus on observable, measurable behavior; reliance on objective measures of behavior change in making treatment decisions; the analysis and manipulation of the environment to understand, predict, and teach behaviors; and learning principles applied to change behavior. In the last decade, behavior therapy applications in neurological disorders have begun in two areas: behavioral medicine, in which behavior therapy and psychophysiology were wedded to assess, study, and treat physiological problems associated with neurological disorders; and applied behavior analysis, or behavior therapy, integrated into rehabilitation service programs for people with brain damage (Burke, 1986; 1988a; 1988b; Burke & Wesolowski, 1987; Wesolowski & Burke, 1988b). In the latter, applications of a wealth of technical knowledge from treatment and teaching people with developmental disabilities were expanded and modified with great success to meet the diverse needs of head injured and neurologically impaired individuals (Burke, 1988b; 1991; Howard, 1988). Interested readers are referred to Burke, Wesolowski, and Blackerby (1988) for a more extensive review of behavior therapy for individuals with brain injuries.

A traditional behavior therapy approach begins with an attempt to identify antecedent, behavior, and consequence as components or steps in interpersonal processes. The underlying principles of learning indicate that behavior that occurs in the presence of certain stimuli and that is rewarded has an increased likelihood of occurring again. This is the basic principle of operant conditioning (Skinner, 1953). Corollary principles are that behavior that is not rewarded extinguishes or goes away, behavior that is punished is suppressed, and behavior that successfully avoids or escapes punishment is strengthened and will recur in similar situations (this is negative reinforcement). A second form of learning, "classical conditioning," occurs when stimuli are associated with autonomic, reflexive responses (fear, emotions) and acquire some control over the response.

In the case of the aggressive patient, a behavior therapy approach begins by attempting to understand how prior learning occurred and how the current environment may be maintaining the behavior. A detailed history must be obtained that identifies behavioral skills, deficits and excesses, stimuli, or antecedents (including people and situations) that reliably predict aggressive responses and consequences of responses, historically and now. A "functional analysis" of current behavior is then conducted, in which the probable relationships among antecedents, behaviors, and consequences are estimated and a plan is developed to further assess and treat the aggressive behavior. The treatment plan generally involves the following steps:

- Identifying and defining behaviors to be assessed and changed (including problem behaviors to be reduced and target behaviors to be increased);
- Measuring the current frequency, duration, and intensity of the problem and target behaviors;
- Developing a functional analysis of each behavior assessed;
- Intervention (a learning/teaching program);
- Programming for generalization, which is the transfer of learning across times, environments, and maintenance over extended periods;
- Ongoing evaluation of data and corrections to the analysis and plan.

In the case of the neurologically impaired client, cognitive, physical, and pharmacological variables must also be considered in analyzing and treating the problem behavior.

Two examples illustrate the importance of a thorough historical review and functional analysis of aggressive behaviors. Two patients exhibit explosive verbal and physical aggression multiple times each day. In both cases, these behaviors are carefully defined and an observation system is set up so that the direct care staff can observe for antecedents and consequences of verbal and physical aggression. In one case, aggression occurs following the patient's requests for cigarettes, beverages, food, and other tangible items, which are initially denied by staff and then provided when the patient begins to become aggressive. This patient is particularly abusive in the presence of his mother. In the second case, aggression occurs in demand situations when the patient is being asked to perform certain therapeutic tasks involving attention and memory. This patient's behavior usually escalates to the point where he is returned to his room and therapies are terminated.

It is likely in both cases that aggression is functioning to produce rewards. In the first case, aggression produces tangible rewards and is likely to occur again when these items are desired. In addition, this patient's mother probably has a history of rewarding aggression and may be a stimulus that sets the occasion for abusive behavior. To decrease aggression, this patient must be taught that aggression does not produce rewards, so the staff must ensure that no rewards are obtained as a result of aggression. Equally important is the need to teach the patient alternative behaviors for obtaining rewards, those pro-social behaviors of asking politely and waiting patiently for reward situations.

In the second case, aggression appears to be reinforced by avoidance or escape from demands, and so it is likely to continue in those situations. This patient must be taught that staying with a task in a demanding situation is rewarding. A positive learning program would break down the demanding task into sufficiently small steps so that rewards could be obtained as the patient progresses through a session. Developing a task analysis (steps required to complete the task) and then shaping responses so that more complex responses or a "chain" of behaviors can be learned more easily is a common behavioral strategy. In both cases, stimulus control of the newly learned behavior would have to be extended to multiple situations and environments and, as possible, to the patient's own control.

In both case examples, neurological damage might significantly complicate the functional analysis and treatment approach. In the first case, for example, patients with orbitofrontal or temporal lobe neurological damage often exhibit impulsivity and explosive aggression. As noted earlier, the neuroanatomical damage may be treated pharmacologically, sometimes with positive results, sometimes with minimal results. Whether or not a pharmacological approach is helpful, patients with impulsive and explosive aggression should be provided with behavior therapy to help them learn self-control and appreciate pro-social behaviors to obtain rewards in the home environment.

Eames (1988) argues convincingly that the use of pharmacological treatments can prepare an individual to learn by altering states of arousal, anger, or attention. However, he stresses that only learning-based treatment strategies will teach more acceptable behaviors. An appropriate behavioral approach might therefore employ the following procedures:

- Protection of the patient, other patients, and staff from harm or aggression by structuring the environment and having adequate and sufficiently well-trained staff to safely handle an aggressive outburst;
- Removing the rewarding effects of aggression so that it extinguishes and loses its response strength;
- Cuing the patient to engage in behavior that is incompatible with aggression, and rewarding that behavior;
- Modeling appropriate pro-social behavior and rewarding the patient for practicing such behavior. For example, rehearsing how to ask politely for a cigarette and how to wait for its delivery;
- Shaping the patient's behavior to enable the patient to wait longer to receive the reward, during both practice and real situations;

• Ensuring that social reinforcers (verbal praise, attention, smiling, staff contact) are closely paired with tangible rewards to increase their reward value and to ensure that appropriate versus inappropriate behavior is reinforced, then fading the tangible rewards as progress occurs;
• Teaching all staff and the family to use those procedures found to be effective;
• Teaching patients to monitor and manage their own behavior program and to feel good about progress.

In the second case example, the possible existence of underlying neuropathology is probable. A multidisciplinary team approach, with disciplines including neuropsychology, speech/language therapy, occupational therapy, and others, is most helpful in constructing a comprehensive picture of how to handle functional deficits. Attention deficit and impulsivity may be complicated by other cognitive dysfunctions, such as a memory impairment. Specification of the exact nature of these deficits is critical so that a task analysis or breaking down of responses needed to function in any setting can be done in a way to maximize the patient's successes in small steps (Burke, 1988).

Unless there is consideration of cognitive dysfunctions and an awareness of the need to develop strategies aimed at correcting them, behavior therapy approaches with aggressive neurological patients may easily fail. However, the use of such simple compensatory devices as a memory notebook may have tremendous influence on a variety of rehabilitation processes, having a positive impact on both retrospective and prospective memory (Zencius, 1991). For example, the aggressive behavior of the neurological patient may well be in response to the frustration experienced due to cognitive impairments. The use of compensatory devices, such as memory aids, task analyses, and visual and verbal cues, often reduces this frustration, thereby reducing the aggressive behavior.

Cognition has been defined as the use of mental processes and the knowledge base needed to make decisions regarding appropriateness and functionality of interacting with the environment, to execute these decisions, to monitor responses to determine the appropriateness and accuracy of these decisions, and to adjust behavior if it is determined to be inappropriate or inaccurate (Adamovich, 1991). Self-initiation, problem solving, and self-monitoring and regulating or modulating behavior are all components of what is defined as "executive function" (Lezak, 1989).

All of these cognitive functions are critically involved in most normal human learning. However, in neurologically damaged patients when learning by instruction is deficient, the patient must be taught by using a combination of repeated trials of practice to learn a given task or behavior. In addition, the use of compensatory strategies to develop cues for self-control of behavior are often essential to reducing aggressive behavior with the neurological patient. For example, for patients with short-term memory impairment or attentional disorders, a higher density of reinforcement and smaller (and shorter) tasks may be key procedures to reduce frustration and increase the likelihood of learning new behaviors. Patients who initially require frequent cues or reinforcers can be shaped to produce longer intervals of appropriate behavior with the frequencies of cues also faded to longer intervals. And, as noted earlier, teaching the patient to self-monitor and self-reward will facilitate self-control so that the patient will transfer and maintain skills across environments and time.

Designing a Transdisciplinary Behavior Program

A well-designed transdisciplinary behavioral approach would therefore expand on the strict applied behavior analysis approach defined above, and would include the following components:
• A thorough history and comprehensive neurological and interdisciplinary evaluations, especially neuropsychological and behavioral, to identify possible neurological and learning contributions to aggressive behavior;
• A thorough inventory of behavioral skills, excesses, and deficits, and a survey and sampling of reinforcers obtained from the patient and caregivers;
• Careful definitions of behaviors to be observed and measured (to allow for reliability) that are developed so that behavioral, pharmacological, and physiological data can be collected concurrently;
• Assessment of responses (defined above) in various situations and times to create a functional analysis of behavior, so that possible antecedent-behavior-consequence relationships may be defined. Experienced clinicians and caregivers will identify possible cognitive or neurological contributions to problem behaviors in their evaluations;
• A treatment program that attempts to teach positive, appropriate, pro-social behavior in both intense situations throughout the day and incidentally as social situations arise provides adequate physical control and protection of patient and staff as the learning process develops; provides decelerative procedures in accordance with legal, ethical, and professional standards; monitors and modifies pharmacological regimens as the data indicate; and uses extensive objective measures to assess progress and modify treatment as needed.

ETHICAL CONSIDERATIONS
The ethics of treating violence and aggression with brain-injured patients has been reviewed by several prominent authors (Haas, 1987; Glenn, 1987). Of particular note are the following considerations for establishing ethical safeguards:
1. The use of pharmacological agents is often considered more restrictive than behavioral procedures that require privilege restrictions or hands-on physical restraint as needed.

2. Policies and procedures that ensure informed consent are appropriate and must be established and regularly reviewed.
3. Decelerative procedures must always be applied after (or in combination with) accelerative treatment designed to teach alternative behaviors to aggression.
4. A hierarchy of authorization/approval for increasingly restrictive procedures and a training and credentialing program should be established for restrictive, risk-related, and especially aversive procedures.
5. Data reviews from the perspective of professional and public acceptance standards should be frequent and documented.
6. An entire risk management system must combine elements 1 through 4 with frequent reviews of supervision policies and practices; the communication among staff and documentation systems in areas of direct care, clinical treatment, and medical/health specialists; a rigorous incident reporting, review, and corrective action system; and an overall clinical and risk management quality assurance system.
7. Elements 1 through 5 must be reviewed for compliance with professional licensing and accreditation, and other legal standards for clinical services and patient rights.
8. The review process should contain in vivo audits of not only documentation, but also actual delivery of services as noted in the documentation.

PRACTICAL CONSIDERATIONS

Many specific practical strategies dramatically influence the efficacy of behavioral medicine treatments. For the practicing nurse, clinician, or caregiver, the most important consideration is that the patient learns something from every interaction. Caregivers are therefore first and foremost teachers; if they are able to systematically teach appropriate behavior, they will dramatically influence their patients. Each time a caregiver interacts with a patient, the patient learns something. If the treatment team is functioning well, these opportunities will be well structured to maximize appropriate learning. Specific practical suggestions are discussed below.

Assessment Scales. Several assessment scales exist that may be helpful to clinicians and caregivers in objectively evaluating individual patients as compared with others and over the course of treatment. The Overt Aggression Scale (Yudofsky, 1986) is particularly easy to use, but provides reliable data regarding the incidence and intensity of violent and aggressive behavior.

Severity Versus Frequency of Aggression. Severe aggression often occurs in the form of an "outburst" or "episode" with multiple verbal and physical responses that may continue into a physical (hands-on) restraint. Indications of treatment success may begin as decreases in the intensity or duration of these episodes, so measuring the time of these "outbursts" as well as their intensity may help provide sensitivity to treatment changes.

That is, a treatment may be succeeding as indicated by decreases in the duration of "outbursts," or the intensity has decreased from physical to only verbal aggression even though the frequency has remained the same.

Antecedents to Aggression. Most patients have identifiable behavioral precursors that reliably precede an act of physical aggression. Breaking the "chain" of responses can be an effective procedure to reduce or limit aggression. This requires measuring components, teaching patients to identify the precursor, produce an appropriate incompatible behavior, and reinforce (self-reinforce) the appropriate behavior.

Anger control programs usually feature self-identification of physical indicators of anger and teach alternative and calming responses, self-instructions to remain calm, production of an appropriate social response ("I am really upset"), self-recording of the response, and self-reinforcement ("I did a good job of controlling myself") (Wesolowski, 1988). Many neurological patients will require checklists and cues to use this type of anger control strategy. Such techniques are typically used in intense training/rehearsal sessions throughout the day in which the patient is asked to role play with staff and data are obtained. Measures of aggression are also taken throughout the day in all situations. The patient is also cued by staff to use the rehearsed anger control procedure. This program should use probes, or "barbs," in which the staff first inform the patient and then proceed to produce a provocative precursor to anger, ie, a criticism, throughout the day and reinforce the patient for appropriate self-control. When the patient exhibits self-control in the face of the typical precursor, extensive reinforcement should occur. Interested readers are referred to a brief "how-to" manual on this topic by Wesolowski and Burke (1988).

Subtle Precursors. Patients with no easy way to identify observable precursors are certainly more challenging to treat. The authors have experience with a number of these patients. The key components to successful treatment have been careful observations by staff and sometimes intense training of the patient to self-identify the subtle precursors to their aggressive behavior.

Reinforcing. Reinforcers are sometimes not easily identified for the patient. A thorough assessment includes a comprehensive survey by the patient and staff to identify tangible, social, and activity reinforcers. Manipulative, cognitively impaired, and psychiatric patients may give verbally incorrect information, so observing for antecedent-behavior-consequence relationships that appear to maintain behavior is important. Many patients will claim that a decelerative procedure such as "time out" does not bother them, but if aggressive behaviors decrease, the procedure is effective.

Time Out. The term "time out" in the behavioral literature has a specific technical meaning: it is defined as a period and situation in which a patient is removed from access to a previously reinforcing environment or event that, when regularly applied as a consequence of a response, produces a decrease in that response. Time out is not simply the act of placing patients in chairs away from the group or having patients go to their room. In fact, if patients are frustrated by a difficult task, explode in violence, and are removed to their room or to a time out room, this may actually be a case of negative reinforcement or escape learning, in which the patient's aggression is reinforced by being removed from an unpleasant situation. Time out must be therefore carefully applied and monitored to ensure that it is not misapplied. Patients with strong responses to social reinforcement are particularly affected by time out. However, for patients who prefer to isolate themselves, alternative procedures must be selected; time away from others may actually be a rewarding privilege for these patients.

Token Economies. A "token economy" technically defined in the applied behavior analysis literature refers to a system of rules and procedures in which materials or verbal or written scores are consequences for specific responses, and those consequences in turn provide the responder access to "primary" reinforcers (tangible reinforcers, preferred activities), also according to specified rules. Token systems have significant use, as caregivers can use them to provide small mediators or indicators of rewards that can be easily applied incrementally, or to reinforce brief periods of appropriate behavior that can be extended into a longer period prior to delivering a primary reinforcer. A common form is a point system or privilege in which clients earn points for certain appropriate behavior and then earn certain privileges, or groups of privileges, for responses sometimes defined as "levels" of performance. Several practical considerations are warranted.

Individualizing treatment is a critical goal for neurological rehabilitation programs. Each client's functional analysis, response repertoire, reinforcer preferences, and projected home residential and work environments should be considered in designing a program. The ease of implementing group token economies with more easily trained and maintained consistency of caregivers must always be tempered by this primary need to individualize treatment. In addition, the use of a token system must always be designed to be either withdrawn or adapted to the home environment.

Although these generalizations and maintenance problems are a key to successful outcomes in all rehabilitation treatments, they are particularly important with token systems. The less artificial and more easily arranged in the home environment, the greater the likelihood the token system will succeed.

For example, creating a system in which an aggressive client must handle artificial tangible tokens or a complex privilege system for outings may be impossible to transfer to a real world work environment. Creating a system in which clients score their own behavior on a score sheet; report to a counselor, home manager, or family member; regulate their own outings according to the level of responsibility they have shown; and weekly review their behavioral scores and real monetary earnings from their job with significant supporters would have a much greater chance of maintaining this over extended periods.

Generalization and Durability of Outcomes. The transfer and durability of learned skills to the home, educational, or vocational environments that are critical for successful outcomes may not automatically occur. In the literature on behavioral technology, there is a growing technology for programming the generalization or transfer of skills from one set of stimuli to another (Burke, 1988a). Learning principles propose that responses reinforced in the presence of a particular set of stimuli will be more strongly controlled by those stimuli if they are easily discriminable and salient. Researchers have also shown that responses reinforced at irregular intervals or frequencies are stronger (they extinguish or stop when reinforcers stop) than those reinforced at each occurrence (more slowly).

In practice, this means that patients can learn inappropriate behavior because an environment or a person accidentally reinforces inappropriate behavior, and that such behavior may be durable and may be demonstrated only in certain specific situations. For example, a client who has learned self-control in a therapeutic environment may exhibit aggressive behavior when a family member comes to visit, because the family member has a previously established history of accidentally rewarding aggressive behavior. The client may have to be taught that this significant person triggers certain behavior, resulting in specific consequences. In addition, the family member must be taught the teaching (maintenance) program. Although it is often difficult to engage family members, this will be critical to a successful return to the home environment.

Because a visiting family member often sets the occasion for a return to aggressive behavior, the family may not see the progress the client has made when they are not around and so will be harder to engage. One helpful technique is to videotape the client exhibiting self-control in what formerly were provoking situations. This often helps the therapist, who must be supportive but direct in discussing how the family may have fed into problems and now must change.

Self-Control and Natural Consequences. Once appropriate pro-social behavior begins to occur at significant rates in the natural environment, it will produce some amount of natural consequences that will reinforce and, thus, help maintain it. However, in addition to setting up families, caregivers, work supervisors, cue sheets, and other strategies in the natural environment, all of which will augment these natural consequences, patients should be taught self-control strategies to monitor and manage their own behaviors. Details on principles and strategies for training self-control in head-injured clients have been provided elsewhere (Wesolowski, 1988b). A few helpful techniques, however, are described here.

The overall strategy should be to position the client to manage more behavior, while reducing the effort that caregivers, supporters, or supervisors expend in setting up and reinforcing self-control programs. For patients with cognitive or executive function problems, daily calendars should be expanded into "memory notebooks" that provide more detailed task-analyzed steps for patients to make it through the day. External cuing devices, such as a wrist watch with an hourly alarm, can be used to teach clients to refer to their memory notebook, which then prompts clients to do certain things. Rehearsing an anger-control self-calming program and recording that it was practiced could be followed by a daily self-reinforcement review initially with the supervisor, then alone; clients would be taught to review their own records for the day and to reinforce themselves with an extra treat (ie, activity) just as most people do if they have performed well. Such programs reduce the burden and costs of care and foster the independence, self-determination, and dignity that people with disabilities often need to achieve.

Risk Management. The authors have had experience in working with patients in a continuum of care that allows very aggressive patients to move from a secure unit to a supported apartment as they demonstrate progress; patients may be moved back into restrictive care for brief periods if violence recurs. These brief returns are usually for regaining learning-based control, not for pharmacological stabilization. However, in all settings, an intense risk management system that protects patients, staff, and others is vital.

Elements of an effective risk management system include policies, procedures, communication systems, training programs, and management that provides:

• A detailed review of history of risk-related behaviors, including records and interviews with caregivers, to identify potential risks and their precursors (as well as consequences for treatment purposes);

• Behavioral monitoring and incident reporting systems that closely monitor not only targeted behaviors, but also potential risk behaviors and precursors, and provide for timely (immediate) notification of professional staff who are competent and credentialed to make supervision and treatment decisions to reduce risk;

• Periodic (daily and weekly) reviews of patient behaviors and incidents to manage individual patient programs and detect systemic problems or trends that require systems changes. More instances of aggression occurring on a certain unit at certain times may indicate patients are not engaging in productive rewarded behavior, so their activity schedule should be reviewed for necessary changes.

• A system that ensures that various staff (direct care, nursing, behavioral, or psychological services) are frequently communicating and alerting each other to potential risks (eg, the patient's levels of carbamazepine are low, increasing the risk for emotional lability; the patient is not sleeping well, is perseverating on a family problem, and is displaying overt/constant signs of anxiety).

• A training program that ensures that staff can competently and safely handle violent behavior given the monitoring and management systems in place to detect and protect against risks.

• A system that relies on teaching and minimal physical or pharmacological restraints; eg, a system that uses frequent staff-intensive, hands-on restraints versus convenient but restrictive mechanical or chemical restraints.

• A clinical management and review process that ensures protection of patients' rights, ensures informed consent, and maximizes independence and self-determination, always with a quid pro quo analysis of restrictions versus risks.

• A system that provides for routine audits, quality assessment, and program evaluation to be self-critical and self-correcting.

Details on this section alone could fill an entire volume. It is the responsibility of program managers to educate themselves and establish such systems. If such systems are deficient, it is the responsibility of staff to actively (urgently, if necessary) advocate for them.

Setting the Tone for Program Management. The role of management in setting the tone for programs for violent patients is a final but critical overriding issue. As noted by Blair (1991), management may unconsciously set a tone of provocation that permeates a program and increases aggression. Proactive systems that use the strategies and techniques discussed combined with a management tone that supports and warmly responds to all patients while teaching them to control their aggression, communication that responds to employee concerns, and self-critical and corrective systems all are essential elements of successful programs. It is the authors' experience that management presence among the patients, modeling warm social teaching interactions and participating in a crisis, can greatly add to this tone. Management staff who do set such a tone and produce such systems and results will have the opportunity to receive the rewards of helping their patients and families achieve goals and the rewards of considerable work.

References

Adamovich, B.L. Cognitive language attention and information processing following closed head injury. In J. Krutzer, P. Wehman (Eds.), *Cognitive rehabilitation for persons with traumatic brain injury.* Baltimore: Paul H. Brookes, 1991.

Baer, D.M., Schnek, L., Benson, M. Increased autonomic responses to neutral and emotional stimuli in patients with temporal lobe epilepsy. *Am J Psychiatry* 1981; 138:843-845.

Baer, D. Neurological perspectives on aggressive behavior. *Journal of Neuropsychiatry* 1991; 3:53-58.

Blair, D.T. Assaultive behavior: Does provocation begin in the front office? *J Psychosoc Nurs Ment Health Serv* 1991; 29(5):21-26.

Brooks, N. *Closed head injury: Psychological, social and family consequences.* Oxford, England: Oxford University Press, 1984.

Burke, W.H. *Head injury rehabilitation: Applied behavior analysis in head injury rehabilitation.* Houston: HDI Publishers, 1988a.

Burke, W.H. Applied behavior analysis in the rehabilitation of brain injured clients. *Rehabilitation Nursing* 1988b; 13:186-188.

Burke, W.H., Lewis, F. Management of maladaptive social behavior of a brain injured adult. *Int J Rehabil Res* 1986; 9:335-342.

Burke, W.H., Wesolowski, M.D. *Applied behavior analysis in brain injury rehabilitation.* Houston: HDI Publishers, 1988.

Burke, W.H., Wesolowski, M.D., Blackerby, W.F. (Eds.). *Rehabilitation and treatment of traumatic brain injury.* Houston: HDI Publishers, 1988.

Burke, W.H., Zencius, A., Wesolowski, M.D., Doubleday, F. Improving executive function disorders in brain injured clients. *Brain Inj* 1991; 5:241-252.

Cardenas, D. Antipsychotics and their use after traumatic brain injury. *Journal of Head Trauma and Rehabilitation* 1987; 2:43-49.

Cope, D.N. (Ed.). Psychopharmacology. *Journal of Head Trauma Rehabilitation* 1987; 2:81-89.

DeKonig, P., Mah, M. Problems in human aggression research. *Journal of Neuropsychiatry* 1991; 3:561-565.

Eames, P. Behavior disorders after severe head injury. *Journal of Head Trama Rehabilitation* 1988; 3:16.

Elliot, F. Propanolol for the control of belligerent behavior following acute brain damage. *Ann Neurol* 1977; 1:189-191.

Fornazzari, L. Farcnik, K., Smith, I., Heasman, G.A., Ichise, M. Violent visual hallucinations and agression in frontal lobe dysfunction: Clinical manifestations of deep orbitofrontal forci. *Journal of Neuropsychiatry* 1992; 4:42-44.

Glenn, M.G., Joseph, A.R. The use of lithium for behavioral and effective disorders after traumatic brain injury. *Journal of Head Trauma Rehabilitation* 1987; 2:68-76.

Haas, J.F. Ethical and legal aspects of psychotropic medications in brain injury. *Journal of Head Trauma Rehabilitation* 1987; 2:6-15.

Horn, L.J. "Atypical" medications for the treatment of disruptive, aggressive behavior in the brain-injured patient. *Journal of Head Trauma Rehabilitation* 1987; 2:18-28.

Howard, M.E. Behavior management in the acute care rehabilitation setting. *Journal of Head Trauma Rehabilitation* 1988; 3:14-22.

Jennett, B., Teasdale, G. *Management of head injuries.* Philadelphia: FA Davis Co, 1981.

Klonoff, P., Prigatano, G.P. Reactions to family members and clinical intervention after traumatic brain injury. In M. Ylvisaker, E.M. Gobble (Eds.), *Community re-entry for head injured adults.* Boston: Little Brown & Company, 1987.

Kluver, H., Bucy, P.C. Preliminary analysis of functions of the temporal lobe in monkeys. *Archives of Neurology and Psychiatry* 1939; 42:979-1000.

Lewis, D.D., Pincus, J.H., Feldman, B., Jackson, L., Bard, B. Psychiatric, neurologic and psychoeducational characteristics of 15 death row inmates in the US. *Am J Psychiatry* 1986; 143:838-845.

Lezak, M. (Ed.). *Assessment of the behavioral consequences of head trauma.* New York: Alan Liss, 1989.

Mysiw, W., Jackson, R. Tricyclic antidepressant therapy after traumatic brain injury. *Journal of Head Trauma Rehabilitation* 1987; 2:34-42.

Namerow, N.S. Current concepts and advances in brain injury rehabilitation. *Journal of Neurological Rehabilitation* 1987; 1:101-114.

Pelco, L., Sawyer, M., Duffield, G., Prior, M., Kinsella, G. Premorbid emotional and behavioral adjustment in children with mild head injuries. *Brain Inj* 1992; 6:29-37.

Prigatano, G.P. (Eds.). Psychotherapy interventions after traumatic brain injury. *Journal of Head Trauma Rehabilitation* 1991; 6:1-61.

Skinner, B.F. *Science and human behavior.* New York: Macmillan, 1953.

Thomsen, I.V. Late outcome of very severe blunt head trauma: A 10-15 year second follow-up. *J Neurol Neurosurg Psychiatry* 1984; 47:260-268.

Tonkonogy, J.M., Giller, J. Hypothalamic lesions and intermittent explosive disorders. *Journal of Neuropsychiatry* 1992; 4:45-50.

Wesolowski, M.D., Burke, W.H. Behavior management techniques. In P. Deutsch, K. Fralish (Eds.), *Innovations in head injury rehabilitation.* New York: Matthew Bender, 1988a.

Wesolowski, M.D., Burke, W.H. *Managing anger and aggression.* Houston: HDI Publishers, 1988b.

Yudofsky, S., Silver, J., Jackson, W., Endicott, J., Williams, D. The overt aggression scale for the objective rating of verbal and physical aggression. *Am J Psychiatry* 1986; 143:35-39.

Yudofsky, S., Stevens, L., Silver, J. Propanolol in the treatment of rage and violent behavior associated with Korsakoff's psychosis. *Am J Psychiatry* 1984; 141:114-115.

Zasler, N. Advances in neuropharmacology rehabilitation for brain dysfunction. *Brain Inj* 1992; 6:1-14.

Zencius, A., Wesolowski, M.D., Krankowski, T., Burke, W.H. Memory notebook training with traumatically brain-injured clients. *Brain Inj* 1991; 5:321-325.

5 | Dynamics and Management of the Violent Patient in Forensic Settings

By Darcy Reeder, RN, MN, CS

The management of violent patients in the forensic setting is influenced by the dynamics of two diverse systems: the correctional system and the mental health system. By definition, the forensic setting is a part of the correctional system, not the mental health system. Individuals committed there are referred to as inmates, prisoners, or offenders instead of patients or clients. However, the correctional system does not have the psychiatric expertise required to manage the violent patient, and, therefore, must collaborate with the mental health system.

The role of the psychosocial nurse in these settings varies from institution to institution, ranging from a limited role such as administering medications and performing basic nursing tasks to functioning as clinical specialists, operating as advanced practitioners and prescribing psychiatric medications. This chapter will use the term "mental health professional" to include all psychiatric staff involved with the forensic setting, including nurses.

A limitation of this chapter is the exclusion of female violent offenders. Although many of the same principles may apply, information regarding their experiences in the forensic setting is limited and is not addressed in this chapter.

Mental Illness and Violent Behavior

Studies indicate the prevalence rate of psychotic mental disorders among inmates in prisons and jails to be from 1% to 7%. The rate for less severe disorders (eg, personality disorders and substance abuse disorders) varies, ranging up to 20% (Bolton, 1976; Guze, 1976; Monohan, 1983). In Guze's (1976) study of 223 male felons, sociopathy, alcohol abuse, and substance abuse were the psychiatric disorders most associated with violent crimes; schizophrenia and major affective disorders were not. Of 365 inmates in a New England maximum security facility described as "disruptive," only 11.5% were assessed to have a psychotic disorder (Uhlig, 1976).

The epidemiological relationship between schizophrenia and violent behavior is not well substantiated in the literature. Many persons, including mental health professionals and correctional workers, tend to associate schizophrenia with violence (Roth, 1987). There are some studies that contend people with schizophrenia are more prone to violence than the general population, but much more needs to be known about that relationship before a causal link can be made. In a review of the literature regarding schizophrenia and violence, Taylor (1982) concluded that there is not enough evidence to use the diagnosis of schizophrenia as a predictor of violent behavior.

The implication of these findings is that to develop programs and policies regarding the management of violent behavior in forensic settings, one cannot assume that traditional psychiatric treatment models will be appropriate for most inmates. Consideration of problems associated with character disorders and alcohol and substance abuse will probably lead to more successful outcomes (Roth, 1987).

Obstacles to Violence Reduction in Prison

DIVERGENT AIMS

It seems logical that in designing a program to reduce violent behavior, there has to be collaboration between correctional administrators and mental health professionals. Although both disciplines are troubled by this population, the historical relationship between the disciplines has been fragile at best and overtly hostile at times, contributing to an environment of mistrust and conflict (Reeder, 1991).

Divergent aims between and among correctional administrators, correctional staff, inmates, and mental health professionals may be (and often is) a source of this conflict. Conflicts arise when the underlying assumptions of the medical personnel and correctional administrators differ. To some extent, how those assumptions are formed is a product of the philosophical orientation of the two disciplines in a specific forensic setting. For example, if the correctional perspective assumes that violent behavior is an intentional act to disrupt the institutional routine and the medical perspective assumes that violent behavior is the result of a mental illness, then conflict over the management of the violent patient is likely. Additionally, procedures about psychological care that affect the correctional environment are based on these underlying assumptions. Although these underlying assumptions create the environment of the correctional setting, certain characteristics of imprisonment serve to further influence the milieu.

SECRECY

Secrecy is a characteristic of imprisonment that is mentioned throughout much of the correctional literature. Knight and Early (1986) describe the geographic and social isolation of detention facilities as contributing to that aura of secrecy. Additionally, the hands-off doctrine of the judiciary, which created laws basically to defer all control in the correctional setting to the correctional administration, contributed to the secrecy surrounding mental health care in the correctional setting. Various sources claim that the seemingly public indifference about standards of care in correctional institutions is partially caused by this secrecy (Knight, 1986; Rudovsky, 1973).

THE FUNCTIONS OF IMPRISONMENT

Additional characteristics of imprisonment that influence the provision of mental health care can be related to the actual functions of imprisonment. The literature supports the idea that there are four major goals of imprisonment; the policy and organization of the correctional setting stem from an application of these goals (Shaw, 1946; Zalman, 1972). These goals are retribution to society for criminal behavior (vengeance), deterrence of future crimes (suffering, deprivation), reformation (reflection and solitude, repentance, and redemption will change behavior and reduce crime), and protection of society.

How a correctional institution functions is based on one or a combination of these proposed aims. For example, if the aims of a specific correctional administration include retribution of crime and deterrence of future crimes, the environment will reflect those aims by its disciplinarian and punishment-oriented nature. This philosophy creates an atmosphere of animosity and antagonism and exists in opposition to the provision of mental health care. Psychiatric intervention may be viewed as unnecessary. Rehabilitation might be considered to be synonymous with following the rules of the institution and conforming to the social controls imposed on the inmates. In the past decade, correctional philosophies have leaned toward this more conservative model.

If, in another situation, reformation is the aim of imprisonment, this could serve as a supportive influence on the provision of mental health care. For example, correctional treatment programs that encourage anger management and improved interpersonal skills may be part of the correctional setting that supports the notion of reformation for violent forensic patients as an aim of imprisonment. Reformation was popular in the late 1960s and early 1970s, echoing trends toward societal change and restoration.

INSTITUTIONAL ENVIRONMENT

Internal sanctions, such as disciplinary segregation and revocation of privileges, are highly prized in correctional settings, distinguished by Goffman (1961) as total institutions in which inmates have minimal contact with the external world. Goffman describes inmates' health-care needs and actual programmatic needs as being used as sanctions in the prison privilege system. This awkward position created by the institutional view of mental health care as a privilege rather than a right is a source of historic and ongoing conflict between correctional and mental health workers.

Furthermore, incarceration impedes the inmate's freedom of choice regarding mental health services. However, seeking psychological care can also be motivated by an inmate's wish for relief from the tedium of incarceration or as a means of seeking drugs. Therefore, assessment of actual mental health needs involves integrating professional conflict (Goldsmith, 1975; Sandrick, 1981; Washington State, 1975). The conflicts are created by the compounding interaction between the closed environment, which limits the inmates' freedom of choice regarding mental health care, and the interpersonal characteristics of the inmate population, which has unclear motivations for seeking health care. For example, if an inmate requires mental health intervention but does not establish a therapeutic alliance with the mental health staff of the setting, then the choice of struggling with a nontherapeutic situation versus discontinuing treatment must be made, whereas outside the institution, the inmate could choose a different provider.

The conflict between mental health care and security functions is germane to mental health practices in the correctional setting. The mental health professional has to struggle with this conflict of priorities, which also affects the relationship with the inmates and other staff, such as correctional officers and administrators (Alexander-Rodriguez, 1983; Fewell, 1988). When correctional staff feel they have ultimate control over the practice of the mental health staff and can deny programs using the guise of a security risk, the mental health professional must decide how to integrate the limitation into treatment programs. Mental health professionals are often placed in the middle of inmate-correctional officer conflicts (Day, 1983). For example, an inmate may perceive a health-care need whereas the correctional officer believes the inmate is seeking unnecessary attention or trying to manipulate the system for drugs or a more comfortable placement. The correctional officer might restrict the inmate from pursuing health care, claiming the inmate would present an unnecessary security risk by being transported to the mental health professional for an invalid reason. In this situation, the mental health professional must decide how best to resolve this dispute without alienating the correctional worker while ensuring that the inmate receives adequate mental health care.

Furthermore,

> . . . since security of the facility and safety of the individuals within it are of
> paramount importance. . . (mental health professionals) may be asked to
> compromise their practice standards by carrying out activities that are not
> related to providing psychological care (for example, performing strip
> searches or interrogating inmates accused of breaking the rules). Or (mental
> health professionals) may recognize a need for. . . stress reduction exercises, or
> health teaching, but gain little acceptance or support. . . from those responsible
> for security (Moritz, 1982).

Mental health professionals who advocate for psychological services may
be seen as "soft" according to correctional staff (Day, 1983). Being "soft" is
seldom considered a positive trait to correctional staff who are taught and
acculturated to the ideas that inmates only respond to invulnerable forces
and will take advantage and manipulate anything less.

Treatment programs for violent offenders and security policies can be
perceived as competing interests in the correctional institution. These
competing interests may also be perceived as sources of conflict, with
procedures related to treatment in opposition to procedures related to
security. Each interest aims toward different goals that may interfere with
the goals of the others. For example, a prisoner who is continually
destructive but is beginning to demonstrate an increase in his control of
aggressive impulses from attending a group to increase problem solving
must be transported from his cell to the therapy area. This movement
creates an increased security risk and could be perceived as counter to
security goals. So the staff and the inmate are involved in a "Catch-22,"
where the approaches that would have the most impact on reducing the
violent behavior (and therefore reduce the inmate's security risk) are also
the approaches that might place the institution at a higher security risk
while the inmate undergoes treatment.

Treatment and Management

The first response to a violent inmate by staff in forensic settings usually
is to institute the traditional disciplinary process for breaking institutional
rules. For some inmates, the punishment associated with the infraction of
rules provides enough structure to allow them to adjust to the routine of
incarceration and additional intervention is not required (Porporino, 1986).

For those inmates who do not respond to conventional sanctions, it does
not make sense to subject them to more of the same. A recommendation
made many years ago by Fox (1958) was to use the prison stay as an
opportunity for this group of men to experience emotional maturation in a
controlled environment. Other philosophical views are stated by Toch

(1989) and include the thought that any resocialization (or for some, socialization) experience is more humanitarian and productive than locking them indefinitely in segregation (isolation). When looking at the idea from the perspective of a society that will include those same violent men at some point, it would seem an incredible waste of resources to not take advantage of the inmates' captivity.

Studies have shown some success regarding rehabilitation programs for violent patients in forensic settings. Frederiksen, Jenkins, Foy, and Eisler (1976) found that they were able to reduce aggressiveness using social skills training. Sarason (1978) reported a study in which subjects were assigned to either an assertiveness training group or a placebo control group. Most of the subjects in the assertiveness training group improved on scales measuring assertion whereas the controls did not.

Toch (1969; 1989) described men with a variety of interpersonal deficits that resulted in violent outcomes. Although being deficient in social skills is not synonymous with being mentally ill, the results of such deficits are an integral part of some illnesses, such as personality disorders. Many programs that are developed in prison reflect this understanding and are designed to repair these deficits. Practical approaches in the form of behavioral and cognitive training are more common than psychotherapy. Social skills or life skills training techniques are the standard for the most successful programs.

The behaviors defined as violent resulting from social skills deficits are fairly consistently reported in the literature. Responding to situations with verbal threats or physical violence is a requirement for the use of social skills training (Kaufman, 1972). Koshy (1986) reported those with impaired social skills and violent behavior had a lack of information, a sense of neglect, an insufficient attention span, and a low frustration level. In one study (Reeder, 1989), violent offenders reported difficulty in almost all situations involving the control of hostile feelings in interpersonal interactions. Kinzel (1970) found that offenders convicted of violent crimes required an average personal space (ie, the distance at which people prefer to have other people remain from them) that was 3.8 times greater than their nonviolent counterparts. The violent offenders became anxious when another person got too close and tended to perceive nonthreatening intrusions as attacks.

SOCIAL SKILLS TRAINING

People often find the concept of social skills difficult to comprehend. One of the reasons for this may be that in ordinary life, these skills are performed almost without conscious thought. Most people go about their lives seldom considering the complex processes involved in the use of social skills or the importance those skills have in their lives. It is only when people are not using social skills in a competent manner that a problem is thought to exist (McGuire, 1985).

Although no single definition of social skills is adequate, there seem to be some characteristics of a basic interpersonal process that may be regarded as prerequisites for successfully meeting social demands (Eisler, 1980; Henderson, 1983b; Liberman, 1982). These include the development of a repertoire of effective social behaviors, an awareness of the social norms governing social behavior in various situations, the ability to select the most effective response from available alternatives, the ability to perceive accurately the feedback from others, and the ability to change one's social behavior based on this feedback.

Basic to the social skills training philosophy are a number of principles that guide the treatment process. Anthony, Cohen, and Cohen (1983) identify seven fundamental principles:

- The involvement of the client is necessary in phases of the rehabilitation treatment process.
- Newly learned skill behaviors are usually situation-specific.
- Each client must have individualized skill goals.
- Reducing a client's personal and environmental discomfort does not automatically lead to improved skills.
- The restrictiveness of an environment is a function of the characteristics of both the environment and the client.
- Increased client dependency can improve client functioning.
- Hope is an essential ingredient of the practice of psychiatric rehabilitation.

The specific content of the programs vary, but in general they address interpersonal and job skills. McGuire and Priestley (1985) list topics they feel should be addressed in any social skills training program for violent offenders: conversation skills, job interview skills, talking to the opposite sex, family interactions and conflicts with parents, encounters with the police, perspective taking, resisting pressure to drink or use illicit drugs, aggression and violence, and attitudes to self and others. Henderson (1983) adds, in more detail, assertiveness training and self-control skills.

Putting social skills training to work with violent offenders requires attention to issues relating to the prison environment. One criticism of using skills training within the institutional setting revolves around what purpose the newly found skills will serve. If the prison administration will only support skills training that will lead to improved inmate compliance with prison rules and not those that can be generalized to situations the inmate might encounter once released, then mental health practitioners teaching the skills must consider balancing the inmate's treatment without falling prey to institutional manipulation.

SHOWS OF FORCE, RESTRAINTS, AND SECLUSION

In even the most forward thinking program, when the inmates have problems managing their anger, there will be times when violence is acted out physically. The behavior of inmates can escalate quickly and some inmates remain unpredictable with little control over their destructive impulses. There is not a prison in the country that does not encounter this scenario on a frequent, and often daily, basis.

How the situation is resolved and who determines that resolution is directly influenced by the prison administrative policy. In retribution or punishment-oriented settings, violence might be countered with more violence. Pain techniques, mace, nightsticks, and guns would not be extraordinary. Rehabilitative models would result in techniques that involve nonphysical interventions to the extent possible. When physical contact is considered necessary, inmates should be restrained based on kinetic means and inoffensive procedures. In the forensic settings of most jurisdictions, the more punitive methods are not the first response. Verbal de-escalation and inoffensive techniques are more routine (Roth, 1987).

The use of a group of organized staff to respond to the violent episode is labeled as a show of force. When done properly, a show of force often induces the inmate to forego a destructive act. It is standard operating procedure for correctional staff to receive training in aggression control, and additional training is the norm for officers who work in special programs. In some programs, mental health professionals do participate in the aggression tactics, but most often that participation is limited to verbal intervention and follow-up after the correctional staff subdue the inmate. In the past few years, it has become fashionable to video tape shows of force. Officially, this adventure into the use of motion pictures is to improve learning and processing of the events, but all involved acknowledge the benefit of this unbiased "witness." It's harder to use unnecessary force when the electronic eye is recording one's actions.

There are elements of a show of force that are designed to reduce the potential for harm to anyone involved (Alexander, 1985). These elements include using verbal intervention whenever possible. Under this precept, staff provide reassurance, offer alternatives, set limits of acceptable behavior, and identify the danger and consequences of the inmate's behavior.

In those instances when verbal intervention is ineffective, a show of force is convened. Other inmates are moved out of harm's way as a minimum of six staff are gathered (one staff member to talk to the inmate, five others for each extremity and the head). A leader is determined. This person is often the correction supervisor on duty. The leader makes assignments for the staff and either talks to the inmate or assigns someone else to the task. It is the leader who decides whether the inmate requires restraints, seclusion, or both.

As the show of force approaches the inmate, the person assigned to talk states the purpose and asks the inmate to return to his cell or other designated area. It is helpful if only one person talks as it is less confusing and provides a sense of confidence in the team. If the inmate does not follow the verbal direction of the show of force, the next step is to place the inmate in restraints.

Restraints consist of a conglomeration of devices from the traditional locked, leather cuffs and belts to metal handcuffs to strips of unbreakable plastic called flexcuffs. Their use is widely varied. Some programs mimic psychiatric wards restraining inmates to beds with leather straps, but it is possible that, unofficially, correctional staff might handcuff an unruly inmate to a drain pipe.

Some inmates require long-term restraint to provide protection to themselves, others, or the environment. How "long term" is defined varies from institution to institution, but generally the definition includes anyone who requires restraints for more than emergent situations. Ambulatory restraints are used to allow the inmate enough freedom of movement to attend treatment, but enough external control to inhibit aggressive impulses. These special restraints are leather anklets and a leather waist belt with attached wrist cuffs that lock and are reasonably comfortable. Perhaps this is not ideal, but it is a tolerable compromise in a world of imperfection.

As recently as a decade or two ago, violent inmates were managed by prolonged solitary confinement. Cells were barren with only the very basics and little sensory stimulation. It is not surprising that this attempt to quell aggressive prisoners was not very successful and was not condoned by the courts. During the years of jail reformation, standards were set for regular periodic review of inmates who were isolated from the prison general population. Inmates are also now required to have scheduled exercise time outside of their cells, regardless of their risk of violence.

A common scenario would be that of the unpredictably violent prisoner who is in a social skills program at a correctional special offender institution. This inmate might be locked in solitary confinement during the hours that he is not in treatment or exercising. When he is out of his cell, he would be fitted with ambulatory restraints. He would have a treatment plan that addressed potential triggers for aggression and methods to manage these incidents. His social skills plan would be developed in collaboration with correctional staff, the inmate, and mental health staff.

Release

By and large, all inmates will leave the prisons to which they are assigned for payment of their debt to society. Regardless of their risk of violence, regardless of how much they matured in prison or how well they responded to institutional treatment programs, the streets of the communities in which we live will be their domain as well. Reports of the man who robbed or killed after spending years being "reformed" in prison can be found in most states. Recidivism of violent offenders is high.

Some states have parole systems that ostensibly assist the emerging inmate with integration into the community. Very few convicts want to regress into a life of crime, but the reality is that it is exceedingly difficult to emerge successfully from the system. In parole states, some efforts are made to set up programs for the offenders to reduce the risk of offending again, but there are inherent difficulties in this system.

Although the inmate comes out of an environment where his every move and decision is in the control of someone else, the parole officer must quickly push the inmate into independence and responsibility. The parole officer must convince other agencies that this dangerous person has the ability to live, work, and exist peacefully. Further complicating the picture are large case loads for the parole officer and a confusing, difficult adjustment period for the parolee. The outcomes of these equations is seldom satisfactory to anyone.

In response to the poor results from parole systems, some states have dropped parole from the criminal justice system. Once convicted, the offender is given a sentence (that can be shortened if the inmate qualifies for time off for good behavior, which most violent offenders do not manage to achieve) and simply completes the sentence and then is released. No follow-up, no monitoring—just released.

The story is not as bleak as it might seem. Attempts are being made to reduce the cycle of destruction for which violent offenders are known. Given a commitment from governing agencies to provide adequate resources, violent offenders can be helped to be productive citizens (Goldmeier, 1980; Reeder, 1990).

Most community treatment programs and residential placements have automatic refusal policies for violent offenders. This is not entirely without justification: fights and property destruction tend to inhibit therapeutic environments. Still, the wholesale dismissal of a population of men in need of mental health services is not good policy.

Hamilton House, a halfway house in Maryland, is designed to meet the special needs of violent offenders leaving forensic settings. The offender "becomes" a patient and is treated in a less structured environment. Staff accept that situations such as loss of a job or relationship dissolution may happen and view it as a learning opportunity for the patient rather than another failure (Goldmeier, 1980).

Intensive community support programs specifically designed for violent offenders can be developed and can be successful (Rogers, 1981). The case management model has already been shown to be effective with mentally ill offenders. Case managers assist the patients in virtually all areas of the patients' lives. For example, the case manager may help the patient negotiate the often confusing state system that frequently provides the patients with their income. A long-term commitment to patients to retain them in the program even when they revert to violent behavior often provides the extra support the patients require to remain in the community. One program reported the success rate of its program during its first 2 years to be more than 500% when using differences in the amount of time spent incarcerated before entry into the program and 1 year after entry as an indicator (King, 1988). With the assistance of the intensive case management program, most of the clients were able to live in the community without engaging in criminal activity. A similar model was described by Rogers and Cavanaugh (1981), but was designed exclusively for violent offenders. The authors reported that the program was enjoying favorable results.

The conception and growth of such a program needs to be nurtured. Those managing the programs need to be sensitive to the special factors that violent offenders bring with them. The problems of social isolation and interpersonal awkwardness are important considerations in their treatment. These men may have learned some living or social skills while incarcerated, but they have not had many opportunities to practice their new approaches and may not know if they have the talent for this game. Their self-esteem will be fragile; they may expect failure and behave provocatively in the beginning. They will not get it perfect without considerable practice, and many will never be more than marginal in their abilities (Frederiksen, 1981; Novaco, 1976; Priestley, 1983).

The professionals involved in the management or clinical activities of the program must have a humanistic, unconditionally positive philosophy. As stated before, it may not be uncommon for the patients to regress to past behavior. This is not to say that staff should accept any outrageous behavior the patient exhibits, but the underlying acceptance of the person must be sincere. Staff will require training in the criminal justice system and aggression control along with basic education in mental health theory and practice. Case managers, optimally, will have case loads not exceeding 15 offenders and would begin to establish a relationship with the offender before the date of release. The pre-release introductions are a key factor to the inmate's formulation of a bond to the program. This population is often suspicious of social agencies.

The content of a program should vary depending on the offenders' particular deficits. Social skills training would continue. This is also the time to consider psychotherapy for those offenders who have issues that respond to such sessions. Job training is extremely important. Studies of recidivism repeatedly find that being unable to hold a job is correlated with return to a criminal life (Twentymen, 1978).

Summary

Studies examining the relationship between psychiatric illness and violent behavior have not been able to report a causal link between the two. In the forensic setting, the management of the violent patient requires a treatment approach that realistically assesses the origin of the violence and develops an intervention program that is appropriate for the individual.

Collaboration between the correctional system and the mental health system has, historically, been minimal. Divergent aims, the secrecy associated with prisons, the functions of imprisonment, and the institutional environment contribute to distrust and conflict between the two systems.

Forensic settings use a social skills enhancement model in the treatment of the violent patient. This psychoeducational approach is practical and seems to enjoy some success in reducing inmates' violent behavior.

The essential mission of any prison rehabilitation program should be to prepare the inmate for re-entry into the community. Anything that may reduce the potential for the inmate to return to his previous lifestyle must be considered. Simply releasing a violent offender to the free world without some follow-up or continuance of treatment is an inefficient use of scarce prison resources and makes recidivism likely. Case management programs can be effective in helping make the streets safer and the prisons less crowded. This strategy may not yield quick results and, admittedly, is costly; Americans are not very patient and have a hard time waiting for long-term profits. Violence, however, does yield instant results and is costly—economically and emotionally. What the future holds for the violent offender should be of concern to more than the prisons and the inmates.

References

Alexander, M. *Aggression control*. Unpublished manuscript, 1985.

Alexander-Rodriguez, T. Prison health: A role for professional nursing. *Nursing Outlook* 1983; 9:115-118.

Anthony, W.A., Cohen, M.R., Cohen, B.F. Philosophy, treatment process, and principles of the psychiatric rehabilitation model. In I. Bachrach (Ed.), *New directions for mental health services: Health deinstitutionalization*. San Francisco: Jossey Bass, 1983, pp. 67-79.

Bolton, A. *A study of the need for and availability of mental health services for mentally disordered jail inmates and juveniles in detention facilities*. Unpublished report. Boston: Arthur Bolton Associates, 1976.

Day, R. The challenge: Health care vs. security. *Canadian Nurse* 1983; 9(79):34-36.

Eisler, J.P., Frederiksen, L.W. *Perfecting social skills: A guide to interpersonal behavior development*. New York: Plenum Press, 1980.

Fewell, C. Successful strategies: Integrating health care and security functions. *Corrections Today* 1988; 9(50):20-22.

Fox, V. Analysis of prison disciplinary problems. *Journal of Criminal Law, Criminology, and Police Science* 1958; 49:321-326.

Frederiksen, L.W., Jenkins, J.O., Foy, D.W., Eisler, R.W. Social skills training to modify abusive verbal outbursts in adults. *Journal of Applied Behavior Analysis* 1976; 2:117-125.

Frederiksen, L.W., Rainwater, N. Explosive behavior: A skill development approach to treatment. In R.B. Stuart (Ed.), *Violent behavior: Social learning approaches to prediction, management, and treatment*. New York: Brunner/Mazel, 1981, pp. 97-124.

Goffman, E. *Asylums*. New York: Doubleday, 1961.

Goldmeier, J., White, E.V., Ulrich, C., Klein, G.A. Community intervention with the mentally ill offender: A residential program. *Bull Am Acad Psychiatry Law* 1980; 8(1):72-82.

Goldsmith, S. *Prison health: Travesty of justice.* New York: Prodist, 1975.

Guze, S.B. *Criminality and psychiatric disorders.* New York: Oxford University Press, 1976.

Henderson, M. Self-reported assertion and aggression among violent offenders with high or low levels of overcontrolled hostility. *Personality and Individual Differences* 1983a; 4:113-115.

Henderson, M., Hollin, C. A critical review of social skills training with young offenders. *Criminal Justice and Behavior* 1983b; 10:316-341.

Kaufman, L.M., Wagner, B.R. Barb: A systematic treatment technology for temper control disorders. *Behavior Therapy* 1972; 3:84-90.

King County Department of Adult Detention Annual Report 1989. Unpublished manuscript.

Kinzel, A.F. Body-buffer zone in violent prisoners. *Am J Psychiatry* 1970; 127:99-104.

Knight, B., Early, S. *Prisoners' rights in America.* Chicago: Nelson-Hall, 1986.

Koshy, K.J. Understanding aggressive behaviour: Role of a nurse. *Nursing Journal of India* 1986; 72(2):41-42.

Liberman, R.P. Assessment of social skills. *Schizophr Bull* 1982; 8:62-83.

McGuire, J., Priestley, P. *Offending behaviour: Skills and stratagems for going straight.* London: Batsford Academic and Educational, 1985.

Monohan, J., Steadman, H.J. Crime and mental disorder: An epidemiological approach. In N. Morris, M.H. Tonry (Eds.), *Crime and justice: An annual review of research.* Chicago: University of Chicago Press, 1983, pp. 26-31.

Moritz, P. Health care in correctional facilities: A nursing challenge. *Health Outlook* 1982; 9(30):253-259.

Novaco, R.W. Treatment of chronic anger cognitive and relaxation controls. *J Consult Clin Psychology* 1976; 44(4):681.

Porporino, F.J. Managing violent individuals in correctional settings. *Journal of Interpersonal Violence* 1986; 1:213-237.

Priestley, P., McGuire, J., Flegg, D., Hemsley,V., Welham, D., Barnitt, R. *Social skills in prison and the community: Problem solving for offenders.* London: Routledge & Kegan Paul, 1983.

Reeder, D. *A comparative analysis of social skills deficits of violent and nonviolent offenders in an urban county jail.* Unpublished master's thesis, University of Washington, Seattle, 1989.

Reeder, D. *A community program for mentally ill offenders.* Presented at the American Psychiatric Nurses' Association Fourth Annual Convention, Washington, DC, October 1990.

Reeder, D., Meldman, L. Conceptualizing psychosocial nursing in the jail setting. *J Psychosoc Nurs Ment Health Serv* 1991; 29(8):40-44.

Rogers, R., Cavanaugh, J.L. A treatment program for potentially violent offender patients. *International Journal of Offender Therapy and Comparative Criminology* 1981; 25(1):53-59.

Roth, L.H. *Clinical treatment of the violent person.* New York: Guilford Press, 1987.

Rudovsky, D. *The rights of prisoners: A basic ACLU guide.* New York: Richard W. Baron, 1973.

Sandrick, K. Behind bars: Health care in US correctional facilities. *QRB* 1981; 1(7):25-29.

Sarason, I.G. Verbal learning, modeling, and juvenile delinquency. *Journal of Counseling Psychology* 1978; 21:442-449.

Shaw, G. *The crime of punishment.* New York: Philosophical Libraries, 1946.

Taylor, P. Schizophrenia and violence. In J. Gunn, D.P. Farrington (Eds.), *Abnormal offenders, delinquency, and the criminal justice system,* vol. 1. New York: John Wiley & Sons, 1982, pp. 269-284.

Toch, H. *Violent men: An inquiry into the psychology of violence.* Chicago: Aldine, 1969.

Toch, H. Violence in prison. In K. Howells, C.R. Hollin (Eds.), *Clinical approaches to violence.* New York: John Wiley & Sons, 1989, pp. 267-286.

Twentyman, C.T., Jensen, M., Kloss, J.D. Social skills for the complex offender: Employment seeking skills. *J Clin Psychol* 1978; 34:320-326.

Uhlig, R.H. Hospitalization experience of mentally disturbed and disruptive, incarcerated offenders. *Journal of Psychiatry and Law* 1976; 4(1):49-59.

Washington State Council on Crime and Delinquency Health Care Committee. *Prison health care: A blueprint for the future.* Olympia, WA: Government Printing Office, 1975.

Zalman, M. Prisoners' rights to medical care. *Journal of Criminal Law, Criminology, and Police Science* 1972; 26(3):185-199.

6 Adult Victims of Domestic Violence

By Alana Dauner, RN, C, BSN

Violence in domestic settings is the most serious problem facing American family relationships today. The US Surgeon General has identified domestic violence as a major health problem for women. Wife-beating is the major cause of injury requiring medical treatment for women more than stranger-rape, auto accidents, and muggings combined (Illinois Coalition Against Domestic Violence, 1991; Stark, 1988). Battering frequently begins or escalates during pregnancy or in the postpartum period (Helton, 1987). Adult female refugees of domestic violence are the fastest growing segment of American homeless. One third of battered women who seek emergency shelter each year are turned away due to lack of facility provisions (Fauldi, 1991). As high as 90% of homeless families are headed by women. Elder mistreatment is increasing as the number of people over the age of 65 live in the family setting rather than in institutions (Tomita, 1990; Quinn, 1990). The newest recognized victim of domestic violence is the gay and lesbian partner, although these victims are less likely than their heterosexual counterparts to seek help because of the stigma and homophobia that pervade our culture and health-care services (Morrow, 1989).

Early identification of domestic abuse has a profound effect on treatment outcome. Nurses are often the first or only health-care contact for these victims of domestic abuse. Nurses are in a unique position to exercise "courageous and visionary direction in proposing, initiating, and implementing interdisciplinary action toward creative community health services of a nature and amount vastly different from those that currently exist" (Rogers, 1972).

This chapter offers an overview of the high prevalence of domestic violence and its effect on adult victims. The reader is directed to the definition of terms in Appendix A. Theories related to domestic violence are reviewed with emphasis on the social learning theory. Characteristics of the adult victims, assessment instruments, and points on nursing-related interventions are identified. A comprehensive reading list (Other Readings) is provided for the readers' more detailed examination of areas of interest.

Prevalence of Domestic Violence

The National Coalition Against Domestic Violence's December 1991 report states that 97% of domestic violence is directed toward women, and 50% of all women are abused at some time in their lives. One in 25 adult women encountered in any health-care setting who live with a man is likely to be a victim of abuse by husband or lover (Campbell, 1984b). Women are six times more likely than men to be assaulted and injured, raped, or killed by intimate partners or ex-partners (Straus, 1990b; US Department of Justice, 1991). Women victims of spouse or ex-spouse abuse are most often between the ages of 20 and 34. Women victims of abuse by boyfriends or ex-boyfriends are most often between the ages of 16 and 24 (US Department of Justice, 1991). Women who are unemployed, in the Armed Forces, and students are most frequently victims of domestic violence. Unemployment among battered women can be as high as 72% (Snyder, 1981). Women college students have an overall rate of rape that is four times that of women who are not students (Bureau of Justice Statistics, 1982).

In relationships with a history of abuse, the severity and frequency of physical assaults are likely to increase during pregnancy and through the postpartum period. Of every 1,000 pregnant women, 154 are assaulted by their partner during the first 4 months of pregnancy. During the fifth through ninth months, 170 of every 1,000 pregnant women are assaulted (National Family Violence Survey, 1985).

Marital rape, an integral part of marital violence, is reported in relationships where no other forms of physical abuse occurs, but it may also occur along with physical and verbal abuse (Fagan, 1984). Spouses commit 14 of 100 attempted or completed reported rapes whereas boyfriends/ex-boyfriends commit 28 of 100 attempted or completed reported rapes (US Department of Justice, 1991).

Incidence of domestic elder abuse was found to be 32 of 1,000 in persons over 65 (Pillemer, 1988a). Elderly men are as likely to be abused as elderly women; however, women sustain more severe physical and psychological injury (Pillemer, 1988a). The elderly female's abuser may be her spouse (58%), her son (16%), or her daughter (8%).

Because the issue of domestic violence among homosexuals is shrouded in silence and distorted by myths, there is, to date, little research in this area

(Morrow, 1989). Such myths that women are not physically assaultive, lesbians have solely egalitarian relationships, or that gay men are effeminate and nonviolent, along with general social homophobia, further isolate this population. One study identifies an incidence of reported rape to be 0.7% among a university student lesbian population (Russell, 1984).

Impact of Domestic Violence

Identified adult domestic violence accounted for approximately $44.4 million in health-care costs in 1989 (McLeer, 1989). Domestic violence results in a range of disguised health-care problems, both medical and psychiatric, not limited to the emergency rooms or acute psychiatric units, and certainly not always identified as being related to any of the varying forms of abuse.

Domestic violence denotes a range of behaviors and motives (Gage, 1991). Typical assaults involve a combination of verbal abuse, threats, and physical or sexual abuse (Browne, 1987).

Minor incidents of violence towards women may involve slapping, throwing something, pushing, or shoving. Injury patterns may include bruises, black eyes, cuts, or swelling. More serious assaults include biting, kicking, punching, choking, beating, being thrown, or the use of a weapon. Injury patterns may include more serious injuries, such as gunshot or knife wounds, broken bones, loss of teeth, internal injuries, loss of consciousness, or miscarriage. Female abuse victims commonly sustain injury to breast, chest, or abdomen and display multiple injuries (Burge, 1979; Stark, 1979). Permanent injuries, such as damage to joints, partial loss of hearing or vision, and scars from burns, bites, or knife wounds, may assist in detection of the battered victim.

Unlike victims of stranger violence, victims of domestic violence have role relationships with the offender that greatly confound their response to the abuse and intensify the psychological sequelae. Domestic abuse is the single most common background factor for patients in psychiatric settings (Stark, 1988). Seriously abused women demonstrate twice the incidence of headaches, four times the rate of depression, and almost six times as many suicide attempts as non-victims (Straus, 1990c). Other frequent primary care complaints include vague medical complaints, sleep and eating disorders, anxiety, muscle aches, abdominal pains, and recurrent vaginal infections. Battered women who abuse alcohol have the highest rate of emergency medical use of any population (Stark, 1981). Adult victims of childhood sexual molestation or incest demonstrate high incidence of self-destructive behaviors including cutting, burning, multiple suicide attempts, and dissociative responses.

Partners involved in relationships with histories of severe battering and sexual abuse are at high risk for homicide (Browne, 1987). Domestic homicide accounted for 17% of all murders in 1986. Male homicide of wives or female lovers account for 3 of 4 murdered women (Campbell, 1984a). Six percent of male homicide victims are killed by their female intimate partners (US Department of Justice, 1986). When women kill, it is likely in response to physical threat from their male victims and follows a severe history of abuse and multiple unsuccessful attempts at obtaining outside intervention (Browne, 1987; Jurik, 1990). The male victim often begins the homicidal incident by threatening the woman with a weapon or striking the woman.

Physical abuse during pregnancy may result in placenta abruptio; antepartum hemorrhage; fetal fractures; rupture of uterus, liver, or spleen; or miscarriage. Various complications of the pregnancy not otherwise "explained" may be as a result of unidentified abuse (Helton, 1987).

Detection of the elderly victim is complicated by the effects of the normal aging process. Physical injuries may be caused by abuse, or falls may be the result of age-related impairments. Within the elderly population, abuse or neglect may take one of four forms. Physical abuse, such as spanking, restraining with injury, or shaking, may result in injuries such as contusions, fractures, or head injury. Physical neglect may result in malnutrition, recurrent vaginal or urinary infection, infestation with head lice, skin breakdown such as pressure sores, or noncompliance with medication due to withholding or unavailability of medication. Emotional abuse or emotional neglect may result in depression, withdrawal, isolation, disorientation, and psychosis (Anderson, 1981). Financial abuse of the elder may include robbing or misappropriation of monies or property by an adult who has legal sanctions or influences financial management. In situations where adult children live with and depend on the elder parent's income, financial abuse of the elder parent may result in neglect of the elder's needs. The elder may be deprived of food, clothing, medication, or assistive devices, such as hearing aids or dentures.

Abuse within lesbian relationships is virtually the same as in heterosexual relationships, although injury may be less severe than among male homosexuals (Morrow, 1989). Verbal abuse to control the partner may include powerful threats to expose the victim's homosexual orientation. Isolation from family and from social resources may further intensify these relationships and contribute to multiple and ongoing incidences of abuse.

Victims of any form of domestic violence demonstrate the same types of responses as do victims of any major trauma (Council on Scientific Affairs, 1992). The *Diagnostic and Statistical Manual* (DSM-III-R) of the American Psychiatric Association (APA, 1980) classifies the trauma response as an anxiety disorder: post-traumatic stress disorder. The essential feature is the development of characteristic symptoms following psychologically traumatic events that are generally outside the range of usual human experience.

Abuse evokes this syndrome of distress with enduring symptoms. Intrusive recollections of the actual events of trauma include vividly detailed nightmares of abusive incidents, instrusive thoughts, and a re-experiencing of an abusive incident (flashback) where the victim loses touch with reality. The debilitating symptom that brings the victim in contact with the health-care system may be recurring intrusive thoughts with associated fears, panic attacks, phobias, or ritualistic avoidant behaviors. In the initial interview with the victim, the nurse will likely discover that the victim has never talked to anyone in detail about the abuse. Additional behaviors indicative of this syndrome are denial, minimization, avoidance, and numbing of the emotional response to the abuse by the victim. Substance abuse as a means of self-medication may have deep connections to this anxiety disorder. Irrational self-blame and guilt about the abuse are themes, and over-controlled patterns of daily behaviors are characteristic of victims. Other presenting symptoms may range from intense startle response to sleeping or eating disturbances (Council on Scientific Affairs, 1992).

Legal Implications

Domestic violence is legally defined differently from violence occurring in public settings. In 30 states, under certain circumstances, it is legal for a husband to rape his wife; only 10 states have laws mandating arrest for domestic violence (Fauldi, 1991). Laws regulating civil protection and powers of police to intervene in domestic situations vary from state to state, as do mandatory reporting requirements by health-care providers. Many women do not report the incidence of violence due to fear of retaliation from the abuser, economic dependence on the abuser, or past experiences with the legal system that did not result in changes in the abuse. Clinicians need to be reminded that referrals and access to shelters or battered women's centers do not require legal involvement.

Laws governing family responsibility for elder members are generally vague unless a guardian has been appointed (Fulmer, 1986). Lack of available respite care support can result in the elderly being left alone for long periods or being abandoned in public places, for example, shopping malls or adult day care centers. Mandatory reporting by health-care providers of neglect or forms of abuse differ among states. Most states have strict laws protecting elders from financial exploitation, such as insurance or home repair scams. Most institutions have policies for reporting patient abuse that occurs within the institution but lack clear definition regarding behaviors that are reportable.

Theory and Research Findings Related to Domestic Violence

There is no single theory that clearly explains domestic violence. Social learning theory, based on cognitive theory, has been the basis for vast amounts of research and model development related to the multifaceted concepts of domestic violence. These have proven valuable in beginning to understand and direct intervention into this profound problem.

Social learning theory identifies the family as the training ground for learning aggressive behaviors. These behaviors are learned and acquired through direct experience and through observing others' behavior (modeling) (Bandura, 1973). Violence in the family then begets violence; that is, violence begins in the cradle but does not end in the grave. It is transgenerational.

A high correlation between aggressive behavior and frequent use of physical punishment by the male parent is found in juvenile males (Campbell, 1984b). There is a positive correlation between the amount of physical punishment experienced by a male child and the subsequent rate of spouse abuse (Straus, 1981). Men who are physically assaultive toward female partners have higher incidences of having witnessed or experienced violence in childhood than do nonabusive men (Browne, 1986). Girls witnessing parental violence during childhood and adolescence consistently are at risk for later experiences of becoming a female victim of partner abuse (Lentzenr, 1980).

Six lessons children are likely to learn from family violence are: violence is an appropriate form of conflict resolution; violence has a place within the family interaction; if violence is reported to others in the community, including mental health and criminal justice professionals, there are few, if any, consequences; sexism, as defined by inequality of power, decision-making ability, and roles within the family, is intrinsic to family systems; violence is an appropriate means of stress management; and victims of violence are, at best, to tolerate this behavior and, at worst, to examine their responsibility in bringing on the violence.

Long-standing patterns of family violence become firmly established in the attitudes and behaviors of family members. Abusive behavior patterns passed on to children from parents extend into adulthood and can be manifested as abuse or neglect of the aging parent. Socially learned behaviors are ingrained into the nature of the family relationships. The abusers become the adult children who did not have satisfying relationships with their parents or who were themselves abused (Pillemer, 1986). They may suffer from developmental factors that further contribute to the likelihood of abuse or neglect of the elder. Dependency of the adult offspring on the elderly parent is identified as socially unacceptable and is a predictor of elder abuse (Pillemer, 1986.) This abuser may be more deviant or pathological than other types of abusers (Wolf, 1986). Such dependency leads to feelings of powerlessness and results in varying forms of abuse and neglect towards the elder. The elder may also become very vulnerable to financial abuse by the dependent adult child.

Social learning theory emphasizes the differences in learned/socialized "roles" of men and women and identifies factors that inhibit this learning (Agosta, 1987). Traditional sex roles reinforce the man's authority, right to violence, and protective responsibilities as is normative in a patriarchal society. The girl is socialized to be passive, submissive, nonoppositional, helpful, and responsible. By virtue of physical size and strength, the woman finds physical confrontation ineffective.

The American culture provides no room for a man as a "victim" (Lew, 1988). The social message given to boys by family, media, schools, and even other children through such comments as "boys don't cry," is that "men are not victims and victims are not men" (Lew, 1988). For the little boy who is victimized in childhood, this translates into emotional numbing, forgetting, distancing, pretending, avenging hurt (Lew, 1988), and setting himself up as a perpetrator to avoid further victimization (Roane, 1989).

Social learning theorists postulate that aggressive as well as passive behavior are products of the cognitive structure (beliefs, values), which either inhibits or disinhibits the performance of the activity. Violence results from learned aggression that is reinforced. Therefore, although the intention of physical punishment may be that a child will learn to change behaviors to avoid physical punishment, the child may also unintentionally learn what will be the roots of future abusive behavior. Physical punishment that is linked with love and violence may teach a moral rightness of hitting a family member or loved one, especially over an important issue, thus justifying the use of physical force. Furthermore, physical violence may be a legitimate way to release stress or anger (Straus, 1990a). These lessons have far-reaching outcomes based on the "role" to which the child is socialized.

Research on the role of alcohol abuse in family violence is inconclusive; alcoholism in and of itself does not appear to cause domestic violence. The effects of alcohol and alcohol abuse have been found to be a social excuse for socially inappropriate or aggressive behaviors (Critchlow, 1986). The rate of alcoholism among battered women is 16% greater than nonbattered women (Stark, 1981). Onset of alcoholism frequently occurs after the onset of abuse, suggesting that alcoholism may be a response to abuse (Stark, 1981).

The central theory that links alcohol to wife abuse is the disinhibition theory, which holds that alcohol releases inhibition and alters judgment. The combination of traits of socioeconomic status (blue-collar), drinking, and approval of violence are associated with a high incidence of wife abuse. This group is found to have 7.8 times greater incidence of wife abuse than the traits of higher socioeconomic status (white-collar), drinking, and disapproval of violence towards a spouse (Kantor, 1990). The social learning of beliefs and values toward violence is the differentiating factor in partner abuse when alcohol abuse is present (Critchlow, 1986).

Additional social learning about family violence takes place outside the family. Political norms, social norms, and media representation that violence is an acceptable way to obtain a desirable result is an inescapable message in our culture. The single best predictor of young men's aggressive behavior at the age of 19 is how much violence they were viewing on television at 8 years old (Campbell, 1984b). Social norms value youth and beauty; there is negative evaluation and treatment of the elderly.

Social learning theory explains learned helplessness (Campbell, 1989), which has debilitating effects on human problem solving. Once abused persons believe they cannot control what happens to them, the perception becomes reality. Learned helplessness results when responses and outcomes seem unrelated (response-outcome noncontingency). Abused women who use passive coping mechanisms and problem solving deficits are in evidence (Launius, 1987; Mitchell 1983). Women exposed to violence in childhood are at greatest risk for developing the three major deficits associated with learned helplessness: apathy, difficulties in problem solving, and depression (Abramson, 1978). The affective component further impairs the victim's perception of available alternatives to the situation such as leaving the abusive situation. Socialization toward passivity and economic dependency, as in the patriarchal family, or perception of acceptable levels of violence influence learned helplessness (Kantor, 1990). This learning appears to occur on a continuum and accounts for women who hold positions of responsibility and are competent and intelligent, but conform to the traditional power dyad within the male-female relationship.

Five major factors related to elder abuse have been identified (Pillemer, 1988). The first factor is intra-individual dynamics of the abuser, which implies some pathological character disorder in adult children, particularly over-dependence on elders. The second factor is the generational transmission of the violent behavior, whereby adult children strike out at their own abuser, the elder. This form of abuse involves the process of retaliation as well as imitation.

The third factor accounts for inequitable levels of dependencies. Financial dependency of the adult child on the elder as well as increased dependency of the elder on the adult child is identified as an important risk factor in elder abuse. Illness or increased financial dependency of the elder on the adult child is a common precursor to elder abuse (Wolf, 1982).

The fourth element, social isolation, is a characteristic of abusers and victims of all forms of domestic violence. Illegitimate behaviors are hidden because detection can result in informal implications from friends and neighbors and formal implications from the legal system. Social isolation limits feedback to victims about their situation and may lead to the assumption that all families or marriages are violent. The resulting compliance becomes a survival mechanism that can be perceived as "approving" the acts of violence.

Social isolation is consistent with elder abuse. Abused elderly are found to have minimal social contact. The major obstacle to early detection of elder abuse is inaccessibility into the home. Isolation as a result of estrangement from family members leaves the elder vulnerable for exploitation by persons other than family members. Younger women can easily exploit elderly men whose ability to attract a partner is diminished, resulting in financial abuse. Elders isolated from their family easily fall prey to other forms of financial abuse ranging from insurance to home repair scams.

The fifth element is high levels of stress either from within family relationships, such as marital conflict, or external stress, such as unemployment or economic conditions.

Situational stress can contribute to elder abuse. Multiple and overwhelming incidences can result in failure of usual coping in the adult-child. Avoiding open conflict by maintaining a distance from the parent becomes an obsolete defense in the face of increased caretaking needs of the aging parent. Role changes in the parent (no longer all-powerful) and increasing dependency on children may result in the elder making constant and unreasonable demands on the adult children, further complicating the stress response. Possible recurrence of continued incest/sexual abuse of younger female children in the family by the elderly male parent may threaten adult children with families of their own.

Stress as a catalyst to domestic violence is a product of social learning. A clear relationship between stress, unemployment rate, alcoholism, assault, and homicide rate exists (Straus, 1990a). Women respond to stress with a clear tendency towards depression. Pregnancy, the addition of a new family member through marriage, caring for an elderly parent, or leaving a family member by divorce, death, or illness are possible situations in which the demands experienced are inconsistent with the response capabilities of the abuser and victim, resulting in an abusive incident or an increase in severity of ongoing battering.

Nurses willing to take up the challenge of building a research-knowledge base assessment and intervention with the abused elderly will be the forerunners in developing methods to assist the elderly in an area neglected by health-care providers.

Research offers nurses insights into the ultimate question: Why do women remain with abusive partners and risk severe injury or death? Some reasons for remaining in an abusive relationship include promises by the abuser to "change," economic dependency; for the sake of the children, religious beliefs, commitment, and fear or lack of ability (or confidence) to be self-reliant (Strube, 1983). The victim is traditionally loyal and has a deep hope that the abusive partner will "change" (Wodarski, 1987). Leaving abusive relationships is a process that occurs over time within the abusive relationship (Ulrich, 1991).

The primary reason cited for women leaving abusive relationships is their own "fear of finally being killed"; that is, as a matter of life and death. When the woman recognizes herself as a victim, her personal growth then involves a process of overcoming self-blame and responsibility for the abuser's behaviors, as well as overcoming the shame and stigma associated with being abused by an intimate partner. Other reasons cited include the "aha"-like experience of "waking up": "It was just that sudden awareness that he had a problem, that he was a batterer" (Ulrich, 1991; Yalom, 1983). The safety concern for children was not found to be a main impetus for leaving (Ulrich, 1991).

Bias in Treatment

Health-care providers are the most likely to see victims of violence and constitute a frontline for identification and intervention (Council on Scientific Affairs, 1992). However, abusive relationships are often unrecognized or are simply ignored by health-care providers (Randall, 1990). Nurses are found to be less likely to believe that domestic abuse is justified than physicians: however, gender rather than professional socialization accounts for this difference (Tilden, 1989). Primary therapy offered to abused women, aside from treatment of the physical injury, is prescription antidepressant medication and tranquilizers (Gayford, 1975). Nurses must first recognize their own past (or present) issues regarding abuse. Nurses must recognize their own attitudes about domestic violence, such as "Do I believe the woman 'deserved' the violence? Do I believe the woman is 'property' of her husband? Do I believe I am incapable of verbal or physical abuse? Do I believe these marital matters are personal and none of my business? Do I believe that parents have the right to use corporal punishment? Do I think the 'old pest' should be put in a nursing home?" If the answer to any of these questions is "yes," the nurse is likely to reinforce the victim's feelings of shame, self-blame, helplessness, and hopelessness.

Maintaining objectivity is crucial in all patient care. However, unresolved ethical questions such as "What is acceptable marital fighting? Is spanking an elderly person an acceptable form of behavioral control?" complicate neutrality, as judgments regarding this highly sensitive issue cannot always be separated from practice. The nurse must be cognizant that the batterer may be a partner of the same sex. Having established a personal and professional philosophy enables the nurse to objectively affect quality health care.

Nurses must identify their conflicts with existing policy or treatment team interventions and participate congruently with management intervention and treatment of adult victims of violence. The serious potentials that are intrinsic to these clients cannot be undermined by conflict within the nurses' working arena. Policies and practices must also be sufficiently congruent.

The nurse can be an effective change agent and peer educator by keeping current in knowledge regarding domestic violence through attending workshops or educational inservice programs reviewing updated research, using skilled supervision and open communication with other treatment team members.

Risk Factors

Persons identified as having risk factors for violent behaviors must be assessed closely and helped to discover, clarify, and alter their beliefs and values toward violence as a viable option for behavioral problem solving. Risk factors which have been identified are sociological, developmental/ psychological, and neuro-psychological (Roberts, 1992).

Sociological factors include involvement in gang activity, drug dealing, and viewing of television violence. Developmental and psychological risk factors include socialized sex role extremes, intergenerational family violence, poor impulse control and psychological disorders involving paranoid thoughts, psychotic thoughts, depression, and/or no self-esteem. The neurological factors include head trauma or epilepsy.

Implications for Nursing

Identifying risk factors associated with violence assists nurses in directing intervention. As a primary intervention, nurses may provide anticipatory guidance, including teaching, effective parenting, nonviolent conflict resolution, avoidance of potentially violent situations, resource development, and techniques for improving impulse control. Secondary level of intervention includes the early detection of (at-risk) clients, crises intervention, and treatment of the response to a violence experience. Tertiary level of intervention is ongoing treatment, the purpose of which is to limit disability and rehabilitate the client to optimum functioning (Roberts, 1992).

Nurses must use knowledge about domestic violence in their work with patients, particularly as data are gathered. Appendix B provides a reference of possible instruments with implications for assessment and monitoring of domestic violence. Feelings of safety and security are basic psychological needs. Disturbed schemas are expressed in feeling states of fear, anxiety, and phobias while behavioral expression is avoidant behavior. Obtaining or providing for the victim's safety is the minimal outcome that must result when the victim comes in contact with health-care providers. Planning for the "next time" may be the most effective initial nursing intervention.

Feelings of confusion and generalized distress most commonly accompany victims seeking health care for domestic injury. Their adaptive defenses may manifest in mistrust, emotional detachment, and inability to make decisions and change, and may impair their ability to form therapeutic alliances with health-care providers.

The psychological aspects of the individual interplay in ways that give personalized meaning to the experiences of trauma and directs adaptive behaviors. Psychological aspects of self, traumatic memories, cognitive schemas (beliefs), and psychological needs are areas of assessment that are vital for gaining insights into the feelings, schemas, and resulting adaptive behaviors.

Dependency and trust are also basic psychological needs and must be distinguished from "passivity." An expression of disturbed schema may be an expectation that a spouse would not be monogamous or that one must "take care of everything" because no one can be depended on. Feeling states include betrayal, self-doubt, and disappointment in being unable to trust others. Behaviors may include inability to make decisions, avoidance of close relationships, suspiciousness, and isolation.

Establishing a therapeutic relationship involves trust and dependency for a victim and even the abuser. By seeking a frame of reference, the nurse may begin by seeking insights into the trauma: "Why did this happen to me? Life just doesn't make sense. I've given up trying to understand." These statements can represent an opportunity for identifying and engaging the victim in treatment. Questions such as "What would it mean to change that belief? What does that behavior mean or achieve?" foster insights necessary to create an optimal opportunity for beginning the therapeutic relationship (Little, 1990).

Listening for themes of abandonment, reluctance to ask for help or support from others, or "being made a fool of" provide clues to the individual's response to experienced trauma. Independence is the ability to control one's own behavior and rewards. The nurse can discover the individual's schema by listening for themes of shame, vulnerability, and helplessness. Discrepancies in disturbed schema may be expressed in a double standard: "I can't tell others of my pain or that I need help. I must be available to others irrespective of my immediate state." Behaviors such as being overcontrolling or overly responsible are characteristic in victims who are abused within a domestic relationship.

Lowered self-esteem is a predominate disturbed schema in both participants of domestic violence. Self-esteem is a basic human need for recognition and validation. Themes of self-blame, worthlessness, badness, feelings of contempt about other people, despair, and futility are feeling states associated with disturbed schema of self-esteem. Beliefs that people do not really care and are out for themselves, or that the self is bad and flawed, commonly exist. Behaviorally, the individual will generally withdraw from the world and may engage in any variety of self-punitive acts, including remaining in or repeating violent relationships.

Any challenge to the detrimental impact of beliefs on behaviors must be gentle. Maximizing the hopes that the abuser will change leaves the victim in a vulnerable position for repeated abuse. Accepting reality, increasing awareness, and integrating opposites are effective goals in assisting the victim of abuse (Harman, 1974; Yontef, 1983). Denial or rationalization of the reality, as in the statements "I know he cares about me," or "He doesn't mean to," can be met with observational "balancing statements" from the nurse, such as "Right now you have a broken arm. Right now we fear for your safety." Increased awareness by the victim can alleviate disabling generalities and bring a clarity about specific beliefs and behaviors. "What can *you* change so that you will be able to get your needs met?" is a question the nurse may pose to begin specific awareness for the victim.

Change by the victim may result in repercussions from the abuser; therefore, the nurse must be highly in tune with possible consequences of treatment interventions. Many abused women feel trapped or are immobilized by fear. Because attacks occur in the home, the woman may have no place to go, particularly if there are children (Wodarski, 1987). They may find little or no social support, such as neighbors, law enforcement intervention, or referrals from the emergency room. Lack of employable skills and economic dependency affects the ability of the victim to leave. Leaving as a process requires interventions aimed at support of the victim even though the victim may leave and return to the relationship many times before final termination of the abusive relationship. During this process, developing a safety plan with the victim for continuing episodes of abuse is vital, especially when there are children in the care of the victim.

Nursing practice with abused women and their families may be guided by a model of three processes: explicating, dwelling within, and moving beyond (Butler, 1991). The goal of the explicating process makes clear the current situation by exploring and clarifying "what is," identifying values and themes for the victim. Victims do not often describe themselves as abused. Paradoxical themes of confusion-clarity, trust-mistrust, hopelessness-hopefulness, or exhaustion-exhilaration may be heard. This process brings new meaning to the victim's situation.

The goal of the dwelling within process is to discover the personal meaning the situation holds for the victim. The dwelling within process begins as enlightenment of the "what is" occurs. Uncovering situational meanings for the victim may also result in work with other family members. Discovery of wishes, desires, and feelings can give a new perspective to the victim.

The moving beyond process explores options within or to the current situation. The victim begins to integrate new ways of being and feeling more capable and worthwhile. Personal responsibility for choices and changes transpires within the victim. Learning experiences that provide feedback on accomplishments and enhance feelings of adequacy and self-esteem promote the victim's personal growth. The nurse may provide direction and support for self-development areas of defining and identifying personal strengths, needs, and limits. Experience in setting one's own goals is valuable practice for the victim.

A major obstacle to early detection of the abused elder is inaccessibility into the home. The abuse often escalates, resulting in severe injury before the elder is in contact with the health-care system. A treatment model for identified elderly victims includes three stages: reluctance, recognition, and rebuilding (Breckman, 1988).

Denial of abuse by the elderly characterizes the reluctance stage. Decreasing isolation through referrals to community services is recommended (ie, Meals-on-Wheels, community health services, visiting nurses, community elderly programs). Decreasing shame, guilt, and self-blame by helping victims redefine their role as elderly parents will assist them in clarifying realistic options. Fear of loss of autonomy, abandonment by children, or death are often foremost fears held by the elderly.

As the elderly's defenses are decreased in treatment, they move into the recognition stage, which may result in a new understanding of the reality and impact of the abuse. The nurse must be skilled in accurate assessment of the elder's existing abilities so that realistic goals and changes can be supported.

In the rebuilding stage, solutions are more imminent and may include new housing, a legal guardian, or family counseling. The nurse should seek the least restrictive alternative in environmental protection for the neglected or abused elderly victim (Quinn, 1990).

The major components in treating victims of any type of domestic violence are intake/evaluation, crisis intervention, advocacy, referral, therapy, education, coordination of treatment, and termination. At the very least, goals must be ensuring the safety of the victim and dependent children; reducing isolation through increasing their knowledge and use of resources and options; increasing their understanding of the origins and impact of domestic violence; assisting them in seeking and making healthier choices for themselves; and facilitating integration and healing.

Conclusion

Early detection and intervention are most vital in treating domestic violence. Nurses are the most prevalent group of providers within a variety of settings to consistently have early and ongoing direct contact with victims of domestic violence. This places nurses in a strategic position for assessment and identification.

Nurses have historically had an impact on social change and must take an active role in the area of domestic violence. Nurse administrators, lobbyists, clinicians, and educators make far-reaching decisions that affect the quality of life for many victims. Most recently, the Kansas State Nurses' Association lobbied to eliminate corporal punishment from schools. The American Nurses Association currently supports the re-establishment of an office of domestic violence within the Department of Health and Human Services, mandatory reporting by health-care professionals of domestic abuse at national and state levels, and an education component within the schools of nursing on awareness and prevention of domestic abuse.

Adding to nursing's knowledge base through practice-based research and education of colleagues through publications are additional means by which nursing can have increased impact in prevention, detection, and treatment of victims of domestic violence.

References

Abramson, L., Seligman, M., Teasdale, J. Learned helplessness in humans: Critique and reformulation. *J Abnorm Psychol* 1978; 87(1):49-74.

Agosta, C., McHugh, M. Family violence. In T. Williams (Ed.), *Post-traumatic stress disorders: A handbook for clinicians.* Cincinnati: Disabled American Veterans, 1987, pp. 253-266.

Anderson, C. Abuse and neglect among the elderly. *Journal of Gerontological Nursing* 1981; 7(21):77-85.

Bandura, A. *Aggression: A social learning analysis.* Englewood Cliffs, NJ: Prentice-Hall, 1973.

Breckman, R., Adelman, R. *Strategies for helping victims of elder mistreatment.* Newbury Park, CA: Sage Publications, 1988.

Browne, A. *When battered women kill.* New York: Macmillan, 1987.

Browne, A., Finkelhor, D. The impact of child sexual abuse: A review of the research. *Psychol Bull* 1986; 99:66-77.

Bureau of Justice Statistics. *Criminal victimization in the United States.* Washington, DC: US Department of Justice, 1982.

Burge, S. Violence against women as a health care issue. *Fam Med* 1989; 21:368-373.

Butler, M., Snodgrass, F. Beyond abuse: Parse's theory in practice. *Nurs Sci Q* 1991; 4(2):76-82.

Campbell, J. Nursing assessment of risk of homicide with battered women. *ANS* 1984a; 8(4):36-51,80.

Campbell, J. A test of two explanatory models of women's responses to battering. *Nurs Res* 1989; 38(1):18-24.

Campbell, J., Humphres, J. *Nursing care of victims of family violence.* Reston, VA: Reston Publishing Co, 1984b.

Council on Scientific Affairs. Violence against women. *JAMA* 1992; 267:3184-3189.

Critchlow, B. The powers of John Barleycorn: Beliefs about the effects of alcohol on social behavior. *Am Psychol* 1986; 41:751-764.

Drake, V. Battered women: A health care problem in disguise. *Image* 1982; 14(2):40.

Fagan, J., Friedman. E., Wexler, S., Lewis, V. *The national family violence evaluation: Final report. Vol. I: Analytical findings.* San Francisco: URSA Institute, 1984.

Fauldi, S. *Backlash: The undeclared war against American women.* New York: Crown Publishers, Inc, 1991.

Fulmer, T., Ashley, J. Neglect: What part of abuse? *Pride Institute Journal of Longer Term Home Health Care* 1986; 5(4):18-24.

Gage, R. Examining the dynamics of spouse abuse: An alternative view. *Nurs Pract* 1991; 16(4):11-16.

Gayford, J. Wife battering: A preliminary survey of 100 cases. *Br Med J* 1975; 1:195.

Harman, R. Goals of Gestalt therapy. *Professional Psychology* 1974; 4:178-184.

Helton, A., Snodgrass, F. Battering during pregnancy: Intervention strategies. *Birth* 1987; 14:142-147.

Jurik, N., Winn, R. Gender and homicide: A comparison of men and women who kill. *Violence and Victims* 1990; 5:227-241.

Kantor, G., Straus, M. The "drunken bum" theory of wife beating. In M. Straus, R. Gelles (Eds.), *Physical violence in American families.* New Brunswick, NJ: Transaction Publishers, 1990, 203-224.

Launius, M.H., Jensen, B.L. Interpersonal problem-solving skills in battered, counseling, and control women. *Journal of Family Violence* 1987; 2(2):151-162.

Lentzner, H., DeBerry, M. *Intimate victims: A study of violence among friends and relatives.* Washington, DC: US Department of Justice, Bureau of Justice Statistics, 1980.

Lew, M. *Victims no longer: Men recovering from incest and other sexual child abuse.* New York: Nevraumont Publishing Co, 1980.

Little, L. Gestalt therapy with females involved in intimate violence. In S. Stith, M. Williams, K. Rosen (Eds.), *Violence hits home: Comprehensive treatment approaches to domestic violence.* New York: Springer, 1990, pp. 47-65.

McLeer, S., Anwar, K. A study of battered women presenting in an emergency department. *Am J Public Health* 1989; 79(1):65-66.

Mitchell, R., Hodson, C. Coping with domestic violence: Social support and psychological health among battered women. *Am J Consult Psychol* 1983; 11:629-654.

Morrow, S., Hawxhurst, D. Lesbian partner abuse: Implications for therapists. *J Counsel Dev* 1989; 68:58-62.

Phillips, L. Elder abuse—What is it? Who says so? *Geriatr Nurs* 1983; 4(3):167-170.

Pillemer, K. Risk factors in elder abuse: Results from a case controlled study. In K. Pillemer (Ed.), *Elder abuse: Conflict in the family.* Dover, MA: Auburn House, 1986.

Pillemer, K., Finkelhor, D. The prevalence of elder abuse: A random sample survey. *Journal of the Gerontological Society of America* 1988a; 28(1):51-57.

Pillemer, K., Suitor, J. Elder abuse. In V. Hasselt, R. Morrison, A. Bellack, M. Hersen (Eds.), *Handbook of family violence.* New York: Plenum Press, 1988b, pp. 247-270.

Quinn, M. Elder abuse and neglect: Treatment Issues. In S. Stith, M. Williams, K. Rosen (Eds.), *Violence hits home: Comprehensive treatment approaches to domestic violence.* New York: Springer Publishing Co, 1990, pp. 277-302.

Randall, T. Domestic violence: Intervention calls for more than treating injuries. *JAMA* 1990; 261:939-944.

Roane, T. *The working handbook: A professional's manual for intervention with sexually abused boys.* Gainsville, FL: Child Care Publishers, 1989.

Roberts, C., Quillan, J. Preventing violence through primary care intervention. *Nurse Practitioner* 1992; 7(8):62-70.

Rogers, M. Nursing: To be or not to be? *Nursing Outlook* 1972; 20:41-46.

Rosenberg, M., Stark, E., Zahn, M. Interpersonal violence: Homicide and spouse abuse. In J. Last (Ed.), *Public health and preventive medicine*, 12th ed. New York: Appleton-Century-Crofts, 1985.

Russell, D. *Sexual exploitation.* Beverly Hills, CA: Sage, 1984.

Sonkin, D., Martin, D., Walker, L. *The male batterer: A treatment approach.* New York: Springer Publishing Co, 1985.

Stark, E., Flitcraft, A. Violence among intimates. In V. Van Hasselt, R. Morrison, A. Bellack, M. Hersen (Eds.) *Handbook of family violence.* New York: Plenum Press, 1988, pp. 293-317.

Stark, E., Flitcraft, A., Frazier, W. Medicine and patriarchal violence: The social construction of a "private" event. *Int J Health Serv* 1979; 9:461-493.

Stark, E., Flitcraft, A., Zuckerman, D., Grey, A., Borison, J., Frazier, W. *Wife abuse in the medical setting: An introduction for health personnel.* Washington, DC: Office of Domestic Violence, 1981.

Straus, M. Social stress and marital violence in a national sample of American families. In M. Straus, R. Gelles (Eds.), *Physical violence in American families.* New Brunswick, NJ: Transaction Publishers, 1990a, pp. 181-201.

Straus, M., Gelles, R. How violent are American families? In M. Straus, R. Gelles

(Eds.), *Physical violence in American families*. New Brunswick, NJ: Transaction Publishers, 1990b, pp. 95-112.

Straus, M., Gelles R., Stinmetz, S. *Behind closed doors: Violence in the American family.* Garden City, NY: Anchor Books, 1981.

Straus, M., Smith, C. Family patterns and primary prevention of family violence. In M. Straus, R. Gelles (Eds.), *Physical violence in American families*. New Brunswick, NJ: Transaction Publishers, 1990c, pp. 507-526.

Tilden, V. Response of the health care delivery system to battered women. *Issues in Mental Health Nursing* 1989; 10:309-320.

Tomita, S. The denial of elder mistreatment by victims and abusers: The application of neutralization theory. *Violence and Victims* 1990; 5:171-183.

Ulrich, Y. Women's reasons for leaving abusive spouses. *Health Care for Women International* 1991; 12:465-473.

US Department of Justice. *Uniform crime reports: Crime reports in the United States.* Washington, DC: US Government Printing Office, 1986.

US Department of Justice. *Female victims of violent crimes.* Washington, DC: US Government Printing Office, 1991. No. NCJ-126826.

Wodarski, J. An examination of spouse abuse: Practice issues for the professional. *Clin Soc Work J* 1987; 15:172-187.

Wolf, R., Strugnell, C., Godkin, M. *Preliminary findings from three model projects on elderly abuse.* Worchester, MA: University of Massachusetts Medical Center, 1982.

Yontef, G. The self in Gestalt therapy: Reply to Tobin. *Gestalt Journal* 1983; 6(1):55-70.

Other Readings

Abrahamsen, D. *The psychology of crime.* New York: Columbia University Press, 1960.

Abrahamsen, D. *Our violent society.* New York: Funk & Wagnalls, 1970.

Anonymous. The battered woman. Breaking the cycle of abuse. *Emerg Med* 1989; 21(11):104-108, 113, 115.

Block, M., Sinnot, J. *The battered elder syndrome: An exploratory study.* College Park, MD: Center on Aging, 1979.

Bograd, M. Family systems approach to wife battering: A feminist critique. *Am J Orthopsychiatry* 1984; 54:559-568.

Chamow, L. The clinician's role in treating spouse abuse. *Family Therapy* 1990; 17:123-128.

Evert, K., Bijkerk, I. *When you're ready: A woman's healing from childhood physical and sexual abuse by her mother.* Walnut Creek. CA: Launch Press, 1987.

Follingstad, D., Laughlin, J., Polek, D., Ruthledge, L., Hause, E. Identification of patterns of wife abuse. *Journal of Interpersonal Violence* 1991; 6:198-204.

Franzer, J. *The many faces of family violence.* Springfield, IL: C. Thomas, 1982.

Fromm, E. *The anatomy of human destruction.* New York: Fawcett Crest Books, 1973.

Gelles, R. Abused wives: Why do they stay? *Journal of Marriage and Family* 1976; 58:659-668.

Gelles, R., Cornell, C. *Intimate violence in families.* Beverly Hills, CA: Sage, 1985.

Gelles, R., Cornell, C. *Intimate violence in families.* Newbury Park, CA: Sage, 1990.

Gelles, R., Straus, M. Violence in the American family. *Journal of Social Issues* 1979; 35(2):20.

Goldstein, J. Brain research and violent behavior. *Arch Neurol* 1975; 30:1-35.

Graham, K. Theories of intoxicated aggression. *Can J Behav Sci* 1980; 12:141-158.

Grubman, A., Black, S. *Broken boys/mending men: Recovery from childhood sexual abuse.* Blue Ridge Summit, PA: TAB Books, 1990.

Herrenkohl, K., Herrenkohl, R., Toedter, L. Perspectives on the intergenerational transmission of abuse. In D. Finkelhor, R. Gelles, G. Hotaling, M. Strauss (Eds.), *The dark side of families: Current family violence research.* Beverly Hills, CA: Sage, 1983, pp. 305-316.

Kaplan, H. *Self-attitudes of deviant behavior.* Pacific Palisades, CA: Goodyear Publishing Co, 1975.

Lorenz, K. *On aggression.* New York: Bantam Books, 1966.

MacDonald, J. *The murderer and his victim.* Springfield IL: Thomas, 1961.

McCubbin, H., Patterson, J. Family transitions: Adaptation to stress. In H. McCubbin, C. Figley (Eds.), *Stress and the family,* vol. 1. New York: Brunner/Mazel, 1983, pp. 5-25.

Monroe, R. *Brain dysfunction in aggressive criminals.* Lexington. MA: DC Heath & Co, 1976.

Moyer, K. *The psychobiology of aggression.* New York: Harper & Row, 1976.

National Center for Women and Family Law. National Coalition Against Domestic Violence, PO Box 34103, Washington, DC, 20043-4103.

Paddock. J. Studies on antivolent and "normal" communities. *Aggressive Behavior* 1975; 1:217-233.

Phillips, L. Elder abuse—What is it? Who says so? *Geriatr Nurs* 1983; May/June:167-170.

Rollo, M. *Power and innocence.* New York: Norton, 1972.

Roy, M. Four thousand partners in violence; A trend analysis. In M. Roy (Ed.), *The abusive partner: An analysis of domestic battering.* New York: van Nostrand Reinhold, 1982, pp. 17-35.

Ryan, W. *Blaming the victim.* New York: Vintage Books, 1971.

Snyder, D., Fruchtman, L. Differential patterns of wife abuse: A data based typology. *J Consult Clin Psychol* 1981; 49:878-885.

Sonkin, D., Durphy, M. *Learning to live without violence: A handbook for men.* Volcano, CA: Volcano Press, 1989.

Stark, E., Flitcraft, A. Violence among intimates: An epidemiological review. In B. Haslatt (Ed.), *Handbook of family violence.* New York: Plenium Press, 1988.

Stinmetz, S., Straus, M. *Violence in the family.* New York: Harper & Row, 1974.

Strube, M., Barbour, L. The decision to leave an abusive relationship: Economic dependence and psychological commitment. *Journal of Marriage and the Family* 1983; 11:785-793.

Stuart, E., Campbell, J. Assessment of patterns of dangerousness with battered women. *Issues Ment Health Nurs* 1989; 10:245-260.

Valzelli, L. *Psychobiology of aggression and violence.* New York: Raven Press, 1981.

Walker, L. *The battered women.* New York: Harper & Row, 1979.

Widom, C. Child abuse, neglect, and adult behavior: Research design and findings on criminality, violence, and child abuse. *Am J Orthopsychiatry* 1989; 59:355-367.

Wilson, S., Cameron, S., Jaffe, P., Wolfe, D. Children exposed to wife abuse: An intervention model. *Social Work* 1989; 70(30):180-184.

Wolf, R. Major findings from three model proeicts on elderly abuse. In K. Pillemer, R. Wolf (Eds.), *Elder abuse: Conflict in the family.* Dover, MA: Auburn Publishing Co, 1986.

7 | *Perpetrators of Family Violence*

Patricia J. Neubauer, RN, PhD

When most people think about wife batterers or child abusers, they envision dirty old men in trench coats hanging around schoolyards or vicious drunks in torn t-shirts whose wives cower in the corner. Rarely do visions feature the neighbor on the corner, the family doctor, or the church pastor. Yet researchers have demonstrated that offenders cross all socioeconomic lines, come from all races and religions, and demonstrate varying degrees of cognitive and social skills. These men are similar by the fact that they experience states of underlying pain and frustration, coupled with profound deficits in coping skills.

Introduction

For the purpose of this chapter, only male perpetrators of violence will be examined. It is likely that the extent to which women perpetrate family violence is underestimated, and that fact is pertinent as the missing link in the cycle of family violence, but that topic is beyond the scope of this chapter. The women's movement freed women to disclose their own rape, incest, and battering. If the men's movement succeeds, men will feel free to expose their pain and humiliation related to childhood abuse. When all individuals no longer need to deny the truth of childhood abuse, then society can begin to make real changes that will break the cycle of violence. For many men, masculinity is equated with toughness and aggression; vulnerability is equated with weakness and failure. When normal coping abilities fail or are never learned, men who hide a history of childhood abuse often resort to violence to regain a sense of power and control.

The statistics that describe child abuse are truly staggering. Recent statistics indicate that 22% of all Americans are victims of child sexual abuse, 27% of women and 16% of men (Crewdson, 1988). Recent studies have noted that one third of abused persons never report the abuse as children. It is estimated that one adult man in 100 will abuse a child. Of these men, 40% were abused as children.

Walker (1979) reported that 50% of women will be battered in their lifetime. One third of these women, and one third of men who batter, beat their children (Walker, 1979). In one review, Steinmetz (1986) reported that 82% of abusive men both witnessed marital violence and were the victims of child abuse and neglect. Lang and Langevin (1990) reported that 50% of offenders who victimize children were subjected to physical or sexual violence as children. The case example will identify many characteristics common to abusive men.

The reader should look for characteristics of low self-esteem, inadequate social skills, and a disturbed marital relationship in the following Case Study. In this family, there are clues that the father may have been conditioned in his family of origin to use physical or sexual abuse as normal behavior. The reader should be able to identify the problems caused by alcohol abuse and inability to cope with life.

Case Example

"Don" was 33 years old when he was arrested for sexually abusing his 16-year-old daughter, "Cheryl." The family included Don's wife, "Jackie," 32, and their son, "Bill," 14. Don's family history included severe physical abuse by his alcoholic father. Don minimized this as punishment for his bad behavior and described his childhood as idyllic. Don's mother and sisters reported that Don's father routinely battered his mother and sexually molested all four of his sisters; Don denied knowledge of this. Both Jackie and Don minimized his actions; Jackie remained aligned with Don until his incarceration. Cheryl was removed from the home by the state child protective services because Don refused to leave after the abuse was reported.

Don physically abused both children from young ages. Cheryl often cooperated with the sexual abuse when it seemed to be the only way to protect her brother from her father's wrath. Don rarely hit Jackie, but they argued frequently and he was verbally demeaning toward her. Conditions improved when Don worked, but he rarely worked. When out of work, Don drank heavily and abuse escalated. Jackie essentially abdicated her role as mother and became the breadwinner. She typically worked 60 to 80 hours a week and distanced herself from her home life. Cheryl cooked all the meals and was responsible for most of the housework. Don often found excuses to keep Cheryl home from school, and Cheryl found herself sneaking out of the house early in the morning to attend school.

Don heavily abused alcohol and marijuana. He used drugs with no efforts to shield the children from his behavior, and he bribed Cheryl with free access to alcohol and drugs. Jackie never objected and seemed oblivious to what was happening. Don allowed Cheryl no privacy; her bedroom was the only room without a door. Don routinely listened to Cheryl's phone calls, searched her room for notes from boys, and would not allow her to date. When Cheryl objected, Don would intensify abuse toward Bill and generally would fly into a rage and claim disrespect from the children.

Cheryl reported that the abuse started when she was in kindergarten or first grade; she was very young when Don started fondling her genitals. Don progressively increased his sexual actions and demands for her participation; he began having intercourse with her when she was 10. Cheryl finally disclosed the abuse after a fight about attending her junior prom. Don would not allow her to buy a dress and Cheryl felt sure he would not, in the end, allow her to attend the event. She told her favorite teacher, who reported the abuse to local authorities. Cheryl never told anyone before this because she believed her father would kill her mother and brother.

Don never denied he molested his daughter, but he minimized his actions. He reported the abuse had occurred for 3 or 4 years. He would explain that he never touched her; he only had her give him "blow jobs." His denial centered on the belief that Cheryl had disclosed the abuse only to punish him. In his mind, Cheryl had long been a willing participant, almost a girlfriend, and he believed that this relieved him of responsibility. Don described himself as a good provider and his family as happy. He reported that his family admired him. When pushed for details, he used alcohol to explain his lack of memory. He had no concept of how his daughter might feel about the abuse. He demonstrated no remorse for his actions.

General Dynamics

To understand perpetrators, the dynamic of denial is of crucial importance and consists of different elements. Some perpetrators will deny all or part of the facts, especially related to extent and intent. There seems to be some ego saved by denying certain actions seen as subjectively more serious. Denial may focus on any extenuating circumstances that alter wrongfulness (Pollack, 1991). The greater the number of elements of denial that are used by an offender, the greater evidence of defensiveness and poorer prognosis for change. Denial serves a protective function and exists on a continuum from defensiveness and minimization to suppression of memory of wrongdoing. Perpetrators use denial to attribute their behavior to external factors or to blame the victim. In situations of wife battering, men tend to project negative traits onto spouses or to blame temporary environmental factors (Overholser, 1990). External attributions center on characteristics specific to the spouse or women in general. As the duration and intensity of abuse fluctuates, the nature of the attributions will also intensify. Offenders often use alcohol to explain violence.

Offenders' distorted thoughts and beliefs serve to initiate and maintain patterns of inappropriate behavior. Often, offenders' denial centers in the question of consent. Perpetrators may perceive that children are consenting to or are benefiting from sexual activity. The offender may believe his wife asks for physical punishment by defying his wishes.

Denial expressed early in treatment may relate to fears regarding potential legal actions. Offenders evaluated as inpatients but not facing legal charges showed more psychopathology on tests such as the MMPI (Grossman, 1990). It is unclear whether this is a sign of greater disturbance or is related to the offenders' openness to gaining help. Both men facing charges and those not facing charges tended to deny more deviant behaviors (Grossman, 1990). Generally, denial serves to maintain some degree of ego strength as offenders are a group of individuals characterized by low self-esteem.

Low self-esteem seems to be a crucial element in the intergenerational transmission of family violence. Briere and Runtz (1990) identified a substantial relationship between self-esteem and psychological abuse, and connected childhood abuse to adult symptomatology. Self-esteem develops as a function of the child's perception of parents' love and acceptance. Childhood abuse fosters a belief that the child is somehow damaged or undesirable.

Psychoanalytic theory proposes that behavior is based on childhood unconscious conflicts, which result in aggressive impulses and anxiety. Rosen (1991) describes some of the psychodynamic concepts that explain victimizing behavior. When childhood abuse results in a fragile or damaged self-concept, real or imagined slights either at home or in the world can trigger aggression. By identifying with the aggressor and acting in an aggressive manner, the perpetrator regains a sense of power and control. Severe childhood neglect and abuse may trigger narcissistic rage. The perpetrator seeks revenge when the object (a person expected to unconditionally meet the perpetrator's needs) fails to meet the offender's expectations. In a narcissistic rage, perpetrators no longer consider right and wrong and behave in a manner that will produce a sense of power and control. In projective identification, perpetrators project painful or undesirable aspects of themselves on either their spouse or children. Childhood abuse is re-enacted when the victim is seen as a rejecting, hurtful parent deserving of retribution. The perpetrator inflicts pain and violation on a weaker being in an attempt to reduce anxiety and regain a sense of self-mastery and control.

Social learning theorists explain intergenerational transmission of violence through the concept that behavior is learned through either direct experience or by viewing behavior. Based on this, with parents acting as models, children grow up to replicate violence. Proponents of modeling theory often blame violent television and movies as teaching aggressive skills and desensitizing viewers to the effects of violence. In frustration-aggression theory, frustration leads to aggressive actions as an innate process. Aggression acts as its own reinforcement by decreasing unpleasant arousal states and resulting in gratification when the object of the aggression acquiesces or is afraid.

In sociocultural models of violence, social pressure promotes aggressive behavior and violence in men who lack the social and coping skills needed to achieve their goals. Boys with physically and emotionally absent fathers turn to athletes and action figures to serve as heroes and models and imitate aggressive problem-solving behavior.

There is some evidence to support a theory of biological origins of violence in men. High levels of testosterone may act as a precursor to violence by lowering frustration thresholds and increasing impulsivity (Medzian, 1991). Langevin and others (1990) have demonstrated an interaction between minimal brain pathology, substance abuse, negative self-perception, and violent offenses. They suspect that alcohol and drug use may produce dysphoria, which is expressed in a paranoid or hostile manner. In this group, 25% of the men demonstrated significant pathology on neuropsychological testing, but showed no deficit on computed tomography scans or electroencephalogram. The authors suggest that the idea of minimal brain dysfunction be applied to aid in understanding violent behavior. Geffner and Rosenbaum (1990) found that 61% of battering husbands in one sample had a history of a head injury and postulated that there was a relationship between the injury and impulse control in offenders.

Child Sexual Offenders

Only perpetrators who victimize biological or stepchildren will be examined in this chapter. The difference between interfamily and intrafamily abuse often relates to the availability of victims. It is believed that pedophiles may serially marry or live with women who bear children of the desired age. A father may only molest one child in the family, only daughters, or children of both sexes. Many perpetrators maintain an apparently satisfactory marital sexual relationship. Based on different values and experiences, a father maintains a set of rules and taboos. Some men may never touch blood-related children, yet molest stepchildren. Some fathers act out sexually only after the child reaches puberty. There is no one theory that definitively explains why men choose to sexually abuse children.

Pedophiles include anyone who has a sustained erotic preference for children, who engages in sexual behavior with a prepubescent child, or who masturbates to fantasies featuring children (Arndt, 1991). Arndt (1991) defines a pedophile as someone who fails to inhibit impulses that are prevalent, but weak, in the normal population. Sexual misconduct includes exposing a child to sexual stimuli inappropriate for the child's age and level of psychosexual development. This definition includes acts such as forcing children to view pornography, watching adults engaged in sexual activity, and engaging in direct sexual contact.

Groth (1979) identifies three ways for a perpetrator to gain sexual access to another person: consent, exploitation, and force. Most state laws remove the issue of consent by legislating that children lack the experience and knowledge to give informed consent. Perpetrators use coercion, threats, or force to gain a child's cooperation. In situations of incest, children often offer no resistance out of fear and lack of understanding. A father uses his power and authority to exploit his relationship with his child. Arndt (1991) estimates that force or threats are used to gain compliance in 30% to 50% of child sexual abuse cases.

Groth (1979) describes anger, power, and sexual dynamics in all sexual misconduct. Angry perpetrators characteristically use physical force. Their anger is rarely premeditated and increases when presented with a vulnerable subject. When an angry perpetrator is confronted with his actions, he may describe events in a manner that presents him as an observer more than a participant (Groth, 1979).

A man who assaults children for the purpose of gaining power is using sex to compensate for feelings of inadequacy. Physical aggression is generally only used to subdue a victim. There may have been significant fantasy and obsessional thoughts prior to any actual action, which can be either premeditated or opportunistic. Sexual dominance serves to validate the offender's masculine identity and bolster self-esteem. This offender often has a stake in seeing his victims as either secretly willing participants or charmed into participation. A sadistic perpetrator combines sex and aggression in a way that gains him pleasure from pain and helplessness. This offender usually fully plans his activities and may pick victims who are seen as exceptionally helpless or vulnerable. This man's sadistic nature often remains otherwise hidden.

Groth describes fixated offenders as men who by virtue of some developmental experience develop sexual interest in children and never mature to a stage of adult sexual relationships. A regressed offender has had age-appropriate relationships and molests others as a result of some sort of internal or external stressful trigger. These categories are no longer widely recognized but still are used in some court systems.

Finkelhor and Williams (1992) have further refined categories of perpetrators. They have identified that there are distinct age preferences that determine the age of onset of abuse. There are many routes to incestuous behavior, and generally a gradual increase in the seriousness or invasiveness of behavior occurs. In their sample, 26% of the fathers were sexually preoccupied. The offender demonstrates obsessive sexual interest in his daughter and may view her as a sexual object from birth. These men tend to view almost everyone in a sexually objectified manner and are likely to be victims of childhood sexual abuse themselves.

In the second group, adolescent regressive, comprising one third of the fathers, the man becomes interested in his daughter when she reaches puberty and his sexual views are similar to that of adolescent boys. This offender becomes transfixed by his daughter's burgeoning sexuality and feminine appearance.

The third group, instrumental gratifiers, made up 20% of the sample. This offender describes non-erotic impulses toward his daughter and acts out of ungratified sexual desires. This offender may feel guilt and be aware of the damage he causes, but denies the seriousness of his actions by blocking awareness of his sexual actions. He may attempt to avoid conscious awareness of his daughter's identity.

Ten percent of the fathers were emotionally needy, lonely, and depressed. These fathers became emotionally dependent on their daughters to offset feelings of failure. This type of offender tends to romanticize and idealize the sexual relationship and feels gratified by the intimate feelings gained from sexual activity with his daughter.

The last group of fathers, angry retaliators, comprised 10% of the sample. These men often had past histories of rape and assault. This type of offender often denies any sexual attraction to his daughter but uses her as a vehicle to punish her, her mother, or women as a group. Such men may derive sadistic pleasure from the violence used to possess or humiliate their daughters.

In trying to understand the motives behind the actions of fathers who perpetrate incest, it is important to understand their fear of their own vulnerable or helpless feelings. Because of childhood neglect and abuse, or perhaps biological instability, an offender ignores the consequences of his actions and lacks compassion or empathy for his victims. Carnes (1989) has identified a process that he labels sexual addiction. In understanding sexual misconduct, Carnes likens the sexual acting out to using drugs and alcohol to numb emotional pain. Some kind of initiation (a man's own sexual abuse, abandonment, emotional and physical abuse or neglect) sensitizes the perpetrator to use sexual activity as a coping tool. Under some kind of extreme emotional or environment stressor (ie, divorce or crisis of self-doubt), the offender moves into an addictive cycle.

The addictive cycle is characterized by ritualized activities, sexual compulsivity, shame, and despair. The preoccupation in the ritualization stage (planning and setting up an activity) is pleasurable, and the sexual release generally produces a period of euphoria. This is followed by a fall into shame and despair and damaged self-esteem coupled with a lessened ability to cope. With each cycle of abuse, behavior becomes more linked to shame, which perpetuates the cycle. Carnes describes a perpetrator's control as episodic with short or lengthy cycles. Alcohol accompanies the cycle by acting as a releaser or disinhibitor. The father engaged in incestual activities is too wrapped up in his pain to consider the consequences of his actions.

In a perpetrator's history, there is most often a disturbed father-son relationship (Lang, 1991). Fathers of perpetrators tend to be aggressive, strict, and unaffectionate. If mothers are aggressive, they tend to direct this more toward sons than daughters. This may set up a negative gender identification, with masculinity and resultant hostility toward women (Lisak, 1991). This also sets up a dynamic that tends to prevent true intimacy and foster only a superficial ability for human relationships.

The perpetrator's confusion about his worth and identity may be expressed in outward religiosity, rigid moral attitudes, and a sense of entitlement. This father views himself as a ruler of his kingdom, but actually depends on his family for all emotional and social support. Fathers perpetrating incest often lack a sense of social competence while appearing quite socially capable. These offenders tend to insist on traditional, rigid family roles (James, 1983). Incest occurs most often in families characterized by social isolation, where fathers are protected from discovery and are assured control (Salter, 1988).

In families where incest occurs, the marital relationship is sometimes characterized by mistrust, lack of mutual time, emotional instability demonstrated in frequent arguments, and loneliness (Lang, 1990). Mothers tend to be emotionally or physically absent. Without the mother to act as a system of checks and balances, severe boundary violations result in role reversal (daughters often become the surrogate wife and mother for the family) and there are expectations for children to nurture parents.

Rigid boundaries around the family maintain the father's sense of control, while inappropriate boundaries between generations serve to open outlets for sexual activity. The family feels chaotic to the child, but often appears quite normal to outsiders. Courtois (1988) describes the symbiotic perpetrator as one who acts out his emotional deprivation, feels distant and isolated, and justifies the use of his child from the depths of his pain. A father who is a sociopath lacks remorse and can justify any means to meet his needs.

Finkelhor (1986) describes four processes that facilitate child sexual abuse:
● The offender experiences emotional congruence in sexual activity with a child. Low self-esteem and inadequate social skills contribute to the perpetrator's inability to relate to other adults. Because of his own childhood trauma, the perpetrator's arrested emotional development seems to require mastering of trauma through identification with aggression against children.
● Sexual arousal toward children may be a product of early conditioning through early sexual contact.
● Blockage from change may exist, preventing normal avenues of mastery of needs and fears. A perpetrator may abuse children as an outlet denied in disturbed marital relationships and insecurity regarding his own worth and desirability.
● There may be some factors that act as disinhibitors, such as an impulse control disorder, alcohol abuse, patriarchal values, or extreme situational stress.

The function of alcohol in abusive situations is controversial. Groth (1979) writes that alcohol is a releaser only for the offender already prone to act out sexually. The affects of alcohol can serve to lower inhibition, impair reasoning and judgment, and distort reality. Estimates place alcohol as a factor in at least 50% of sexual assaults (Courtois, 1982; Groth, 1979).

Treatment for perpetrators of incest is most successful when there is minimal denial and the offender can demonstrate empathy for his victim. Treatment is most successful when the whole family becomes involved and treatment facilities use a combination of group, family, and individual therapy. Treatment should be aimed at changing cognitive distortions, gaining insight into the offender's family history of abuse or neglect, gaining insight into any sexual addictive cycles, understanding of feelings, and improving coping ability through social skills training, stress management, and learning assertiveness and nonaggressive expression. Treatment of depression and anxiety is often an important component of treatment. Treatment will not be successful if abstinence from drugs and alcohol and treatment of addictions is not initiated early in therapy.

Wife Batterers

Many of the elements that describe child sexual offenders also describe men who batter. A man who suffers from low self-esteem may use aggression against his wife to exert a feeling of dominance and power. The American culture promotes the idea that a man's home is his castle. Men who lack positive coping skills to combat stress, loss, and pain may compensate with aggression. Some men's denial systems rely on patriarchal values—traditional sex roles that enable a husband to feel entitled to obedience, sex on command, total control of financial assets, and unconditional gratification of his emotional needs.

A typical man who batters his wife suffers from low self-esteem and feels devalued by the world and in his own eyes. A perception that a man's wife does not view him in an unconditionally positive manner may cause him to explode in rage. Not only does the battering husband need to feel perfectly admired, even feared, but he also needs to view his wife as a representation of his idealized woman. Aggression serves as a way to gain revenge for his disappointment and to provide the offender with a feeling of mastery and dominance. A batterer tends to be pathologically jealous and to blame his wife for his assaults. He does not believe he should be sanctioned for his actions. Following violence, he is apologetic, minimizes his actions, and does not fathom why others do not believe his vows to never repeat violent cycles. This offender lacks the ability to cope with life stressors and uses alcohol and aggressive acting out to cope.

Geffner and Rosenbaum (1990) have demonstrated that perpetrators lack verbal and assertive skills and require greater experiences of being in power. Hurlburt and Apt (1991) noted that perpetrators often show an external locus of control and are more impulsive. These men feel a sense of entitlement that is born out of insecurity and low self-esteem. They demand frequent ego gratification. Men who batter generally are incapable of empathy for their wives.

Burgess and Draper (1989) have shown that marital communications tend to be more negative in content and affect in these couples. A battering husband may coerce his wife into remaining with him through threats of suicide. Freidman (1985) noted a 10% incidence of husband suicide in marriages in which battering occurs. Rosen (1991) reported an investigation of marital homicide that revealed that 44% of all murdered women are killed by husbands or lovers. Men who batter come from all socioeconomic levels, ages, and races. An early finding that men batter more when their wives make more money or have higher status jobs has not been borne out. Claes and Rosenthal (1990) suggest that men of higher status and educational level may demonstrate more severe violence.

In understanding battering men, again the role of alcohol becomes pertinent. A husband's misuse of alcohol significantly increases his risk for aggressive behavior. Geffner and Rosenbaum (1990) write that alcohol is neither a necessary nor sufficient variable in wife abuse, but alcohol may serve a releasing function or merely provide an excuse. Their research demonstrated a link between incidence of head injury and alcohol use in battering men. Burgess and Draper (1989) noted that battering husbands are likely to abuse both when drunk and when not drunk, but when there is significant alcohol abuse, violence tends to be more frequent and more serious. Men who drink are less likely to voluntarily enter treatment. They suggest that alcohol may lead battering men to misinterpret others' actions, or merely may serve as an excuse for aggressive behavior (Burgess, 1989).

Men who batter often grow up in violent homes. If there is no outright physical abuse, there is often lack of respect for women and children. These men often are loners and unable to maintain intimate interpersonal relationships. In battering men's histories, dynamics of negative attribution occur when parents invest children with negative feelings and critical attitudes. Battering men describe that they never felt loved and cared for as children (Rosen, 1991). Milner and others (1990) found that contact with any caring adult moderates the potential to abuse. More severe and chronic abuse tends to increase a perpetrator's potential to abuse his family.

Although battering can occur at any time, there definitely seems to be a cycle when assaultive behavior is most prevalent. Clearly, there is a link between battering incidents and the presence of stressful life events. In some battering relationships, men never lay a hand on their mates prior to marriage, but violence also can begin in the dating phase.

Battering incidents have many similar features (Walker, 1979). Initially, women are startled by the battering incidents. When aggressive tendencies coexist with gentleness, women find it hard to believe when they are the victim of a brutal attack. It is not always possible to predict precarious times and incidents for battering. Battering men tend to be jealous and possessive.

Women often have vivid recall of the events and incidents of battering. Baumeister et al (1990) noted substantial differences in the accounts given by victims and perpetrators. Perpetrators tend to see violence as discrete events in time with minimal negative consequences. Perpetrators rarely understand victims' negative responses that relate to multiple incidents.

Women often conceal the abuse to protect their spouse. Physical abuse is generally accompanied by severe verbal degradation and criticism. Assaultive men are often quite astute at finding a woman's vulnerable areas and directing their attacks to these sensitive areas. A battering man tends to use extremely aggressive coercive techniques to keep his wife from reporting abuse or leaving the marriage. A man will threaten his children and extended family with harm. These battering men tend to keep collections of guns and knives and use them to intimidate women. Battered wives frequently reveal a belief that their husbands are quite capable of killing. Battering men convince their wives that they are omnipotent (Walker, 1979).

Walker (1979) describes a cycle of violence with three phases that can vary in time and intensity. The first tension-building phase consists of minor incidents of verbal and physical abuse. The wife generally assumes the blame in this stage as a way to keep her husband from exploding. Early in the cycle, the wife has some power to limit the violence and becomes astute at recognizing the signs of a brewing storm of violence. Toward the end of this phase, the wife tends to become exhausted and withdraw from her mate, which may lead to escalation of violence.

The second phase includes an acute battering incident. Some event, either triggered by external stressors or a man's internal state, will lead to out-of-control rage. In this phase, a woman has no power to change the tide of the assault and has a limited ability to predict the violence. The battering man often rationalizes his behavior as a need to teach his woman a lesson.

The third phase is characterized by kindness and contrite loving behavior. In this phase, a woman sees her mate as everything she ever wanted in a man and his love and attention becomes sufficient to keep her in the dysfunctional relationship. The husband makes promises to never repeat the violence, and the wife wants to believe this is true. Something always happens: the battering husband, stretched beyond his coping ability by daily life, will view some of his wife's behavior or statements as insulting or disrespectful, and the violent cycles begin again.

Treatment is best effected with psychological, social, and educational interventions that divert battering men out of formal criminal justice systems. Treatment is more successful when the couple both become involved in individual, group, and marital treatment. Learned behaviors are changed with programs that emphasize making choices and learning appropriate responses to aggressive feelings. Men need to evaluate their beliefs about traditional masculine roles and learn a collaborative marital style. Skills training is essential and often includes relaxation training, assertiveness training, cognitive restricting, and communication training.

Conclusions

Even with the wealth of research involving family violence, it is still difficult to evaluate and describe the extent of the problem. Most of the data come from self-report material based on memory of childhood and data gathered from persons who get involved in either treatment programs or the criminal justice system. Because some researchers guess that as few as 1 in 10 victims report their abuse, one can only begin to guess about the violence that goes unreported.

There is no one profile of men who abuse their wives and children. Generally, there is no clear evidence of psychopathology in perpetrators. Men who are incarcerated tend to be more aggressive and more likely to demonstrate antisocial behavior, but these men are not necessarily representative of the whole group. Men who assault their family members are likely to have grown up either witnessing or experiencing sexual, physical, or emotional violence. It is believed that the presence of one caring, involved adult can soften the inevitability of the cycle of violence.

A man whose self-esteem is shattered in homes characterized by abuse or neglect is likely to require a greater sense of power and control to compensate for his sense of shame and humiliation or emptiness and worthlessness. It seems likely that without a clear one-to-one relationship between childhood violence and adult acting out, the effects of neglect need to be more closely scrutinized.

Alcohol and drug use is a significant factor in family violence. It cannot be viewed as an explanatory variable, but with early detection and treatment, it is one variable that can be modified so that the more pure roots of violence can be identified. To break the cycle, men must become aware of the consequences of their abusive actions and find some way to empathize with the pain of abused wives and children. When all children are loved, protected, and nurtured, maybe the cycle of violence will be broken.

References

Arndt, W.B. *Gender disorders and the paraphilias.* Madison, CT: International Universities Press, 1991.

Baumeister, R.F., Stillwell, A., Wotman, S.R. Victim and perpetrator accounts of interpersonal conflict: Autobiographical narratives about anger. *J Pers Soc Psychology* 1990; 59:994-1005.

Briere, J., Runtz, M. Differential adult symptomatology associated with three types of child abuse history. *Child Abuse Neglect* 1990; 14:357-343.

Burgess, R.L., Draper, P. Explanation of family violence: Role of biology, behavior and cultural selection. In L. Ohlin, M. Tonry (Eds.), *Family violence.* Chicago: University of Chicago Press, 1989.

Carnes, P. *Contrary to love: Helping the sexual addict.* Minneapolis: Complare Publishers, 1989.

Claes, J.A., Rosenthal, D.M. Men who batter women: A study in power. *Journal of Family Violence* 1990; 5:215-224.

Courtois, C.A. *Healing the incest wound.* New York: WW Norton & Co, 1988.

Crewdson, J. *By silence betrayed. Sexual abuse of children in America.* New York: Harper & Row, 1988.

Finkelhor, D. *A sourcebook on child sexual abuse.* Beverly Hills, CA: Sage Publishers, 1986.

Finkelhor, D., Williams, L.M. In H. Vanderbilt (Ed.), Incest: A four part chilling report. *Lears* 1992; 4(12):49-77.

Friedman, L. Wife assault. In C. Guberman and M. Wolf (Eds.), *No safe place: Violence against women and children.* Toronto: Women's Press, 1985.

Geffner, R., Rosenbaum, A. Characteristics and treatment of batterers. *J Interpers Viol* 1990; 5:131-140.

Grossman, L.S., Cavanaugh, J.C. Psychopathology and denial in alleged sex offenders. *J Nerv Ment Dis* 1990; 178;739-744.

Groth, A.N. *Men who rape. The psychology of the offender.* New York: Plenum Press, 1979.

Hurlburt, D.F., Apt, C. Sexual narcissism and the abusive male. *Journal of Sex and Marital Therapy* 1991; 17:279-289.

James, B., Nasjleti, M. *Treating sexually abused children and their families.* Palo Alto, CA: Consulting Psychologists Press, 1983.

Lang, R.A., Langevin, R. Parent child relations in offenders who commit violent sexual crimes against children. *Behavioral Science and the Law* 1991; 9(1):61-71.

Lang, R.A., Langevin, R., Von Sahten, V., Billingsley, A., Wright, P. Marital relations in incest offenders. *Journal of Sex and Marital Therapy* 1990; 16:214-229.

Langevin, R., Ben-Aran, M., Wortzman, G., Dickey, R., Handry, L. Brain damage, drug substance abuse among violent offenders. *J Interpers Viol* 1990; 5:215-227.

Lisak, D. Sexual aggression, masculinity, and fathers. *Signs* 1991; 16:238-262.

Medzian, M. *Boys will be boys. Breaking the link between masculinity and violence.* New York: Doubleday, 1991.

Milner, J.S., Robertson, K.R., Rogers, D.L. Childhood history of abuse and adult child abuse potential. *Journal of Family Violence* 1990; 5(1):15-34.

Overholser, J.C., Mol, S.J. Who's to blame: Attributions regarding causality in spouse abuse. *Behavioral Sciences and the Law* 1990; 8:107-120.

Pollack, N.L., Hashmal, J.M. Excuses of child molesters. *Behavioral Sciences and the Law* 1991; 9:53-59.

Rosen, I. Self-esteem as a factor in social domestic violence. *Br J Psychiatry* 1991; 158:18-23.

Salter, A.C. *Treating child sex offenders and victims.* London: Sage Publications, 1988.

Simkins, L., Ward, W., Bowman, S., Renck, C.M., DeSouza, E. Predicting treatment for child sexual abusers. *Annals of Sex Research* 1990; 3:21-57.

Steinmetz, S.K. The violent family. In M. Lystad (Ed.), *Violence in the home: Interdisciplinary perspectives.* New York: Brunner/Mazel, 1986.

Walker, L.E. *The battered woman.* New York: Harper & Row.

8 | Elders "At Risk": Understanding and Managing Aggression/ Violence in Institutionalized Older Adults

By Kathleen C. Buckwalter, PhD, RN, FAAN; and Marianne Smith, MS, RN

Agitated, aggressive, and acting out behaviors are troubling to staff, other patients/residents, and family members, and management of the verbally or physically aggressive elder is both a challenge and a source of much frustration to nurses. Appropriate management of the aggressive elderly client depends on accurate assessment and preventive care. This chapter highlights specific assessment and intervention strategies designed to assist staff in understanding and managing a variety of difficult behaviors common in the institutionalized elderly.

Identifying "At Risk" Elderly

It is important to remember that any person can be provoked to verbal or physical aggression to protect themselves if they are sufficiently threatened. The threat may be something real or it may be something only "imagined," as in the case of hallucinations and delusions. In either case, the threat is real to the person, and attempts to prevent or manage potentially aggressive or violent behavior are best approached from that perspective (Figure 1).

FIGURE 1
Residents "At Risk"*

Physical Illness and Disability
Any illness that interferes with the ability of individuals to understand and use information from their environment (reality) will put them at risk. For example:

Sensory loss and impairment: misinterpretation of real-life events increase the risk that the person will feel threatened;

Aphasia: loss of the ability to understand the spoken word or to express oneself may frustrate or frighten the person to the point of aggression.

Mental Illness and Disability
Organic and psychotic mental disorders are highly associated with aggressive behavior in institutionalized elderly.

Organic mental disorders: loss of mental abilities (due to the death/destruction of brain cells) interferes with the person's ability to think, reason, use judgment, remember, explain needs or wants, and accurately interpret reality. Some of the more common diagnoses include Alzheimer's disease, multi-infarct dementia, organic brain syndrome, organic delusional syndrome, delirium (acute confusion), and organic hallucinosis.

Psychotic disorders: interfere with the person's ability to accurately interpret reality; false fixed beliefs (delusions) and unreal sensory experiences (hallucinations) frighten, mislead, or otherwise interfere with the person's ability to get along. Some of the more common diagnoses include schizophrenic disorders, paranoid disorders, schizoaffective disorder, atypical psychosis, depression, bipolar affective disorder, and mania.

Threats to Mental Health
It is also important to remember that any person who is sufficiently threatened may respond with aggression if he or she feels the need to protect him/herself.

Loss of control (powerlessness): acting out or aggression in the attempt to "take back" control.

Loss of self-worth: attempts by individuals to make themselves feel better by putting others down.

Long-standing personality traits: the use of aggression as a way of coping is a long-standing pattern that extends into late life.

Situational stress: cranky, crabby, "on edge" because of difficult life situation can lead to verbal outbursts.

Modified from Smith, 1990

Those most at risk for aggressive episodes are persons with some type of mental illness or sensory impairment, both of which interfere with the person's ability to take in and use information from the environment. For example, elders who are unable to accurately interpret what is said or done because of visual or hearing loss may respond in an "inappropriately" aggressive manner. Factors such as memory loss or acute confusion will interfere with the person's ability to process information, making attempts to reason or solve problems with these persons virtually useless. And like people of any age, elders who are experiencing delusions or hallucinations may become anxious, upset, and frightened for no "apparent" reason as they respond to their "internal reality." Any diagnosis of mental or emotional disorder, or severe sensory loss, should alert nurses to the potential for aggression.

Although most nurses are aware of the potential for violence in persons with diagnoses such as schizophrenia or paranoid disorders, many fail to appreciate that older persons suffering from organic brain disease are also at great risk, especially those with problems such as Alzheimer's disease, multi-infarct dementia, or other dementias. The characteristic loss of memory, judgment, impulse control, language, and abstract thinking associated with the dementias interfere with the person's ability to think, reason, and respond. As the disease progresses, the person becomes more likely to misinterpret stimuli, feel over-whelmed and anxious, and become agitated or aggressive (cross reference to Burke Chapter).

The Progressively Lowered Stress Threshold (PLST) model of care (Hall, 1987) provides valuable insight regarding the aggressive behavior so often seen in Alzheimer's disease and other dementias. The PLST model describes the increasing inability of persons with dementia to cope with stress due to progressive cerebral pathology and associated cognitive decline (Figure 2A). The major premise of the PLST model is that the demented person's ability to tolerate all forms of stress becomes progressively lower as the disease progresses (Figure 2B) and they therefore need environmental demands modified because of their declining cognitive and functional abilities.

Both environmental and internal stressors are demands that cause the person with dementia to become anxious and agitated. If the stressful stimuli are allowed to continue or increase, the behavior becomes increasingly dysfunctional, and often catastrophic (Figure 2C). The PLST model suggests that reducing stress by modifying environmental demands promotes functional adaptive behavior (Figure 2D). Importantly, factors like fatigue, multiple competing stimuli (noise, activity in the environment), changes in routine, physical illness or discomfort, or demands to achieve beyond their abilities can all lead to anxious, dysfunctional, and cata-strophic behaviors, including verbal and physical aggression. As a result, effective management relies on accurate assessment and the use of preventive methods in this population.

Although many staff who work with institutionalized older adults may believe that aggressive or violent behavior "comes out of nowhere" and cannot be predicted, this is rarely the case. In reality, changes in the autonomic nervous system cause physical changes that can actually be observed as the person becomes more threatened. The increased tension may appear either in verbal or nonverbal behaviors and is commonly referred to as the "fight or flight" response. Figure 3 outlines some of the more common physical manifestations that may be observed in a person whose body is prepared to attack.

In addition, there are typically a host of identifiable factors that lead up to the act of aggression, whether verbal or physical in nature. The goal of nursing

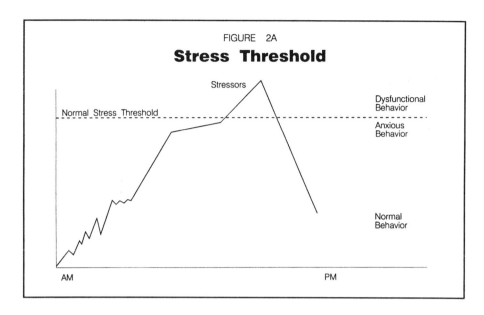

FIGURE 2A
Stress Threshold

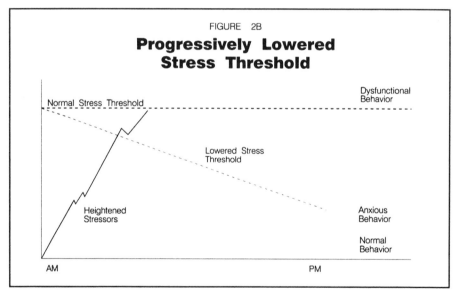

FIGURE 2B
Progressively Lowered Stress Threshold

care is to identify those components, whether social, personal, or environmental, that contribute to the aggressive or violent behavior and to act preventively to reduce the risk that aggression/violence occurs in the first place. Because our focus is on prevention, accurate and comprehensive assessment is the key.

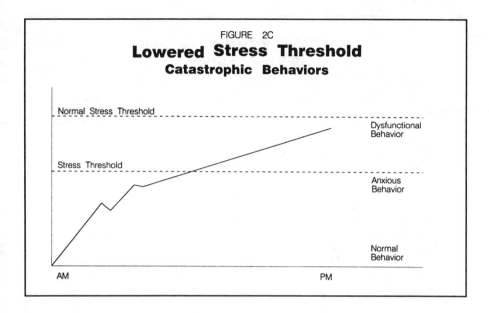

FIGURE 2C
Lowered Stress Threshold
Catastrophic Behaviors

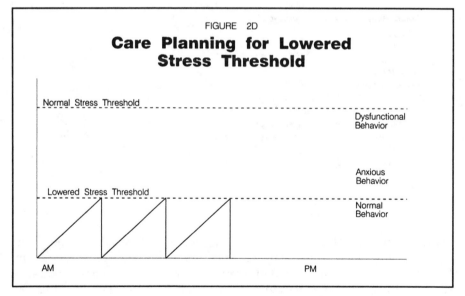

FIGURE 2D
Care Planning for Lowered Stress Threshold

Assessment

The A-B-C approach to behavior management (Cohn, 1990) helps staff to "sift out" what is going on with their elderly clients so that they can devise ways to reduce or eliminate the patient's discomfort and thus reduce the potential for aggressive/violent behavior. The A-B-C model stands for antecedents, behavior, and consequences. The "A" refers to things that

---

FIGURE 3
Behavioral Cues*

Remember: aggressive behavior is a response to some type of discomfort or threat. The perception of threat is real to the person, even if it is not real to us. The physical reaction, called fight or flight, causes visible signs of increasing tension that we can observe in the person.

Verbal cues
   Direct verbal warnings; eg, "Get out of my way!"
   Demanding, threatening, loud
   Clipped or pressured speech
   Morose (surly, brooding) silence
   Short yes/no answers
   Logical thought decreases; becomes more and more irrational
   Negative to rules or requests from staff, others
   Easily frustrated by "no"
   Curses, uses coarse language

Nonverbal Cues
   Jaws tense, teeth clenched, biting, pursed lips
   Frowning
   Eyes look vigilant (alert, watchful, wary) and intent
   Look directly at you or "through you"
   Flushing or blanching
   Dilated pupils
   Quivering lips
   Pulsating carotid
   Fists clenched, knuckles white
   Shift from "relaxed" to "tight" body position
   Discharge movements: pounding fists, kicking
   Breathing becomes shallow and rapid
   Body attitude: ready for action versus restless/pacing versus "stony" withdrawal

---

Modified from Smith, 1990

---

preceded the violent event that may have triggered the behavior. The "B" is the behavior, which must be described in detail regarding its nature, frequency, duration, location, and intensity. The "C" is the consequence, or what happens after the behavior occurs; that is, what the elder may be "getting out of it" and what the staff do in response to the behavior that may, in fact, be "fueling the fire" (Figure 4).

DESCRIBING THE BEHAVIOR

The first step in the A-B-C approach is to describe the behavior in detail. Violent or aggressive episodes cannot simply be taken at face value. Rather, staff must be urged to stop and question the behavior, to look for clues about what is going on and why, and to listen and talk to others in an effort to get the whole picture. It is not enough to chart "Mr.

Jones is agitated and combative," or "Mrs. Smith appeared confused and was aggressive when approached." These general observations do not contribute to our understanding and management of the negative behaviors and may actually reinforce negative stereotypes about the patients and their problems.

Effective management relies on the identification of a comprehensive problem list, with each difficult behavior described as a separate challenge. Within that framework, the description should note precisely what the patient/resident is doing, where the behavior is happening, how often, for how long, and how intense the behavior is. The behavior must be evaluated in terms of issues of safety versus danger. Furthermore, it is important to consider for whom the behavior is really a problem: The resident? Other residents in the facility? The family? Or the staff? Likewise, we must question if our and their expectations are realistic, or if the staff, family, or even the individuals themselves want more than is practical, given the person's limitations.

DESCRIBING THE ANTECEDENTS

Once the behavior has been observed and described in detail, we want to investigate all possible causes of the behavior, the antecedents. Unfortunately, with the elderly, staff often assume there is no reason for the behavior and that older persons are simply "senile" or "set in their own ways." However, effective management relies on a comprehensive review of all possible components that contribute to, or precipitate, the aggressive behavior. This includes both external and internal antecedent conditions.

In the arena of external antecedents, it is necessary to evaluate events in both the physical and social environment of the facility. For example, does a certain nurses' aide always seem to trigger the behavior? Does it happen every time the family comes to visit? Is the dayroom too noisy or confusing for cognitively impaired residents to make sense of? Are residents not hearing, seeing, or understanding what is going on? How might residents be misinterpreting the environment? Have there been too many demands to achieve (from staff, family) beyond their abilities? Are they responding to changes in the environment (eg, relocation), changes in caregivers, or changes in routine?

Nurses also need to think about internal antecedents that are of physical, mental, or emotional origin, especially with cognitively impaired elders. For example, is there evidence of pain or discomfort that cannot be articulated? Could the aggressive episode be the result of an adverse side effect from a new medication? Are the residents hungry or thirsty? Are they fatigued, bored, lonesome, or feeling left out? Do they have an infection or undiagnosed illness? What is the older person not getting that he or she wants or needs? And what unmet needs motivate individuals to keep repeating this behavior?

FIGURE 4
Application of the A-B-C Model to a Demented Person*

Common "Problem" Behaviors
Confusion: disoriented to time, place, person, thing; says things that do not make sense
Psychotic behaviors: evidence of hallucinations or delusions
Fearfulness: becomes frightened for no clear cause, as seen in facial expressions, body posture, spoken words and phrases
Repetitious behaviors: calling out, clapping, rocking, wandering, pacing, getting lost
Agitation: increased physical movements, restlessness, "worked up," often accompanied by verbal expressions of distress
Combativeness: striking out at others
Night waking: episodes of confusion, wandering, and sleeplessness that are linked to daytime stress

Common Antecedents
Medication side effects
Sensory loss leading to misinterpretation of events
Episodes of acute illness (urinary tract or respiratory infections)
Pain or discomfort, including hunger, thirst, constipation
Fatigue
Being asked to exceed real-life abilities
Being given too many choices
Overstimulation (noise, confusion, too many people)
Understimulation (lack of attention by staff, family, friends)
Delusions and hallucinations
Changes in environment (relocation, movement to a new room)
Changes in caregivers (new or unfamiliar staff)
Changes in routine (going to physician, other outings; family visits; holiday activities)
Dehydration, electrolyte imbalance

Common Unhelpful Consequences
Ignoring the behavior
Scolding or yelling at the person
Mocking or embarrassing the person (often by other patients)
Telling individuals they are "wrong" (in response to delusions)
Yelling at individuals to "stop it" or "straighten out"
Trying to reason with the person
Getting angry at the person
Feeling that the person is "manipulating" staff
Labeling the behavior or the person as "unmanageable"
Restraining the person (either physically or chemically)

Alternative Helpful Consequences
Paying attention to the person, making eye contact
Talking to the person in a soothing tone of voice
Speaking in simple, easy to understand language
Giving one command or asking one question at a time
Waiting for responses and listening carefully for meaning
Avoiding any type of confrontation or challenging the person
Reassuring individual that they are safe with you
Redirecting or distracting individuals to another place or activity
Providing needed assistance or relief from discomfort
Offering opportunities to rest or relax
Reducing environmental stress to calm the person (eg, number of people, noise)
Reducing misleading stimuli (eg, television, radio, public address systems)
Reducing stimulation (eg, by taking the patients to their rooms or a quiet place)

*Modified from Buckwalter, 1990

DESCRIBING THE CONSEQUENCES

The final step in the assessment process is to describe the consequences of the behavior, analyzing the situation from the perspective of the patients/ residents. Are they getting something positive from the behavior, such as attention or relief from discomfort? Or are they getting something negative, such as being restrained? What does the resident do next? How do other patients and staff respond to the behavior? Thinking carefully about the consequences of a behavior is important, because often staff unconsciously resort to unhelpful consequences, such as avoiding the resident, becoming defensive or indifferent, or "paying them back" by "forgetting" to respond to requests in a timely way.

Interventions

Development of a care plan to reduce undesirable aggressive behaviors and increase healthier behaviors can proceed using the A-B-C approach as well.

SETTING BEHAVIORAL GOALS

To set realistic goals, nurses first need to ask what it is we want the resident to do. Do we want to eliminate the aggressive behavior, or simply to decrease the frequency with which it occurs? Again, priorities need to be set and only one problem can be worked on at a time (eg, what is the most distressing behavior? Which one is actually a matter of resident safety? What can be ignored or dismissed?)

Sometimes this is difficult to do, particularly as staff become aggravated and burned out with a particular patient/resident with whom they have recurrent and unresolved care problems. However, it is critically important to differentiate between behaviors that have the potential for violence and those that are simply a nuisance in care management. As noted earlier, nurses need to consider if their goals are realistic and specific, or whether their expectations should be adjusted. Finally, nurses must examine whether the goal can be accomplished in a single step, or whether it needs to be broken down into incremental steps to get the job done.

CHANGING ANTECEDENTS

Referring once again to the A-B-C model, nurses must review the list of antecedent conditions that may have precipitated the aggressive behavior and decide which triggers can be eliminated or changed. Likewise, nurses need to consider what new triggers or cues can be added to prompt different and more desirable behaviors. This step is enormously important in the management of cognitively impaired elderly patients, and yet is frequently neglected. Too often staff allow the patient to escalate to the point of aggression instead of identifying early warning symptoms, or known precipitants, that signal the need for early and preventive interventions.

CHANGING CONSEQUENCES

Next, nurses should examine how they can change the consequences of the behavior, keeping in mind those things that keep the behavior going or that may even be making it worse (ie, reactions that "fuel the fire"). Nurses are challenged to think creatively about what they can do differently in response to aggressive behaviors, and about ways to reinforce adaptive (nonaggressive) behaviors on the part of their elderly clients.

The process of reinforcement falls in the domain of behavior modification. However, it is important to recognize that "pure" behavior modification relies on the person's ability to learn new ways to behave. That is, over time, consistency and repetition teach the person to do, or not do, certain things. The reinforcement can eventually be discontinued and individuals will continue the behavior on their own.

Unfortunately, many aggressive or potentially violent elderly are cognitively impaired. Their ability to learn new behavior is lost and consequently they cannot be expected to perform in the absence of a stimulus or cue to prompt the desired behavior. Behavior modification principles may still be applied to cognitively impaired patients, but with an understanding that staff cannot expect patients to eventually "do it on their own." In this case, nurses may wish to refer to the strategy as behavior management, which implies that the interventions must be ongoing.

Although the term "reinforcement" is classically used in reference to the response to a certain behavior (the consequence), these principles can easily be used to conceptualize ways that nurses can change antecedent conditions as well. Successful management of aggressive behavior in elderly clients requires that nurses place as much emphasis on changing the antecedent conditions as they do on changing the consequences. Staff responses, whether conscious or unconscious, planned or unplanned, verbal or nonverbal, involving action or inaction, do influence what the resident does next. Those responses may be categorized as antecedents or they may be seen as consequences, and yet the goal remains the same. Our response to patients should increase their comfort, decrease their perception of threat, and, thus, reduce the risk of aggressive or violent behavior.

Staff who are inexperienced with behavior modification and management techniques frequently fail to see their part in the process. An emphasis must be placed on what the staff is doing or not doing in response to the negative behavior. For example, if nurses ignore individuals, hoping that they will eventually calm themselves, we may be actually contributing to the aggressive behavior by not attending to their needs before they become severely distraught. Likewise, if nurses are angry or rude to the resident, even without meaning to be, we may further threaten the person and trigger acts of violence. The following case scenario illustrates the effect that staff responses may have on the patient's behavior.

> Mrs. S. is a chronic complainer. She puts on her call light several times an hour, sometimes for important things but mostly for "little" things. She has called Jane, the nursing assistant, five times in an hour: to bring her a box of tissues, to ask for pain medication, to complain that she is chilly and that wants a sweater, to suggest that the nurse call the doctor about her illness, and to help her dial the phone to call her daughter.
>
> Each time Jane goes in to see her, Mrs. S. frowns and moans softly about how awful she feels. Each time her light comes on, Jane takes more and more time to get there, figuring she can wait because it is probably another "false alarm." Each time Jane feels a little more angry with Mrs. S. for bothering her when she has other residents to help. And each time Jane is a little more short and to the point, doing only what Mrs. S. has asked her to do and then leaving.
>
> Jane caught herself sighing, frowning, and shaking her head as she left the room the last time. When Jane walked into the room on the sixth call, Mrs. S. said, "You took 9 minutes to get here! Nine whole minutes! I timed you. I have to go to the bathroom, and I need to go now! What's wrong with you people?" Jane's face turned red. She was furious. She said nothing, grudgingly helped Mrs. S. to the bathroom, and walked out of the room, leaving her sitting on the stool.

In this case, the unplanned consequence, avoiding the patient by being slow to respond, resulted only in verbal aggression. However, the same type of unplanned and unthinking reactions can precipitate physical aggression as well. To shape behavior and move the potentially violent resident in a stepwise fashion toward more healthy and adaptive ways of coping, we must carefully examine both their needs and our responses.

RULES OF REINFORCEMENT

The process of reinforcement is actually quite simple. As mentioned above, a nurse's response to the behavior influences what the person does next, and that, stated simply, is the crux of reinforcement. When reinforcement is done thoughtfully and with a plan, nurses can shape the person's behavior, moving the person away from aggressive or other maladaptive ways of coping and toward healthier behaviors.

The first step is to find reinforcers that are valued by and meaningful to the older adult. The most powerful reinforcers are those that are individualized, given only when the desired behavior occurs, immediately after it occurs, and every time it occurs (Figure 5). The last of these, consistency in response, is of utmost importance in managing behaviorally impaired elderly. Failure to follow through with the designated response to the problem behavior is likely to perpetuate the problem. That is, if one staff member responds one way and another responds differently, the lucid

FIGURE 5
Rules of Reinforcement*

Reinforcement: the stepwise movement of behavior; behavior followed by a response to the behavior, and then either more or less of that original behavior.
Behavior → Response A → Behavior repeats itself
Behavior → Response B → Behavior does not reoccur
Reinforcement may be positive or negative and it can involve either giving something or taking something away.

		Giving	Removing
	Increase Behavior	Giving (+) Positive Reinforcement	Removing (−) Negative Reinforcement
Effect on Behavior	**Decrease Behavior**	Giving (−) Punishment	Removing (+) Penalty

Positive Reinforcement: Giving Something Positive
A patient is obviously trying very hard to do as much of his own self-care as possible despite multiple limitations. You said, "Gosh, you are really doing a good job!" (You gave something positive, a compliment.)

Negative Reinforcement: Taking Away Something Negative
A depressed and dangerously anorexic patient typically resists eating because food "tastes like paste." This day she has eaten well, but at supper withdraws, saying that she has always hated Italian food, which is being served. You said, "You've been cooperative even when the food doesn't taste good, so I'm not going to 'twist your arm' tonight. You eat what you want." (You removed something negative, the usual request to eat at least part of the main course. You also gave something positive, a compliment.)

Punishment: Giving Something Negative
When asked to finish breakfast and get dressed, the patient threw orange juice on you. You said, "I am really disappointed in you, sir. That was both childish and unnecessary!" (You gave something negative, a reprimand.)

Penalty: Taking Away Something Positive
The patient complains that she is too sick to come out of her room for meals but comes out to smoke cigarettes. You say, "You may have dinner in your room, but if you're feeling that badly, I don't want you to come out to smoke, either." (You removed something positive, the privilege of smoking.)

The most powerful reinforcer will be:
Individualized: something valued by the person
Immediate: right after the desired behavior
Contingent: only after the desired behavior
Consistent: every time the behavior occurs
Consumable: something disposable or temporary, preferably not food (eg, staff time, outings, special activities, decision-making rights for the group, other privileges; cigarettes, prizes, other material rewards).

*Modified from Smith, 1990

patient remains uncertain about what the consequences actually are, and thus the behavior continues.

These same principles must also be applied to interventions that are designed to change the antecedent conditions. Once a known precipitant has been identified, staff must consistently implement the individualized protocol to reduce the risk that the patient will escalate to aggression. This is particularly true for demented residents who are ignored or avoided by staff, then become catastrophic when approached and strike out.

As shown in Figure 5, nurses can combine giving and removing with positive and negative responses to derive four basic responses to aggressive behaviors—two that tend to encourage behaviors (giving something positive, taking way something negative), and two that tend to discourage behaviors (giving something negative, taking away something positive). These concepts may be used to examine what nurses currently do and to think about what they could do differently to shape behavior in elderly patients. However, nurses must remember to use them in accordance with the person's cognitive abilities. That is, these principles may be used with demented elderly, but they cannot be expected to understand that they are being "rewarded" or "penalized." This emphasis must be reserved for lucid patients who can comprehend and remember the meaning of the message.

To increase desirable, nonaggressive behaviors, nurses can either take away something negative, such as a restriction or a task the older person dislikes, or give something positive, making sure that the person understands this is a reward for improved behavior (in lucid patients). Consider concrete reinforcers for positive (eg, nonaggressive) behaviors. These might include money, food, special times together, privileges, or a hug. Remember that reinforcers can be combined. For example, something negative may be taken away (from the resident's perspective; eg, you don't have to go to bingo this week) and at the same time, something positive may be given (eg, a compliment about how well-behaved the person was during lunch).

Similarly, punishment and penalties serve to decrease negative behaviors and may be used to diminish aggressive responses. Although there are fewer opportunities to use punishment or penalty in patient care, these concepts may be still be applied. For example, lucid and attention-seeking elders may be informed that their "special time" with staff will be taken away (which is a penalty) if they become verbally or physically aggressive. In other instances, nurses may give elderly a time out, isolating them in their rooms (a form of punishment) for being verbally or physically aggressive, acting out, or other behaviors that nurses wish to reduce.

A number of interventions are needed to effectively manage aggressive or potentially violent behavior in elderly patients. Comprehensive assessment is required to develop interventions that address various levels of the problem. Careful observation and description of the antecedents and consequences of the difficult behavior present opportunities to devise methods to change both the precipitating events and reactions to the problem behavior. Self-awareness among staff is critically important, as well

FIGURE 6
Managing the Crisis*

1. Tune in to your own attitudes and feelings about what is going on. Getting angry won't help and will probably make things worse. Remember: being caught off guard puts you at risk.
> You may be tempted to "fight back."
> Anger and resentment will make you ineffective.
> Your reaction can actually make things worse.

Try to remain calm, cool, and collected, at least on the outside. Use positive self-talk to get yourself under control. For example, remind yourself:
> "This person is 'uncomfortable' and needs my help."
> "I can handle this. I don't need to get upset, too."
> "They're not really angry with me. They're just upset and I'm in the way!"

Avoid words or actions that might threaten the person even more. If you cannot get your own feelings under control, leave the area immediately, alerting other staff if needed.

2. Keep track of what you are doing with your body and what that might mean to the elderly.
> Don't surprise them; move slowly and steadily.
> Keep your hands out where they can see them, palms up and open, which is nonthreatening.
> Respect their "personal space"; the more threatened they are, the more distance you should give them.
> Do not stand squarely in front of them, which is confronting and threatening; turn slightly to one side.
> Be careful to not stare, glare, or otherwise challenge them with eye contact.
> Do not turn your back on the person.
> Always leave yourself an escape route.
> Avoid standing over persons if they are sitting or reclining, which can be very threatening.

3. Think about what you say and how you say it.
> Speak in short, simple phrases.
> Use a normal tone of voice and talk at a normal rate.
> Communicate concern and caring while being firm.
> Avoid sarcasm, insulting remarks, and even humor, which can easily be misinterpreted.

4. Use directions or explanations that are appropriate for the person and the situation. For example, if the person is acting out, you might say things like:
> "I'm sorry if I upset you, that wasn't what I meant to do."
> "Your behavior worries (frightens, upsets) me."
> "How can I help you be more comfortable?"

If the person is demented and having a catastrophic reaction, you may want to redirect or reassure the person:
> "Mr. S., let's go to your room (a quiet place)."
> "It's all right now. You are safe with me. I won't let anything bad happen to you."

5. Listen carefully to what they are saying and try to respond to the message they are trying to communicate.
> Check for meaning, "You're saying that. . ."
> Avoid giving advice.
> Respond to the content of the message (the actual meaning), not the way it is being said.
> Try to understand what the person is upset about and respond to that unmet need or feeling.

FIGURE 6 CONTINUED

Do not assume that the person has heard or understood you. People become narrowly
focused when they are anxious.

6. Try to calm or soothe the person, remembering that the first priority is to protect
yourself and others.

Leave the room or area if the person continues to threaten you.

Get assistance, even if you are unsure if you really need it.

Use physical control only as the last resort. Try everything else first.

---

*From Smith, 1990

---

as appreciation and understanding of the patient's underlying disabilities
and deficits (eg, cognitive impairment, mental illness, sensory deficits).
Reinforcement techniques may be used to change the behavior of lucid
elderly patients who act out and become aggressive, and these principles
may also be applied to assist cognitively impaired patients to be more
comfortable, thus reducing the risk of aggressive/violent behaviors in this
population.

MANAGING THE CRISIS

Although prevention is always the "best medicine," nurses must be
prepared to manage a person who has escalated to the point of physical
aggression (Figure 6). Staff must immediately assess their own attitudes and
feelings about what is happening. Being caught off guard puts staff at risk
for further aggravating the person by responding with anger or defensive
actions. Encourage staff to remain calm and collected, at least in their
outward presentation. Positive self-talk can help reduce their stress and
reframe the situation in a way that allows them to help the person (eg, "This
person is uncomfortable and needs my help"). Staff members who cannot
control their own feelings and emotions should leave the area immediately
and find someone else to intervene with the patient.

Staff must also be cautioned to be aware of what they are doing with their
body. The more threatened the person is, the more space he or she should be
given. How staff move, position themselves, and look at the patient carry an
important message. Staff can be threatening and precipitate violence if they
are not alert to their body language.

What nurses say and how they say it is also of critical importance. As
patients become more anxious and threatened, their ability to focus and
attend becomes more limited and narrow. Speaking in short, simple, easy to
understand language helps them process the message. Communicate caring
and concern while being firm, and be certain that enough backup is
available to intercede physically if that becomes necessary. Use directions or
explanations that are appropriate to the individual and to the situation,

taking into consideration the individual's cognitive level, the presence of hallucinations or delusions, and environmental factors that may be contributing to the distress. Listen carefully to what patients are saying and try to respond to the message that they are trying to communicate. Every effort should be made to calm the patient and reduce the perception of threat. Threats, angry gestures, or even advice typically aggravate anxious and agitated people further and often makes the situation worse. Physical control of the person should be used only as the last resort and should be executed with the assistance of enough people to avoid injury to either the resident or to staff.

EVALUATION

As with any intervention strategy, it is important to examine both successes and failures by asking whether or not the plan (or any part of the plan) worked to reduce aggressive behaviors. Why or why not? What interfered, if anything? Perhaps the interventions (either changing the antecedents, changing the consequences, or providing reinforcement) were not performed consistently by all staff members.

Likewise, it is important to critically evaluate the management of a "crisis" situation in which the person has already become violent (eg, in post-hoc crisis management meetings). Staff must be encouraged to critically examine both the series of events leading to the crisis and techniques that were used once the aggression occurred. The goal of this retrospective analysis is not to "blame" or find fault with the staff's performance, but to examine what occurred and why. Without evaluation of interventions, staff do not know where to proceed to find a solution that does work.

Conclusion

Anyone, including the elderly, can become aggressive or violent if feeling threatened enough. Persons with dementia are at special risk because the disease process lowers their stress threshold and at the same time renders them unable to accurately interpret their environment. Prevention is always the "best medicine" when it comes to aggressive behaviors. Assessment, using the A-B-C model, is a key ingredient to help identify both internal and external factors that may trigger the violent behavior, as well as to examine consequences of the behavior. Nurses are in an ideal position to apply the principles of behavior modification and management, increasing the comfort of the resident (as well as other residents, family, and staff in the facility), and thus diminishing the potential for aggressive and violent behaviors.

References

Buckwalter, K.C., Smith, M. When you forget that you forgot: Recognizing and managing Alzheimer's type dementia. In M. Smith, K.C. Buckwalter, S. Mitchell (Eds.), *The geriatric mental health training series*. Cedar Rapids, IA: The Abbe Center for Community Mental Health, 1990.

Cohn, M.D., Horgas, A.L., Marisiske, M. Behavior management training for nurse aides: Is it effective? *Journal of Gerontological Nursing* 1990; 16(11):21-25.

Hall, G.R., Buckwalter, K.C. Progressively lowered stress threshold: A conceptual model for care of adults with Alzheimer's disease. *Arch Psychiatr Nurs* 1987; 1:399-406.

Smith, M., Buckwalter, K.C. Acting up and acting out: Assessing and managing aggressive and acting out behaviors. In M. Smith, K.C. Buckwalter, S. Mitchell (Eds.), *The geriatric mental health training series*. Cedar Rapids, IA: The Abbe Center for Community Mental Health, 1990.

9

Reframing: Using the Positive Intention Behind Violent and Disruptive Behavior

By Daniel J. Pesut, PhD, RN, CS

This chapter is a brief description and discussion of selected techniques developed within the model of human behavior and communication known as neurolinguistic programming (NLP). As psychiatric nursing textbooks introduce students to the concepts of NLP (Burgess, 1990; Wilson, 1992), it is important that nurses in clinical settings have some fundamental information about the model and examples of the application and usefulness of selected NLP techniques (Brockopp, 1983; Knowles, 1983; Pesut, 1989; 1991). NLP techniques such as pacing and leading, meta-model challenges, reframing, and visual-kinesthetic dissociation are useful as one works with patients who are disruptive or violent. In addition, NLP interventions have proven effective with victims of violence and assault. Knowledge about NLP complements and expands a practitioner's repertoire of communication skills and enables one to facilitate remedial and generative (creative) changes with patients.

Neurolinguistic Programming

NLP is a model of human behavior and communication that was developed by Bandler (1975) and Grinder (1976) in the mid-1970s. NLP is a systemized set of techniques that provide clinicians with strategies to decode and unpack the sensory components of perceptions and ways people represent experience. To some, NLP is a comprehensive theory and original contribution to communication theory. Others believe that NLP is merely a compendium of techniques that have been gleaned from a variety of counseling practices (Sharpley, 1987).

Based on their observations and studies of master communicators, Bandler and Grinder (1975;1976) determined expert therapists consistently demonstrated four skills. These experts were skilled at establishing rapport with their clients, were adept at specifying outcomes with their clients, were resourceful and flexible in their behavior, and had an ability to detect nuances in behavior. This sensory acuity enabled them to use the verbal and nonverbal feedback they received from their clients and to respond differently and effectively in therapeutic contexts.

Many NLP concepts and interventions are designed to help clients develop insight into their own thinking, feeling, and behaving. NLP techniques can be used to deal with past issues in a remedial way or develop resources and new patterns of behaving in a creative way with patients. The ability to establish rapport, calibrate responses, define outcomes, and be flexible are skills vital to the success and effectiveness of any health-care practitioner, especially those who work with disruptive or potentially violent individuals. Helping patients develop behavioral responses and choices other than violence is one example of the generative possibilities associated with using NLP techniques in clinical practice.

Framing Experiences

Thinking, feeling, and behaving are greatly influenced by the frames, beliefs, and contexts in which one lives and works. How one "frames" events has a great deal to do with an individual's responses to events given specific contexts. For example, when confronted with stressors, does one "frame" them as threats or challenges? Beliefs guide actions. Contexts provide rules and boundaries for behavior, feelings, beliefs, and actions.

Analyzing the frames, facts, and meanings associated with violence and disruptive behavior can help staff, patients, and victims of assaultive and violent behavior develop insight, choices, and different ways to respond in clinical situations that are often difficult to manage. It is periodically useful to take stock and reflect on how events are reframed in clinical practice.

What do nurses believe to be the antecedents, etiologies, dynamics, and consequences of disruptive or violent behavior? How they "explain" violent and disruptive behavior gives one insight into the "frame of reference" nurses use to understand, intervene, and treat this human response. What implications does a nurse's personal "explanation" have for nursing practice?

Reflections

Once a person is labeled "violent and disruptive," how do staff members frame their perceptions and feelings about that person? How do they act toward that person? What do staff expect from the person? How are the expectations different given the contexts of a locked inpatient unit versus a community mental health center or a victim support group? While asking themselves the following questions, nurses should consider if they "reframe" their thinking about disruptive and assaultive behavior.

• When experiencing violent episodes of behavior on an inpatient unit, what specifically do you think and feel at the time? What mental images (pictures), internal dialogue (what you say to yourself), or feelings do you have going on inside your head or registering in your body?

• Is disruptive behavior ever useful? Can you think of a time, place, or context in which assaultive or disruptive behavior could be motivated by some positive intention? Given a patient's history of child abuse or neglect, does violence as a response become "understandable"?

• Should perpetrators of violence be prosecuted or treated? Do you believe violence and assaultive behaviors are conscious, premeditated behaviors, or unconscious, habitual default responses to threatening situations?

• In your clinical work with victims of assault, are they incapacitated by the pain, fear, and anguish of the event? Do victims ever consider the experience of surviving an assault a positive resource that will help them at some future time?

• Given violence and assaultive behavior as problems, what, specifically, should be goals or outcomes associated with interventions and treatment of perpetrators as well as victims of violence?

Reframing: Creating Multiple Meanings

O'Hanlon (1987) observes that therapists work with patients who report both facts and meanings of situations. Facts are sensory-based observations that can be perceived by the senses and are descriptions of what actually happens or has happened. In contrast, meanings are interpretations, conclusions, and attributions that are derived from or related to the facts. Reframing is possible because individuals develop their own models of the world based on a combination of facts and meanings.

By definition, "to reframe" something means to change the conceptual or emotional setting of some event or thing, or to place it in another frame that fits the facts of the same concrete situation equally well or even better. Its entire meaning is changed or reframed as a result (Watzlawick, 1974).

Hartman (1990) defines reframing as the process by which information is exchanged with a patient that facilitates the patient's (or staff person's) ability to take a negatively identified situation and put it in terms that increase the patient's sense of mastery and control through choice and options. Other definitions of reframing are to "think about things a different way"; to relabel and redefine behavior; or to find the "positive connotation" of a behavior or situation (Berger, 1984; Citrenbaum, 1985; Erickson, 1983; Fenyes, 1976; Grunebaum, 1980; O'Hanlon, 1984; 1987; Stanton, 1986; Watzlawick, 1974; Weeks, 1979; 1982).

Weeks (1977) suggests several examples that illustrate how a behavior can be reframed or redefined to find the positive intent behind the behavior. Withdrawal can be construed as "taking care of oneself." Passivity can be relabeled as a way to "accept things as they are." Insensitivity can be redefined as a way to "protect oneself from hurt." Disruptive behavior, too, may be construed as a way to "protect oneself," "keep others at a distance," or "maintain control."

In some clinical settings, the fear of violence often limits interaction among nurses and patients. Some patients use the threat of violence to get their needs met because they are impoverished and have not learned alternative ways of dealing with anxiety or need gratification. Some nurses limit their interaction with patients who have been labeled violent because the nurses are concerned for their own safety and well-being.

Blair and New (1991) note that taking something away from a patient drastically increases the likelihood of an assault. Increases in assaultive episodes are also associated with provocation. An increase in assaults on a unit may also be a statement about a dysfunctional milieu or an indication of how staff are treating patients. In these instances, from the patient's perspective, a violent reaction could be framed "defending or protecting one's own space or territory." From the staff's perspective, it is likely that disruptive or violent behavior is framed as a patient's "failure to comply with the rules" or the "treatment plan," or may be an indication of "manipulative behavior."

Knowing the risks associated with assault, namely history of assault, diagnosis of dementia or organic brain disorder, intoxication from drugs or alcohol, and detrimental characteristics of the milieu or treatment itself can reduce the incidence of assault (Blair, 1991). In addition, developing more effective interaction styles and interventions that complement current therapeutic practices is also a worthwhile goal for those who work with disruptive and assaultive patients. Learning about NLP and reframing is likely to be useful because many NLP techniques provide new and different ways to approach age-old problems.

Assumptions and Values of the NLP Model

The NLP model is comprehensive and complex. A detailed explanation of the model is not possible in the context of this chapter; for more information, contact the International Association of NLP (IANLP). Laborde

(1984) offers a good introduction to the model. Listed below are several assumptions on which the NLP model of human behavior and communication is based. Assume a nurse has adopted the values and beliefs described in the assumptions (Dilts, 1983). While reviewing the assumptions, nurses should think about their most recent experiences with a "violent or disruptive patient." They should ask themselves if their thoughts, feelings, beliefs, and experiences with the patient change as they process the experience in the context of these assumptions.

NLP Practitioners believe:

• An individual's reality is based on his or her subjective experience, not on objective experience.

• People make the best choices they can for themselves at any given moment.

• The meaning of communication is the response that the communication elicits.

• Because a person cannot not respond, to a degree nearly everything one does can be influenced.

• All behavior is useful in some context.

• It is better to have choices than no choice.

• The person with the most flexibility will be the most controlling element in the system.

• Individuals possess the psychological resources they need to make changes they want.

• Anything one can pretend, one can master.

• There are no mistakes, only outcomes.

On reflection, it is clear these assumptions complement nursing care models that have a positive orientation built on a foundation of trust, client goal-orientation, learning, growth and development, mastery, a focus on client strengths, and the promotion of client control. Several NLP techniques are especially useful when applied in clinical situations. Below is a brief discussion of selected NLP techniques that are useful when working with actual or potentially violent or disruptive patients.

Pacing and Leading

Experienced nurses pace and then lead or "talk down" agitated patients. How do they acquire these skills? Experienced nurses are skilled at predicting or anticipating violent behavior before it occurs. How do they recognize this pattern? Is this intuition or is it a highly developed sensory acuity coupled with keen pattern recognition skills? Or are they unconsciously pacing the preassaultive state of the patient and finding that they themselves are beginning to experience an increased state of arousal? Can such acuity be developed in a systematic way, or does one have to rely on years of experience? The NLP model suggests learning and insights can be accelerated by helping clinicians recognize and systematically use strategic verbal and nonverbal cues.

Pacing involves matching a person's language, emotions, posture, breathing pattern, tone, tempo, and rhythm and rate of speech. The ability to pace gives information about a client's internal feeling states and thinking processes. Such insight and understanding can be used clinically to intervene and reframe potentially difficult situations.

Pacing and leading are key concepts in the NLP model. The NLP model is built on the premise that people operate on the environment, using the primary senses of seeing (vision), hearing (audition), feeling (kinesthesia), tasting (gustation), and smelling (olfaction). These sensory channels transmit the raw data that help create representations in our minds. These representations are stored in memory and become reference experiences as we go through the world. The way an individual experiences and reacts to a given situation or environment begins to be understood in the context of these experience-based internal structures or representations.

One can assume violent or disruptive behavior is learned. People who exhibit such behavior have thoughts, feelings, and beliefs that violence is a means to get what one wants or needs in specific contexts that elicit this response. One could argue that violence as a behavioral response is so well-learned that in many instances it is impulsive and spontaneous and represents a habitual, reflexive way of responding in stressful situations.

Connecting and communicating with violent and disruptive persons involves establishing rapport with them and pacing their thoughts, feelings, and behavior in a congruent way. Once rapport is established, one can lead the person to less violent or disruptive ways of meeting needs.

Pacing involves recognition and use of cues. For example, the cues involved with a preassaultive tension state include anxiety, breathlessness, rigid posture, clenching of fists and jaw, hyperactivity, pacing, verbal profanity, changes in verbal content, pressured speech, loudness, overreaction, and threatening stances (Blair, 1991). If one experienced (acted out) some of these behaviors, chances are that increased arousal would be felt and a preassaultive tension state would be experienced. NLP is rooted in the belief that mind and body is a cybernetic system. A change in emotion or mood is reflected in the body, and changes in the body are reflected in emotions and moods. Rossi (1986) has developed a model that suggests learning and behavior can be conceptualized as state-dependent. States are created because on the neurophysiological level, the brain is responding to information substances that trigger old learning.

Dilts (1983) summarized pacing applications of NLP in clinical practice. Specifically, when working with any individual, one is more likely to establish rapport if one can identify and match the client's most common sensory based words and predicates to create rapport and ensure understanding between the therapist and client. Pace qualities of the client through the matching of postural, gestural, and facial positions and movements, as well as voice tone and tempo, to create, enhance, and sustain rapport; and translate experiences expressed in one sensory modality to another to help increase understanding and choices among clients, staff, family members, couples, or individuals.

For example, if someone's preferred sensory channel (visual, auditory, kinesthetic) is identified, information or ideas may be presented to that person in the preferred system (Knowles, 1983). The outcome of such a "match" is to help the person understand the information or idea more quickly than if a foreign description or another's projection of that person's perception were used.

Identify someone's preferred representational system by listening to the choice of words, verbs, adjectives, and predicates. By listening with a "third ear," nurses will quickly develop ideas as to which sensory modality a patient uses most frequently. For example, a patient may say "I can't 'get a grip' (kinesthetic/feeling) on things," "I feel like I'm going to 'explode' " (kinesthetic/feeling/visual), "I cannot 'contain' (kinesthetic) my rage." "I have a difficult time 'holding' (kinesthetic) my temper." "The only 'release' I feel is when I 'knock some one's block off' " (kinesthetic/feeling). Such clients may feel "pressured" and want "space" if people get "too close" and start "pushing them around." So it is important to "keep their guard up" and "fight back" if they feel like they are being "pushed around." As one listens to a client's language, one gains clues about the way in which the client thinks, feels, and behaves.

Using a client's own words is a better "pace" than interpreting the client's state with a different set of words. One is more likely to establish rapport and communicate effectively by first matching the client's reality and then leading the client to a different way of thinking, feeling, or responding, given the context.

Talking to a patient who is in the pre-assaultive tension state, one might say "I know you are feeling anxious/angry now. You have probably felt this way in the past. I know that it helped you to talk about your anger then, and it will help you to talk about it now. Look around and see there are many people here for you to talk with. As you pick one of us, you will feel less angry." Such an approach acknowledges the patient's model of the world (a pace) and provides a lead to a more effective and, it is hoped, a less disruptive outcome. This response also employs the technique of using an embedded directive (Kersey, 1984).

Communicating with patients using the patient's most preferred sensory channel is more effective than using one's own. The guiding principle is to start where the client is; once a nurse establishes rapport, the client can be led to a more resourceful state of choice or the next step in the plan.

Meta-Model Challenges

A person's model of the world evolves as a result of three universal human modeling processes: generalization, deletions, and distortion (Bandler, 1975; Bandler, 1978; Grinder, 1976). Generalization is the process by which elements or pieces of a person's model becomes detached from the original experience and instead represent the entire category of which the experience is an example. For example, a patient might say, "Everyone around here is cruel and heartless." A useful response to such a generalization might be to emphasize the word "everyone." Such a response challenges the generalization and opens the possibility that at least one person may escape the generalization of being "cruel and heartless," thus helping to identify an ally for an alienated patient.

Deletion is a process by which people selectively pay attention to certain dimensions of their experience and exclude others. For example, someone might say, "I'm scared." Obviously, the person has not provided or has deleted some essential information. A useful response to such a deletion might be, "Scared about what, specifically?" Asking for specifics about deleted information reveals the connection of experience and feelings with events and opens up exploration of options, choices, and the possibility of control and mastery.

Distortions tend to limit a person's view of reality because of the underlying structure of the assumptions. One type of distortion is a presupposition. For example, some people hold a fixed belief that perpetrators of violence should be prosecuted and not receive treatment. Another example of a distortion is a language pattern referred to as "mind reading." For example, "I know the staff hates me." To recover information about the specific way in which this person is processing the event or experience, a useful response to this type of distortion would be "How do you know the staff hates you?"

People build representations or models of the real world out of their perceptions. To discover what that model of the real world is, it is necessary to create a model of their model, or a meta-model. Meta-model violations demonstrate how words limit, distort, delete, and generalize experiences and actions due to limited information processing capabilities. As one can see from the examples presented above, strategic use of questions or meta-model challenges can clarify the deletions, distortions, and generalizations individuals make based on their experiences in the world.

The meta-model is a set of questions designed to reveal how a person's language is connected to experience. In her book, *Solutions*, Cameron-Bandler (1985) does a superior job of explaining the meta-model and provides many more examples of meta-model challenges. Another valuable reference is the work of Hartman (1990), who has developed an excellent discussion of the meta-model and illustrates how it can be used as part of the therapeutic process in a variety of clinical nursing situations. Finally, the work of Neizo and Lanza (1984) illustrates how selected aspects of the meta-model and meta-model challenges were used to process episodes of violence with patients after the episode had occurred on an inpatient psychiatric unit.

Reframing

Patients report their experiences through the language they use. The language people use gives clues to the types of generalizations, deletions, and distortions they make, helping them to realize that several meanings can be associated with a set of facts. When patients report their complaints to therapists, they report both the facts and added meaning.

O'Hanlon (1987) defines deframing as the process that occurs when a therapist challenges the meanings patients associate with the situation without providing a new frame. As a result of deframing, patients are left to create or discover alternative meanings for themselves or to accept the situation without any particular meanings. For example, confronting violence and assaultive behavior with violence and assaults, be it physical or chemical, often serves to reinforce a patient's model of the world. It confirms what has been experienced. It may reaffirm patients' powerlessness or generalization about how people interact and what one needs to do to protect oneself.

Pesut (1991) suggests that the development of reframing skills among nurses is an important clinical focus for psychiatric nursing in the '90s. Nurses can provide new or alternative frames of meaning for many situations. A reframe may be the stimulus for insight and future behavior change. For example, is it possible that a violent episode could be construed as a patient taking care of himself the best way he knew how at that moment?

A nurse might acknowledge that the patient used violence when out on the street and, in fact, it may have been a way to survive in gang wars. However, in the hospital, there are other ways to effectively communicate with people and get one's message across. The patient is in the hospital to learn about having more choices for responding in situations. Nurses are in a position to help patients gain insight, choice, control, and mastery through the use of at least three types of reframing techniques. Content, context, and the six-step reframe technique are described below.

CONTENT REFRAMING

A content reframe exists when one leaves the content of a situation or event the same and puts another piece of meaning around it. Bandler and Grinder (1982) suggest using the following four questions to guide the internal cognitive process nurses can use to develop reframes of specific situations. After each question is an example related to assault and violence.

- Is there a larger or different frame in which this behavior would have positive value? For example, in some contexts, if someone takes something away from another, the expected reaction is fighting and standing up for what is rightfully owned. On a psychiatric ward, this behavior may be labeled disruptive.
- Are there other aspects of this situation that are not apparent to the person that could provide a different meaning? For example, if violence on a ward is provoked by staff, how does that change the frame or focus of the intervention and care of the patient?
- What else could this behavior mean? For example, are increases in the incidence of violence on a particular ward a message about a dysfunctional milieu?
- How else might this same situation be described? For example, was a patient's violent response related to a violation of that patient's rights?

CONTEXT REFRAMING

Context reframing flows from a presupposition that all behavior is useful in some context. A context reframe can be developed by using the internal cognitive process of asking the following questions: In what context would this particular behavior be useful? In what context would the behavior that the person is complaining about have value (Bandler, 1982)? For example, violence in a gang war might mean the difference between life and death in a big city; a similar violent response in a locked psychiatric ward has different meaning and consequences.

THE SIX-STEP REFRAME TECHNIQUE

The six-step reframing technique was developed by Bandler and Grinder (1982) and grew out of the assumptions of the NLP model. One way to approach change is to separate or split old associations about behavior and link the split patterns to new patterns or beliefs that focus on a desired change. O'Hanlon (1987) described this Ericksonian technique as "splitting and linking." This is one of the fundamental dynamics of the six-step reframing technique. Habitual mental associations, beliefs, and unwanted behaviors are split into parts, creating new resourceful parts. The therapist facilitates interaction and dialogue among parts. As a result of the interaction that takes place, new associations that lead to constructive change are developed.

Specifically, the steps are:

1. Identification of a pattern of unwanted behavior;
2. Establishing communication with the part responsible for the pattern of behavior or symptom;
3. Discovering the positive intention behind the behavior or symptom;
4. Creating a new creative part that can generate new or alternative ways to achieve the positive intention of the part responsible for the unwanted behavior or symptom;
5. Negotiation between the responsible part and the creative part so that the

original part accepts the new choices and responsibility for activating the choices; and

6. Testing the ecology of the new choices so that the system maintains its integrity. This is accomplished by a survey or internal dialogue with all of a person's "parts." If any part objects to the new choices, then one must reframe each objection until agreement is reached.

For purposes of this discussion, if a nurse had the opportunity to work intensively with a patient in a one-to-one relationship, the opportunity to use a six-step reframe might present itself. In this instance, the nurse could ask the client to get in touch with the "part" that is responsible for generating the violent or disruptive behavior.

After establishing communication with the part, the client and therapist could explore together possible positive intentions of the behavior. Such exploration answers the question "what are you (the part) trying to do for me?" The answer to such a query often involves issues of maintaining safety, equilibrium, or integrity at some level. Other ways to achieve the same intention are generated through the development of a "creative part" that the patient can use as a resource. If the possible alternatives are acceptable to patients, then they have any number of suitable ways to fulfill the positive intention behind the disruptive behavior.

Use of this technique is best done with patients who are competent, verbal, and have some degree of insight. Breaking the person into discrete parts is a form of dissociation. Splitting and linking helps the patient develop new associations and patterns of responding (O'Hanlon, 1987). An important aspect of the intervention is the patient's analysis of the "ecology" of the alternative behaviors. This is accomplished by having patients focus their attention internally and conducting a survey of any parts that might object to the new behaviors identified by the creative part to meet the identified positive intention.

Citrenbaum, King, and Cohen (1985) offer a specific example of how this technique has been used in clinical practice. These therapists observe that the use of the six-step reframe technique is respectful of, surprising to, and refreshing for patients. In addition, they note that most of the work is left up to the patients, not the health professional, and that this type of reframing allows the patients to use their own inner power and resources to construct alternative patterns of behavior. Obviously, to use these techniques, patients need to be competent and not organically or chemically impaired. Psychotherapeutic skill is required to guide a patient through these six steps. Moreover, the successful use of this technique requires a context of rapport and a well-specified outcome identified jointly by both the client and the therapist. Finally, a therapist must be prepared to deal with the responses clients elicit from their parts just as the therapist deals with client issues that arise during the therapeutic process.

NLP Interventions With Victims of Violence

Reframing is also a useful technique when working with victims of violence. Other NLP techniques that are especially helpful in work with victims of violence include the three place visual-kinesthetic dissociation (VKD) technique (Bandler, 1978; Cameron-Bandler, 1985). This is a way to work through, process, and reframe a past traumatic event.

The VKD technique has also been called the theater technique (Stanton, 1988). A show or performance can be viewed from a variety of perspectives in a theater: on stage looking at the audience; as a member of the audience; and watching from the projection booth, which would allow one to watch the people in the audience as they watch the performance. These different perspectives expand and contract frames of reference.

Victims of violence who have not learned to dissociate may indeed feel the trauma of a violent event as if they were experiencing it as a performer on the stage. If they were able to view the event as a spectator rather then a victim, how might that perspective change their experience? Additionally, if they could watch themselves from a projection booth watching themselves in the audience watching the traumatic event on the screen, this would create a situation in which the victim is three times removed from the original traumatic event; that is, once out of the event and into the spectator position, then out of the spectator position into the projection booth.

Bandler (1978) provides an excellent example of how she used this technique with a rape victim to rework the trauma of the incident. From this dissociated perspective, one can work with patients to add resources, change perspectives, and work through issues associated with the event. Use of this technique requires skill, talent, and supervision. Koziey and McLeod (1987) and Shelden and Shelden (1989) provide detailed information about the techniques and clinical case studies that use this change history technique.

Summary

NLP is a comprehensive model of human behavior and communication. Many of the techniques developed within the NLP model are useful in a variety of settings with different clinical patient populations. The techniques of pacing, leading, meta-model challenge, and reframing have been described and introduced in this chapter. NLP technology is a valuable complement to the repertoire of communication skills psychiatric nurses already possess.

Interested readers are invited to learn more about the model and expand the frames through which they filter their practice. Reflecting on the framing and reframing of situations and events can generate choices in difficult clinical situations where one may not have realized the multiple meanings and different ways to frame the situation.

References

Bandler, L. *They lived happily ever after: A book about achieving happy endings in coupling.* Cupertina, CA: Meta Publications, 1978.

Bandler, R., Grinder, J. *The structure of magic,* vol 1. Palo Alto, CA: Science and Behavior Books, 1975.

Bandler, R., Grinder, J. *Reframing neurolinguistic programming and the transformation of meaning.* Moab, UT: Real People Press, 1982.

Berger, M. Across the corpus callosum with Chris Columbus; Or, how to put enough information in your left brain so that when your right brain intuits, it does so intelligently. Some ideas for the learning of reframing. *Journal of Strategic and Systemic Therapies* 1984; 3(2):22-28.

Blair, D.T., New, S.A. Assaultive behavior: Know the risks. *J Psychosoc Nurs Ment Health Serv* 1991; 29(11):25-30.

Brockopp, D. What is NLP? *Am J Nurs* 1983; 83:1012-1014.

Burgess, A. *Psychiatric nursing in the hospital and community,* 5th ed. Norwalk, CT: Appleton & Lange, 1990.

Cameron-Bandler, L. *Solutions.* San Raphael, CA: Future Pace Inc, 1985.

Citrenbaum, C., King, M., Cohen, W. *Modern clinical hypnosis for habit control.* New York: WW Norton, 1985.

Dilts, R. *Applications of neurolinguistic programming.* Cupertino, CA: Meta Publications, 1983.

Erickson, H., Tomlin, E., Swain, M. Modeling and role modeling: A theory and paradigm for nursing. Englewood Cliffs, NJ: Prentice Hall, 1983.

Fenyes, C. Kiss the frog: A therapeutic intervention for reframing family rules. *Family Therapy* 1976; 3:123-128.

Grinder, J., Bandler, R. *The structure of magic,* vol 2. Palo Alto, CA: Science and Behavior Books, 1976.

Grunebaum, H., Chasin, R. Relabeling and reframing reconsidered: The beneficial effects of a pathological label. *Advances in Family Psychiatry* 1980; 2:199-208.

Hartman, C. Communication and the therapeutic process. In A. Burgess (Ed.), *Psychiatric nursing in the hospital and community,* 5th ed. Norwalk, CT: Appleton & Lange, 1990, pp. 261-288.

Kersey, B., Protinsky, B. Reframing and embedded directives: A complementary intervention strategy. *Journal of Strategic and Systemic Therapies* 1984; 3(2):17-20.

Knowles, R. Building rapport through neurolinguistic programming. *Am J Nurs* 1983; 83:1011-1014.

Koziey, P., McLeod, G. Visual-kinesthetic dissociation in treatment of victims of rape. *Professional Psychology: Research and Practice* 1987; 18:276-282.

Laborde, G. *Influencing with integrity.* Palo Alto, CA: Syntony Publishers, Inc, 1984.

Neizo, B., Lanza, M. Post violence dialogue: Perception change through language restructuring. *Issues in Mental Health Nursing* 1984; 6:245-254.

O'Hanlon, B. Framing interventions in therapy: Deframing and reframing. *Journal of Strategic and Systemic Therapies* 1984; 3(2):1-4.

O'Hanlon, B. *Taproots: Underlying principles of Milton Erickson's therapy and hypnosis.* New York: WW Norton, 1987.

Pesut, D. Aim versus blame: Using an outcome specification model. *J Psychosoc Nurs Ment Health Serv* 1989; 27(5):26-30.

Pesut, D. The art, science and techniques of reframing in psychiatric mental health nursing. *Issues in Mental Health* 1991; 12(1):9-18.

Rossi, E. *The psychobiology of mind-body healing.* New York: WW Norton, 1986.

Sharpley, C. Research findings on neurolinguistic programming: Nonsupportive data or an untestable theory? *Journal of Counseling Psychology* 1987; 34:103-107.

Shelden, V., Shelden, R. Sexual abuse of males by females: The problem, treatment modality, and case example. *Family Therapy* 1989; 16:249-258.

Stanton, H. The removal of phobias through ego-state reframing. *Int J Psychosom* 1986; 33(4):15-18.

Stanton, H. Treating phobias rapidly with Bandler's theater technique. *Australian Journal of Clinical and Experimental Hypnosis* 1988; 16:153-160.

Watzlawick, P., Weakland, J., Fisch, R. *Change: Principles of problem formation and problem resolution.* New York: WW Norton, 1974.

Weeks, G. Toward a dialectical approach to intervention. *Human Development* 1977; 20:277-292.

Weeks, G., L'Abate, L. A compilation of paradoxical methods. *American Journal of Family Therapy* 1979; 7:449-453.

Weeks, G., L'Abate, L. *Paradoxical psychotherapy: Theory and practice with individuals, couples, and families.* New York: Brunner Mazel, 1982.

Wilson, H., Kneisl, C. *Psychiatric nursing,* 4th ed. Menlo Park, CA: Addison-Wesley, 1992.

For more information on the International Association for Neurolinguistic Programming (IANLP), contact 342 Massachusetts Avenue, 200 Marriott Center, Indianapolis, IN 46204.

10 Art Therapy: Facilitating Treatment of the Long-Term Effects of Sexual Abuse

By Janis J. Bowers, RN, MSN

Much has been written about the long-term effects of sexual abuse. These effects can include depression, dissociative symptoms and disorders, impulsiveness, drug and alcohol abuse, somatic complaints, generalized anxiety, phobic responses, sexual problems, difficulty with trust and interpersonal relationships, and personality disorders of varying severity (Courtois, 1988; Gelinas, 1983; Finkelhor, 1985; Meiselman, 1990).

Courtois (1988) points out that at least half of the sexually abused clients who seek therapy request relief from depression or some other Axis I diagnosis rather than for working on issues related to having been sexually abused as a child. Although the client may fit any number of Axis I diagnoses, there seems to be a growing consensus that post-traumatic stress disorder (PTSD) should be the primary diagnosis (Courtois, 1990; Ellenson, 1986; van der Kolk, 1987), and other Axis I and II diagnoses should be secondary.

Post-Traumatic Stress Disorder

PTSD is a constellation of symptoms that develop in response to overwhelming and uncontrollable life events that create intense fear, terror, and helplessness. Van der Kolk (1987) describes the response to psychological trauma as a biphasic reliving and denial of the trauma, characterized by alternating intrusive and numbing responses. The intrusive symptoms may include recurrent dreams of the event; sudden, intense feelings that the event is actually recurring (which may include a feeling of reliving the experience, hallucinations, illusions, and dissociative or flashback episodes); or intense psychological distress over events that symbolize some aspect of the trauma. These reactions lead to further symptoms, such as sleeping problems, exaggerated anger responses, difficulty concentrating, and general anxiety. Victims may display hypervigilance, an exaggerated startle response, or extreme physiological symptoms when exposed to symbolic stimuli (APA, 1987).

The intrusive symptoms alternate with numbing symptoms, such as avoiding thoughts, feelings, or activities associated with the trauma and an inability to remember all or some aspects of the trauma. Also seen are depressive symptoms, including a decreased interest in daily activities, feelings of depersonalization, and greatly restricted affect (often due to a fear of losing control) (APA, 1987).

It is important to understand why these alternating symptoms occur. Under extreme and overwhelming stress, basic psychological defenses are used to preserve the ego. A splitting or dissociation of self occurs, and in an attempt to maintain a positive sense of self and life, most or all aspects of the trauma are eliminated from consciousness (Johnson, 1987). However, sometimes a certain stimuli or situation triggers a memory, and parts of it may break through into consciousness, causing intrusive symptoms. The anxiety this causes leads to the need to further deny or repress the memories involved. The result is an overall psychic numbing that is often character-ized by an inability to attach words to feelings (alexithymia), partial or full amnesia for the traumatic event, and dissociative episodes in response to the anxiety caused by repressed memories coming too close to consciousness. This chapter will address art therapy as a way to gain access to repressed traumatic memories of sexual abuse and as a way to facilitate the processes of therapy and healing.

Gaining Access to Traumatic Memories Through Art Therapy

Generally, memories from early childhood are few; this may be due to the fact that infants and preverbal children encode memory through visual and sensorimotor channels rather than through cognitive processes (van der Kolk, 1987). If abuse occurs during these early years, cognitive memories may not exist. Johnson (1987) suggests that there is evidence that in later years, at times of overwhelming stress and terror, the cognitive memory system may be bypassed; the event is recorded in photographic form and is not integrated with other memories through the usual cognitive processes. This process, in combination with the dissociative process discussed earlier, contributes to the amnesia and alexithymia sometimes experienced by incest survivors. The problem lies in finding a way to translate these visual and sensorimotor memories into meaningful symbolic and verbal representations and then integrating them into a healthy life schema.

Because the traumatic memories were neurologically encoded through visual and sensorimotor pathways, art therapy offers a visual and sensorimotor medium that may more easily allow traumatic memories to come to the conscious level (Greenberg, 1987; Johnson, 1987). Through therapeutic recreation and discussion of the visual memories, sensorimotor memories also may surface, in turn stimulating new memories. Gradually, feelings can be recognized, and more memories often surface in response. Furthermore, the dreams and nightmares that seem to be so much a part of PTSD can be recreated visually, just as they are usually experienced. While memories are stimulated, the artwork allows the client more control over, and distance from, the memories. The artwork can be approached at whatever depth at which the client is comfortable. Resistance is lowered, and gradually the memories become owned and integrated into the self (Wadeson, 1980).

Art therapy has been used frequently with children and adolescents to overcome resistance, build trust, reduce tension, and stimulate memory. Because children's verbal and cognitive skills are not as highly developed, art therapy is often a more developmentally appropriate way to approach the sexually abused child (Burgess, 1990; Kelley, 1985; Powell, 1990).

Even though many adults are more cognitively and verbally adept, the adult may still have a child's concept of the traumatic event because repression of material occurred at a much earlier stage of development. These conceptualizations may be more apparent through the use of a medium with which the person was more familiar during the actual time of abuse. Also, the frightened inner child of the adult may respond more willingly to an art therapy approach for the same reasons as children. Finally, for victims who were cautioned not to talk about the abuse, creative arts may allow more freedom to express the sexual abuse "symbolically or realistically. . . in modalities not perceived to be covered by the cautionary injunction" (Naitove, 1988).

Case Study: Emily

This author found a paucity of published literature on the use of artwork to enhance therapy with adults who were sexually abused as children. Spring (1985) wrote about using artwork with sexually abused, chemically dependent women. Green and van der Kolk (1987) used a client's artwork to illustrate how early childhood sexual trauma can be accessed and worked through using a nonverbal medium.

The following case study illustrates how art therapy was used with a client who had few concrete childhood memories and who was experiencing chronic symptoms of PTSD resulting from early childhood sexual abuse.

For the purpose of this chapter, the client chose the pseudonym "Emily." She agreed to the discussion of her history, therapy, and artwork in the hope that other therapists could learn more about effective treatment modalities for working with survivors of sexual abuse.

BACKGROUND DATA AND ASSESSMENT

Emily was a pretty, quiet, thin, fragile-looking 24-year-old who seemed very ill at ease when she came to therapy; she had great difficulty articulating her problems and history. She is the second of four children and the oldest girl. Her father is an alcoholic and her mother is a recovering alcoholic. Although she graduated from college, Emily had spent the past 3 years at a variety of temporary jobs for which she was overqualified. Emily stated that because of the difficulties she was presently having with relationships and with her life in general, a good friend suggested she might have been sexually abused as a child. In the past, two other therapists had also proposed this possibility to Emily and she had fled from therapy each time. Her older brother had also wondered whether their father might have sexually abused Emily and her sister, but when he and Emily asked their sister, she tensely and vehemently denied the possibility.

Emily presented with symptoms of depression with suicidal ideation (without a plan) and fear (extreme revulsion) that she may have been sexually abused by her father. She denied any actual memories of sexual abuse, although she commented that both she and her sister could not bear to be around their father.

Generally, Emily's interpersonal relationships were superficial and she felt detached from others. She was unable to form intimate relationships with men or women. The one exception to this was a long-term platonic friendship with the young man who encouraged her to come to therapy. Although this friendship was platonic, a part of Emily mourned her inability to have a total relationship with him, but her disgust over anything sexual overruled this possibility. Any type of physical intimacy caused her to recoil and withdraw emotionally.

Emily frequently had violent dreams and generally slept poorly. Concentration was often a problem and she was hypervigilant. When she was in college, she went through a long period of excessive sleeping to the point where she would fall asleep frequently throughout the day. She had a neurological evaluation, which proved negative. She stated that she came out of this period by making a conscious decision to live. Emily had feelings of helplessness and hopelessness, as well as feelings of derealization and depersonalization. Her self-concept and body image were extremely poor.

Emily wanted two things out of therapy: relief from her depression and to learn whether she had been sexually abused.

PLAN

Emily was told that the depression could be managed through therapy and perhaps medication as well, but Emily was never comfortable with the

Figure 1. Emily's self-portrait.

idea of medication, so we worked at alleviating the depression through therapeutic work. We also agreed that interpersonal relationships and self-esteem were problems for her, and decided that these would be areas

Figure 2. Emily's portrait of her father in a rage.

we would explore in therapy. Her lack of concrete memories, her intense difficulty verbalizing feelings and thoughts, as well as her anxiety and dissociative responses to emotionally laden content were a challenge to the normal verbal mode of therapy. This also pointed to the need to carefully monitor and titrate her retrieval of and responses to any memories.

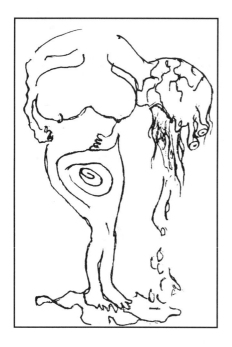

Figure 3. Emily's depiction of her feelings the morning after her father had climbed into her bed.

INTERVENTIONS

In working with children and adolescents who have been sexually abused, I usually ask them to draw a picture of themselves, of their family, and of the person who molested them. This seemed like it might be worth a try with Emily, given her difficulty with verbal communication. Emily had never mentioned having any artistic tendencies, so I was dumbfounded when she produced extraordinarily powerful and emotionally articulate drawings. She was able to discuss them to varying degrees.

Her self-portrait revealed a Picasso-like, bony, misshapen, sad-faced person in a defensive posture (Figure 1). She related how as a child, school peers would make fun of her bony back. There were signs of power, however; her leg looked as if it were kicking out, and she shyly, and a bit proudly, described a finger that was sticking out as her "fuck you" finger. Her mouth was drawn back and down in a sad position, and her eyes were without pupils, reflecting an inner deadness or void, a theme that was to recur in her artwork. We talked at length about what her portrayal of her eyes meant to her.

The picture of her father was shocking in its intensity (Figure 2). It was a close-up of his face in an absolute, wild rage. She used black and red crayon to draw the picture, and even though the crayon strokes were bold, it was extremely detailed, down to the veins on his neck. The rage in his eyes and mouth was frightening, and Emily said that this is frequently how he would look when he became angry, even over inconsequential things. For example, if she or a sibling could not give ready answers to her father at mealtime, he

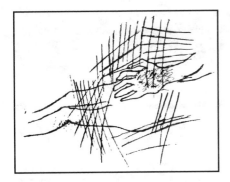

Figure 4. This sketch released a vivid description of a hypothetical experience of sexual abuse. When it was suggested that Emily removed herself from the memory to protect herself from pain, she answered, "Maybe."

would fly into a rage. (Another time that we looked at this picture, Emily remembered that he also looked this way whenever he would get angry and throw the family cat against the wall.) These recalled incidents certainly gave a more vivid portrayal of what growing up was like for Emily. Hearing her own words also seemed to help Emily see how abnormal the "normal" was at home. These drawings opened up a new avenue of therapy with Emily as I realized she was able to access and express her feelings eloquently through her artwork.

From then on, at least half of our work together was accomplished through Emily's artwork. She never felt comfortable drawing during a session, but I frequently suggested a theme or idea for her to draw, and more often than not, a week or two later she returned with a drawing in hand. When I asked her how it felt to do these drawings, she said that she generally drew them very quickly, and sometimes felt like she was almost in a trance-like state.

Many of the drawings had violent and self-destructive themes, and I tried to monitor carefully how she was reacting to this process, especially because her ego-functioning seemed fragile. Emily said that doing the drawings gave her a sense of relief; they made vague, overwhelming feelings more concrete, real, and manageable. She progressed from drawing on 8X11 art paper to the next larger size to an even larger size, saying that she needed more space to draw. I took that as a sign of opening up and needing to get things out. Her drawings ranged from pen or pencil sketches, often quickly drawn in an almost driven, primitive way, to elaborate charcoal sketches or crayon drawings with immense detail. She and I began to see certain themes emerge, and even though she was not always able to integrate them or "own" them, she began to become aware of these issues for the first time.

Many of her drawings pointed to incest. She had one memory of a time when she was about 14 and had been very sick. She called out for her mother, but her older brother got her father, who came into her bedroom with a glass of orange juice for her. Then he got into bed with her with his front to her back, wrapping his arms around her. That was the end of the memory. Later, Emily brought a picture to therapy that showed how she felt the next day when she awoke from that experience (Figure 3). She depicted

Figure 5

Figure 5. Emily's rendering of a dream.

herself as an almost reptilian human figure, doubled over, vomiting, with her head cracking open; over her genital area was a spiral that resembled a target. She had written underneath: "I couldn't tell anyone and the sun was out and my family eating breakfast and I had been killed." Her memory was jogged a bit more by this; she remembered her father caressing her hair and how she had practically hugged the wall.

Another sketch (Figure 4) showed a recumbent female from waist to ankles and a hairy hand coming down over her genital area. Immediately after Emily drew the picture, she wrote: "feel like it's all of me—I mean this image—how can I get around it—men control me—I'm sick and at mercy—defined by between my legs—flat on back—*no hope*—and this is horrible *murder*—just before the hand comes down completely—after that it's too *sick.*"

In describing the picture, Emily commented that, "This is how it would have been if it had happened." I asked her to describe the room it hypothetically might have happened in, and she proceeded to give a detailed and dispassionate description of the room, how he would have come in, what would have happened, what it would have been like, and finished with ". . . if it had happened." This seemed like a remarkable description, and I suggested that sometimes the first way memories come back is in a "removed" way, without the emotional component, so our emotional selves can be protected from the pain, and that might be a

Figure 6. A sketch of Emily's sadness. She did not specify her age in this drawing.

possibility for her. She remained thoughtfully silent for a while, and then, nodding slowly, said, "Maybe. . .."

The aforementioned example is the closest we ever came to an actual cognitive memory of an event, but all of Emily's pictures pointed to themes and issues seen in cases of child sexual abuse. Penises frequently appeared; several drawings even had "hidden" penises, much as a "find the hidden picture" drawing in children's books.

For several weeks Emily brought a picture but was unable to show it to me. Finally she gathered considerable courage and unrolled a 2-ft×3-ft picture (Figure 5). She had difficulty even looking at it, although it was obvious she had spent much time working on it. She did not know what to say about the picture, so I gently asked questions. The face with the tongue hanging out is her father; she laughed nervously and commented on how disgusting it was. (Another time she commented that it looked like a flaccid penis or that he might lick something with it.) The figure in the center of the drawing is a representation of a dream Emily had: a man who (in reality) was a child molester tried to get into her house (he is not seen in this picture). She fought to keep him out by nailing down a window. In a "Freudian slip" (or visual pun), the nail is actually a screw.

Emily has one eye open and one closed, she said, to keep watch and stay on guard just as she did in real life. Her throat is full, and when looked at carefully, just behind her clenched teeth there is a hidden penis going down

Figure 7. Emily's fantasy of what she would like to be. An earlier, smaller drawing did not show enough anger and power, said Emily.

her throat. (This theme of feeling her throat filled up and wanting to gag came through several other pictures as well.) There is a terrible wedge-shaped wound going from her stomach to her genital area, and this, too, is a frequent theme. Smaller versions of the wound appear down her forehead and in her chest area, and Emily said softly, "It was as if my chest would break open." Spring (1985) discusses the frequent use of the wedge shape in drawings by sexually abused children.

Emily did not want to identify the tube-like object with the sharp pincers, but she indicated that it came out of curly hair and went back into a fold with curly hair, and this was particularly disgusting to her. I suggested that it might feel like terrible stinging if one had been sexually abused as a child, and Emily nodded.

We also talked about the strange head on the right. At first Emily did not say much about it except that it was her father, but I had a hunch and observed that the stalk sticking out from the head looked rigid and penis-like. Emily chuckled wryly and said, "I told you he was a penis head!" (Another time she was able to talk more about that characterization, and very matter-of-factly said, "That's how he'd look when he wanted to have sex with me. I don't know how I know that, but I do. And that's

Figure 8. The "family secret." Emily explained that the family had to work hard to keep the beast in its cage, and later said that it lived in her parent's bedroom.

slobber coming out of his mouth.") His open eye is the bloodshot eye of an alcoholic. Again, in an ironic and unconscious touch, Emily shows herself "screwing" his head; while he was not technically part of the dream sequence she had drawn in the center, he ended up very much included.

Finally, Emily described the cross-hatch background as a malevolent atmosphere or miasma that permeated her father, her home, and her growing up years. This malevolent atmosphere is seen in many of her other drawings. She spent an enormous amount of time drawing in this background, and it obviously was an important part of her perception of her father and her life as a child.

There were other pictures of Emily with her mouth gaping wide open, and when she described the feeling that went along with it, she described a terrible gagging, full feeling in her throat. A sketch of what her "sadness" feels like shows a figure lying on its stomach with its head pulled back and its mouth open and distended; there is a feeling of terrible despair to the picture (Figure 6). Emily could not say how old she was in this picture, but she drew another in which she depicted herself as an infant with something going into her mouth. The drawing itself was primitive, and she admitted in an ashamedly voice that she had drawn a penis and then had crossed it out.

As Emily began to see the developing theme of oral sex, she was revolted and incredulous, and frequently questioned her sanity, saying that she must be very bad to make up such sick things. Besides wondering aloud if she might have been told something like that frequently as a child (the answer was yes), I pointed out other more objective, cognitive data that corroborated some of these "memories": her brother's "guesses," her sister's reaction when Emily and her brother asked if she had been sexually abused by their father, her mother's questions to Emily about her relationship with her father, her other therapists' "hunches," her inability to have physical intimacy, and the themes of her other drawings. There came a day when,

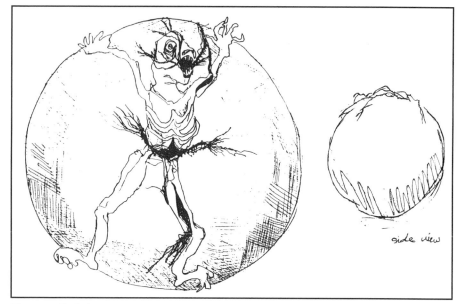

Figure 9. Emily's struggle to keep the "family secret" in control so that it would not destroy her.

with tears streaming down her face, she said that she knew what all the pictures meant, but she could not bear to say it out loud. After that she seemed a bit more at peace with herself—at least less self-doubting—and therapy seemed to enter a new working phase.

Other themes from her pictures included immense anger and rage, betrayal, sorrow, a family secret, denial, and feelings of being "damaged goods." One picture was a drawing of what she would like to be; she drew a vicious-looking, snarling, long-fanged, cat-like animal. She said that that picture did not show enough of the anger and power, and she pulled out a second larger, even more intense drawing (Figure 7). Emily always shied away from getting into that anger, and we talked about that; she was afraid if she let the anger out, it would be all-consuming. This is not an uncommon feeling in victims of sexual abuse (Curtois, 1988), but it is certainly terrifying and overwhelming. I frequently suggested that the anger would indeed come out, but that she would be able to let it out in a way that was manageable for her at her own pace, and that it would happen only when she was ready for it. In fact, the pictures were a safe beginning to try out a little of the inner rage she works so hard to suppress.

One day Emily brought in a picture of a dream she had of the "family secret": it was a sketch of a creature with long sharp fangs and even longer, sharp talons that "everyone in the family had to work very hard to keep in its cage; it kept trying to get out all the time" (Figure 8). (In another session, Emily said that this animal lived in her parent's bedroom.) After drawing the picture, Emily said she became dizzy and she wrote words that she

Figure 10. The family's denial symbolized by a gash on Emily's foot.

heard a little girl saying in her head: "Did your Daddy cut you? Do you have to go to the bathroom?" Hearing the voices frightened Emily, and it was important for her to know that hallucinations are not an unusual response to stress; it was her way of dealing with the stress of confronting the family secret. It must have taken tremendous energy to control the secret, and a related picture shows the terrible stress and despair Emily felt as she tried to balance the "family world" so it would not roll over and crush her (Figure 9). She does not look human; the wounds are obvious and terrible and the effort is literally killing her.

Denial was an associated theme. Emily drew a picture of a dream in which her foot was badly cut and dripping blood (Figure 10). She knew she had to go to the hospital, yet everyone in her family kept telling her it was okay, that she was making a big deal of nothing, and she was wrong. She wrote on the picture: "Me aghast—have to believe it? Can't go if they don't think so."

We talked about the feeling of powerlessness and the issue of family denial this picture triggered. Much discussion and insight came of relating this picture to her life as a child in her family. Along with the feelings of denial came feelings of betrayal and lack of protection. She drew a Madonna-like portrayal of her mother shielding Emily from a skeleton reaching out for her, when in reality her mother was "tricking her about her whole life and what was out there."

"Damaged goods" was another obvious recurring theme. Many of Emily's drawings showed a large gash with blood dripping from it. This could be taken on several levels; Emily did not interpret it in a sexual way as much as having been "so damaged that I should have died." She also portrayed herself in terribly disfigured ways. Her cognitive perceptions of herself have been drastically distorted by her early experiences, and this is an area that will need to be reworked repeatedly.

Although working with Emily's art occupied much of therapy, I needed to use other interventions to help Emily cope with the process of dissociation. She would often come into therapy feeling extremely tense and anxious. This feeling might abate somewhat, but sometimes it would escalate and she would enter a panicked, dissociative state (especially when the content of the session was heavy or when she was getting closer to affect or memory). When this happened, she was unable to concentrate on my words, but it was important to talk her down to a calmer state through the use of calm, firm suggestions that she would be all right; she was safe now; her reaction was the reaction she experienced as a child trying to cope with her abuse and that it allowed her to survive then, but she did not need that reaction now.

We also worked on ways to decrease her anxiety. Emily voiced concern that I might touch her (nonsexually, but even that was frightening to her), and I promised her that I would not touch her in any way without her permission. I also suggested that it might be more comfortable if our chairs were farther apart, and she agreed. Because Emily felt her prior experiences with therapists had been negative, I checked with her frequently about how therapy was going: if we were going too fast, if it was too intense, if I was pushing too much or not enough, if she was generally feeling worse or better. It was a sign of trust and strength that Emily was able to respond honestly, and I reinforced that sense of inner control as frequently as possible.

EVALUATION

Emily and I worked together for 8 months. Therapy terminated because I moved to another state. Although retrieval of childhood memories was a large part of our work together, we also worked at various levels on her relationships with others and on realistic goals for improving her life and relationships. Emily has re-established her relationship with her older brother and younger sister. Her brother has given her support and much feedback about how violent their father could be. She and her sister visit, write to each other, and support each other, and Emily values that relationship dearly.

She decided to participate in a group therapy experience for adults who were sexually abused as children; she was very apprehensive about that experience, but afterward said that although she did not participate much, she learned a great deal, received good support, and did not feel so isolated. Considering that she entered therapy hardly able to tolerate thinking about having been sexually abused, this was indeed progress. Emily finally has a job she loves working with animals. She bought a new car; in the past, she never felt "grown-up or worthwhile" enough to own a car, much less a new one.

Emily has also resumed therapy and continues to make progress; although she remains frustrated by the lack of concrete cognitive memories, she has begun to work on her anger as well as on her feelings about and relationship with her mother. She no longer feels the need to keep up a smiling front or talk to family members she cannot tolerate. Emily still fights various levels of depression, and her artwork remains an important monitor for her level of depression, as well as a safe outlet for strong feelings. Therapy is painful for Emily; integrating the visual-sensory memories, the emotions, and the cognitive understanding of these memories and emotions is a slow process. More painful memories continue to surface, yet Emily persists and grows, and her determination is often a study in courage.

Clinician Considerations

Many excellent books and articles have been written about conducting art therapy with children and adults, and indeed, there are graduate degree programs that lead to a master's degree in art therapy. Oaklander (1988) encourages professionals from other disciplines to use the principles and techniques of art therapy to enhance their work with and understanding of children. Oaklander's gestalt approach, profound respect for the client's inner wisdom, and her belief in the therapeutic endeavor as a partnership were important guidelines for this therapist. Although she wrote mainly about conducting art therapy with children, many of the principles involved and exercises employed are just as applicable (or are easily modified) to working with adults. Her book is a practical and readable book about using the creative arts in therapy. The following are some practical suggestions useful in facilitating working with a client's artwork:

• It is important to convey to the client that this is not an art test. No art talent is required; life-like shapes need not be used and the drawing will not be judged. It is simply another way to find out more about the clients' thoughts and feelings about self and their world. Together the therapist and client can explore its meaning.

- Have clients describe the picture in their own way.
- Ask the client to tell more about specific parts of the picture, making parts clearer, describing actual forms, objects, and people. Had I not asked Emily to describe her pictures, I could easily have misinterpreted them. Also, as she described them, new feelings and thoughts would often be triggered.
- Ask the client to describe the picture in the "first person" and focus on describing parts of it in the first person as well. The client can dialogue between parts of the picture, whether the parts are persons or shapes or objects. However, Emily was unable to do this; I suspect it was too threatening and brought the affect too close to the surface. I respected that and reinforced her sense of control by reiterating that she would get into strong feelings only when she was actually ready and able to handle them.
- If a client does not know what something means in a drawing, an explanation or interpretation can be tentatively suggested, but that interpretation should be checked out with the client's sense of its "rightness." When Emily blocked while describing Figure 8, I offered the suggestion to her that the picture might be a metaphor for her life, and she nodded vehemently. Another time I made a tentative interpretation, but Emily's response was only lukewarm. Even if I was correct, she was not ready for the interpretation.
- Encourage the client to focus on the use of colors. What do they mean to the client? Even if she does not know, it opens up a new awareness. Emily's use of color in her self-portrait drew the viewer to specific parts of her body that were an important part of her self-concept.
- Watch for cues in the client's voice, tone, body posture, expression, and breathing. Use these cues to encourage further exploration or to back off from material that is produces too much anxiety. Sometimes when we were exploring the meaning of a picture, Emily would show signs of dissociating; it was important to back away and ground Emily in the present when this happened.
- Help the client "own" what has been said about the picture or parts of it. Carefully and gently ask how the picture, or the interpretation of it, fits with any part of the client's life. When I asked Emily about the picture of what she would like to be (Figure 7), she said that she would like to have as much power as the animal in the picture; she could protect herself that way.
- Watch for missing parts or empty spaces. Emily frequently drew pictures in which the lower half of her body was missing or bleeding out; we talked about what this meant to Emily. Sometimes it was a way of avoiding the sexual part of herself; other times it was a definite message about how damaged she felt.
- Sometimes take the picture literally, but sometimes go for the opposite of what is there, especially when the opposite seems more likely. Emily drew a picture of her mother protecting her from a skeletal figure. Although her mother looked protective, in reality Emily said it was a picture about betrayal and denial, and it was an important step in Emily's ability to identify her anger at her mother.

- Have the client share the experience of drawing: feelings about doing the drawing before, during, and after the process. Had I not asked Emily how she felt when she drew some pictures with extremely self-destructive themes, I might have assumed the art therapy was too anxiety provoking. After carefully assessing her reactions, the pictures seemed to provide a safety valve.
- Let clients work at their own pace. Although I frequently suggested themes for Emily to draw, I trusted that she would draw only what she was ready to draw (and confront), that she would show it to me only when she was ready to trust me with that part of herself, and that she would talk about it at the depth that she could handle. If I decided to try for a deeper level of understanding, I monitored her response and comfort level carefully.
- Look for patterns and themes in and among pictures. For Emily, major themes that emerged included sexual abuse, oral sex, betrayal, denial, anger, sorrow, and damaged goods. Although it was stressful to concurrently look at several pictures with the same theme, it was also important in helping Emily believe her own perceptions and hunches. We spent much time on these themes and the emotions they reflected and elicited.

Conclusion

Art therapy can be an important tool to access repressed memories and emotions and to work through conflicting feelings and relationships, especially when the client has difficulty expressing emotion or articulating thoughts and feelings. It can also help establish a therapeutic and trusting relationship between the client and therapist, often a difficult process for persons who have been sexually traumatized as children. Although art therapy has been successful as a treatment modality for sexually abused children, its use with adults who were sexually abused as children does not seem to have been well explored. This is only one case history, and only one artistic medium was used; however, the author hopes it will encourage others to learn more about art therapy as a treatment modality and to try this modality with adult survivors of sexual abuse.

References

American Psychiatric Association. *Diagnostic and statistical manual of mental disorders*, 3rd ed, rev. Washington DC: Author, 1987.

Burgess, A.W., Hartman, C.R., Howe, J.W., Shaw, E.R., McFarland, G.C. Juvenile murderers: Assessing memory through crime scene drawings. *J Psychosoc Nurs Ment Health Serv* 1990; 28(1):26-34.

Courtios, C.A. Healing the incest wound: Adult survivors in therapy. New York: WW Norton & Co, 1988.

Ellenson, G.S. Disturbances of perception in adult female incest survivors. *Social Casework: The Journal of Contemporary Social Work* 1986; 67:149-159.

Finkelhor, D., Brown, A. The traumatic impact of child sexual abuse: A conceptualization. *Am J Orthopsychiatry* 1985; 55:530-541.

Gelinas, D.J. The persisting negative effects of incest. *Psychiatry* 1983; 46:312-332.

Greenberg, M.S., van der Kolk, B.A. Retrieval and integration of traumatic memories with the "painting cure." In B.A. van der Kolk (Ed.), *Psychological trauma.* Washington, DC: American Psychiatric Press, Inc, 1987, pp. 191-216.

Johnson, D.R. The role of the creative arts therapies in the diagnosis and treatment of psychological trauma. *Arts in Psychotherapy* 1987; 14(1):7-13.

Kelley, S.J. The use of art therapy with sexually abused children. *J Psychosoc Nurs Ment Health Serv* 1984; 22(12):12-18.

Meiselman, K.C. *Resolving the trauma of incest: Reintegration therapy with survivors.* San Francisco: Jossey-Bass Inc, 1990.

Naitove, C. Art therapy with sexually abused children. In S.M. Sgroi (Ed.), *Handbook of clinical intervention in child sexual abuse.* Lexington, MA: DC Heath & Co, 1988, pp. 269-308.

Oaklander, V. *Windows to our children.* Highland, NY: The Center for Gestalt Development, Inc, 1988.

Powell, L., Faherty, S.L. Treating sexually abused latency age girls. *Arts in Psychotherapy* 1990; 17:35-47.

Spring, D. Symbolic language of sexually abused, chemically dependent women. *American Journal of Art Therapy* 1985; (24):13-21.

van der Kolk, B.A. *Psychological trauma.* Washington, DC: American Psychiatric Press, Inc, 1987.

Wadeson, H. *Art psychotherapy.* New York: John Wiley & Sons, 1980.

Reprinted with permission from the Journal of Psychosocial Nursing and Mental Health Services 1992; 30(6):15-24.

11

Juvenile Murderers: Assessing Memory Through Crime Scene Drawings

By Ann Wolbert Burgess, RN, DNSc;
Carol R. Hartman, RN, DNSc;
Judith Wood Howe, MS, ATR;
Edward R. Shaw, PhD;
and Gloria C. McFarland, MS

Psychiatric nurses have focused considerable attention on eliciting information through interviewing techniques and helping patients to verbally communicate. Images are equally as important as words and actions in therapeutic efforts and evaluation. The use of material to structure images—whether it be painting, drawing, sculpting, or drama—is part of the informational system out of which people react and are motivated. To advance the science, we have been studying the storage of information in memory and techniques to access the memory system.

Human figure drawings provide a means of exploring the personal constructs individuals have about themselves, others, and events in their lives. Drawings permit the expression of emotion through both motor and visual representations of experience. The products allow for the expression of the association between symbols and their meanings as construed by the artist.

There is beginning literature on the use of children's drawings following traumatic events such as hospitalization (Crowl, 1980), death of a parent (Raymer, 1987), sexual abuse, (Burgess, 1981; Hibbard, 1987; Kelley, 1984), running away from home (Howe, 1987), and witnessing family violence (Wohl, 1985). These drawings help explain the sense of distress experienced by children as they recall the event.

Neglected in the literature, however, are how drawings aid in stimulating a person's memory to recall aggressive acts. In an attempt to contribute to the clinical literature on violence, we used a series drawing technique, in which youthful killers were asked to produce five drawings. As part of a substudy of a larger ongoing project examining possible links between childhood sexual abuse and exploitation, juvenile delinquency, and criminal behavior (Burgess, 1987), data were collected on incarcerated juveniles who had committed murders. The 15 juveniles in this sample were part of a previously reported sample (Grant, 1989). After being provided with a description of the study and the opportunity to ask questions, juveniles consented to make a series of drawings and complete a research protocol (Faulkner, 1986).

The conceptual framework of information processing guided the drawing analysis. We previously conceptualized a phase-specific model in the information processing of trauma, from which post-traumatic behavior emerges (Burgess, 1987; Hartman, 1986; Horowitz, 1976). This processing model helps explain how a child victim attempts to modify the sensory, perceptual, and cognitive alterations that occurred during abuse, whether it was physical or sexual. It hypothesizes how these behavioral adaptations, at these three levels, emerge in overt behavioral patterns specifically reflective of how the abuse itself and the memory constructs over time are influenced by the psychological survival mechanisms. These behaviors, reflecting how the event is stored in memory and processed, are referred to as "trauma learned." This learning is characterized by actions that are a symbolic repetition of the trauma processing.

These behaviors can be direct re-enactments of the trauma, in which case the victim responds to others as if the old trauma is ongoing (eg, an intrusive image or a flashback), or, in another case, the behavior is a repetition of the trauma as experienced by the victim with the victim vacillating between his own perceived behaviors and the behaviors of the offender. The repetition characterizing early abuse experiences underscores the violent acts of some juvenile offenders. If the expression of the trauma learned process is not disrupted, it is reinforced by the offensive behavior, and the violent and/or sexual offending behavior becomes habituated. As this process continues, the ability to distinguish between victim and offender becomes blurred and the behavioral identification is almost entirely with the offender. The attitude toward subsequent victims is without empathy or recognition of the earlier abuse.

This framework focuses on how individuals organize their thinking or reconstruction of a critical event. At times, the perceptions and behaviors associated with the victimization dominate, and at other times, perceptions and behaviors regarding the perpetrator rule. A third aspect of trauma learning is displacement of fear and rage to others. We hypothesized that the drawing of the event (ie, the crime) would allow us to understand how the juvenile perceived himself in relation to the victim. By combining the drawings with the juveniles' statements relating their motives for the murderous acts, we speculated that we would derive some notion of the reconstructive and memory processing of the juveniles and their violent actions. This chapter illustrates the use of crime scene drawings as a technique to access memory for critical information in planning nursing care.

Crime Scene Drawings and Assessing Memory

The use of the drawing series provides a noninvasive way to access perceptions, memories, and recall. The juvenile is asked to make a series of drawings, using whole figures (not stick) in the following order: self younger; current self; family doing something; event (crime); and house/tree. A sixth drawing is optional as a free drawing. The event drawing is requested by saying: "Draw what brought you here." There usually is some dialogue by the juvenile, all of which is important in assessing psychological defenses ("I can't remember" or "I can't do that") and affect. The nurse may need to encourage and reassure the juvenile that he can produce such a drawing. A full interpretation of the drawing series includes all the drawings, but for the purposes of this article, only the crime scene drawings will be discussed.

Although the interpretation of crime scene drawings requires considerable experience and background in forensic psychiatric nursing, there are two basic areas that can be used by inpatient or residential staff to assess the juvenile's memory and recall of the crime for planning therapeutic interventions. These areas are crime and phases of murder, and motivational dynamics.

Crime and Phases of Murder

The first step in understanding the juvenile's crime is a thorough review of official records and reports. This should be done prior to an assessment. Facts provide a base against which the defensiveness and/or truthfulness of the juvenile can be measured and the drawing content can be filtered.

The request to draw the crime scene or murder event requires the juvenile to reconstruct from memory an image influenced by emotions, thinking patterns, and motivations. Because murder is a behavior constructed in phases, it also requires the juvenile to select a phase or point in time to draw, that is, before the action that led to death, during the killing, or after the murder.

The crime scene drawing is observed for the phase of the crime that is presented: is it before, during, or after the murder? The drawing itself gives information about gaps in the juvenile's emotional state that need to be filled. One never gets an entire memory for emotional states, but rather extraneous details of dresser drawers or tiles on a wall. The subject can be

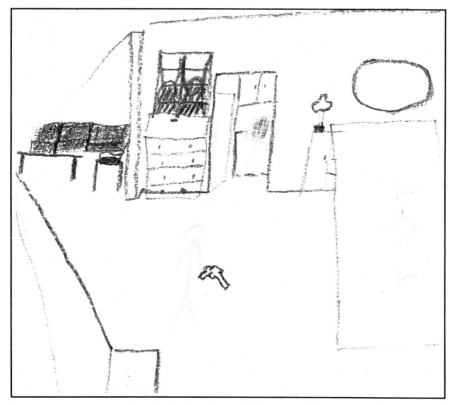

Figure 1. The crime scene drawing in Case 1 prior to the murder. The merging of the victim and offender is illustrated by the use of the same color and the likeness of the two figures. The victim (mother) is talking on the telephone while the juvenile advances through the dining room with a gun. The fact that the picture is drawn the moment before the juvenile decided to pull the trigger indicates premeditation.

asked to fill in more details specific to the time phases. As the rationale, image, and emotions that led to the crime unfold, the events during and after the crime can be elicited. A better understanding of the crime develops that directs the intervention.

CASE 1: SCENE BEFORE THE MURDER

Case 1 illustrates the crime scene of a 14-year-old youth prior to the murder. The youth was known to the juvenile courts for "incorrigible and assaultive behavior" to his mother and had stated in court on one occasion, "I want to take Daddy's gun and do in my mother, father, and grandmother." It was an English composition written by the juvenile about a fantasy of killing his teachers that precipitated parental agreement to obtain psychiatric treatment.

This family violence crime scene drawing illustrates merging of the victim and offender through the use of the color yellow and the likeness of the two

Figure 2. The first drawing, depicting the murder in Case 2, is before the murder. The offender (the stick figure coming through the doorway) showed himself as being smaller than the victim. The second drawing, after the murder, shows the victim on the bed and the juvenile in the kitchen lighting newspaper on the stove. The important aspect in these drawings is not only the merging brown color, but also the alteration in size.

stick figures (Figure 1). The mother is making a telephone call as the son advances through the dining room to the kitchen carrying a large gun.

The important point in this drawing is the phase in which the juvenile depicts the crime; it is just before he decided to pull the trigger and kill his mother. There was an elaborate chain of events that led to this murder, which indicates premeditation. It is important for the staff nurse to recognize that this boy is dangerous: he planned and thought out the murder; it came in the context of someone setting limits on him; and there is a high level of vindictiveness and little remorse. From the milieu standpoint, the nurse needs to observe and assess his relationships with people and how he handles frustration and challenge.

CASE 2: SEQUENCE OF THE MURDER

In a second case, a 16-year-old juvenile drew the murder in several phases; that is, he sequenced the acts before, during, and following the murder. He stabbed and then burned the bed and body of a 31-year-old female neighbor.

In drawing the crime scene, the juvenile claimed that the victim had invited him into the apartment, and an unidentified man solicited a sexual act. After the man left the apartment, the victim grabbed for the defendant's crotch and then hit him several times with a metal pipe (which was not found). The youth pulled a screwdriver from his pocket and hit the victim several times. When asked what happened next, he drew a second picture of the victim on the bed, a doorway, and himself in the next room lighting paper on the stove.

The first drawing is before the murder (Figure 2). The juvenile depicted himself as smaller than the victim (the juvenile is the stick figure coming through the doorway; the victim is larger and standing beside the bed). The defendant holds a metal pipe and has an exaggerated attribution to his mouth.

In the second picture (Figure 2), after the murder, the offender is larger than the victim (lying on the bed) and separated by a doorway, lighting

Figure 3. Note the artistic skill and drawing of the murder act in Case 3. The figures are well-differentiated and there is strong use of color and an emphasis on detail. The underwear covering the juvenile's hand and gun indicates he is sneaky, hides weapons and drugs, and feels the act was justified. Although the juvenile will be a model patient on the ward, he will most likely resume criminal behavior when he is discharged.

newspapers on the stove. The important aspect of this sequence is not only the merging brown color but also the alteration in size.

This sexual homicide has an elaborate story accompanying the drawings that suggests the emotional difficulty and confusion over aggression and sexuality that is projected onto the female victim. The juvenile's ability to lie and view the victim as the danger is linked to his personal sense of being damaged, as noted in the drawing of self and in his distortion of his own aggressive and sexual impulses. The arson is a specific method of destroying evidence of sexual contact. In the sequence of drawings, he uses only the color brown.

Motivational Dynamics

Although the juvenile may provide a verbal statement of motive, it is also useful to examine the crime scene drawing for the relative size of the victim to the offender to speculate on motivational dynamics of power, anger, and displacement of emotion.

The question regarding motive may be verbally asked: "How did it happen?" The motives of the juveniles in this study were categorized in two ways: the victim provoked an argument in ways that challenged the offender and, thus, the victim was seen by the offender as responsible for the act of rage; or, the offender perceived that the victim was going to physically overtake or overpower him.

CASE 3: VICTIM-PROVOKED MURDER

Eight of 15 juveniles emphasized disagreements and arguments as the basis for the violent acts and viewed the victim as having unjustly provoked the offender, and thus responsible for the offender's rage towards him. The victim-provoked motive is illustrated in Case 3. The mother of a 15-year-old youth, hearing a firecracker-type noise, went upstairs to her son's room where four boys had gathered. She was told a boy had been shot. Then, three boys ran out and the mother found the victim lying on the floor. A second boy came back to the apartment when he realized he had been shot; he found part of a bullet protruding from his chest. Both boys were taken to the hospital, where one died. The juvenile who had fired at the boys denied possession of the gun, denied loading or firing it, and stated he was merely holding it in his hand when another boy slammed the cylinder shut and it went off. The autopsy report suggested otherwise, and after 2 years of incarceration, the juvenile admitted the murder of his cousin. "We were dealing and doing drugs. There was an argument over money. He swung at me and I came up with [the gun]."

Note in the crime scene drawing the artistic skill and drawing of the murder act (Figure 3). There are full, well-differentiated figures; facial anger; strong use of color; emphasis on detail; and underwear covering the gun. This drawing with the hand and gun covered indicates the youth is sneaky, hides weapons and drugs, and feels the act was justified. The important points for the staff nurse to recognize are that he will be a leader on the ward and will be able to avoid facing up to what he did. He will ingratiate the staff, be a model patient, and yet resume criminal behavior once he leaves. He has no sense of attachment.

CASE 4: VICTIM AS A PHYSICAL THREAT

In contrast with the victim-provoked motive for the act, 7 of 15 juveniles represented the reasons for their violent act as being linked to a fear and expectation that the victims were somehow going to physically assault, hurt, or overpower them. In Case 4, a girl, returning home after school, found the body of her 15-year-old brother. The only item missing from the home was the victim's radio/cassette player, which was his 15th birthday present. The police investigation continued over several months. Four months after the murder, a 16-year-old youth was convicted of the stabbing death of his best friend. The youth was identified when a pawnbroker

Figure 4. The juvenile in Case 4 depicted himself and the victim as similar in size; in reality, the victim was physically larger. The hurried lack of detail suggests denial and avoidance. The juvenile's story as to the nature of the assault and his behavior is a cover for the complex sexual relationship between the two youths.

supplied police with the name and address of the person who had placed the victim's stolen radio in pawn.

The juvenile first denied his guilt and then told police he had gone to the victim's home after school, where he was shown the new radio. He said the victim went into the kitchen and returned with two knives, loosened his belt, and told the juvenile to take down his pants. The juvenile claims he took one knife away from the victim and stabbed him. He said he took the radio because the victim had borrowed his radio and never returned it. Following the victim's death, the juvenile acted like any other student, showed no remorse or noticeable behavior change, posed no different problems, and attended the funeral.

Note the drawing before the murder (Figure 4). The size of the victim and offender match; in reality the victim was physically larger than the offender. The facial expressions are emphasized, and the hurried lack of detail to the drawing suggests denial and avoidance. His story as to the nature of the assault and his behavior is a cover for the complex sexual relationship between the youths.

CASE 5: SIZE DISTORTION

Regardless of whether the juvenile can provide a verbal motive for the murder, the drawn sizes of the victim and offender should be observed and measured against the official records to determine if the sizes match reality or if they are distorted (eg, the victim is larger than the offender or the two figures merge).

When the offender believes himself to be under the victim's power and control, the victim may take on a larger size than the offender. This is noted in Case 5, where a 16-year-old youth reported a murder to a neighbor stating that he found bags near the china closet and had seen a man running from the house. Upon questioning by police, he admitted telling a false story because he was scared and nervous about what would happen. He

Figure 5. The drawing of Case 5 shows the scene after the murder with size distortion (the offender was in reality much larger than the victim). Although the juvenile clearly illustrates his hatred toward his sister (through strong use of color), he justifies his anger by minimizing the vulnerability of his sister by distorting who was more powerful. On the surface he appears to have admitted to the murder, yet he continues to deny the real ingredients of the murder.

pled guilty to the murder of his 11-year-old sister. The youth said he and his sister were at home while their parents were out. They had fought that morning ("she tested my authority") and kept calling each other names. "She accused me of not being right, of doing wrong, and threatened to tell the folks about my sexual things and smoking marijuana. I lost my cool and did it. Then I focused back and fixed it to look like a burglary." He stabbed her 143 times while she was combing her hair in the bathroom.

Note that the crime scene illustration is drawn after the murder and there is size distortion with victim and offender (Figure 5): the offender was 6'2" and weighed 191 lbs; the sister was 5' and 92 lbs. The youth drew himself with emotional attribution contrary to his lack of remorse following the incident. There is considerable detail to the background, the victim, and the stab wounds; there is strong use of color.

The important point in the drawing is the violence toward the sister and the distortion of who was more powerful. Although this juvenile showed how much hatred he felt toward his sister, he minimized his act by denying his sister's vulnerability, suggesting that in some respect he feels his act was right and justifiable. The nurse can expect that on interview he will move quickly away from the murderous act and focus on himself. This may be confusing because although he appears to have admitted to the murder, he is denying the real ingredients of the murder. The post-murder drawing has to be matched with the information from the evidence. The fact is he was left alone with his sister, she was smaller than he, and there was fighting and struggle before he killed—that phase of the crime is omitted in the drawing. The drawing shows his sister bigger and the juvenile's rage through the blood. Distraction is noted in the details of the bathroom. This youth's potential for danger needs to be kept in mind, especially in the areas of frustration and being held accountable for his behavior. He has poor self-monitoring abilities and sees little connection between antecedent aspects to behavior and consequences.

CASE 6: ROLE REVERSAL OF VICTIM AND OFFENDER

When there is a merging of victim and offender, there is a tendency to use the same colors for both the offender and victim, or the colors are reversed between the victim and offender as in Case 6 (Figure 6). A 16-year-old youth stabbed and sodomized a 13-year-old close friend. Although the offender claimed to be under the influence of drugs, there are aspects of the crime sequence that indicate there were many points where the action could have been reversed.

The juvenile drew three frames of the crime on one piece of paper. In the first frame, he drew himself in black holding a knife and a downcast victim in brown trying to ward off the assault. The second frame depicts the offender, now in brown (reverse of victim color), and the victim in black being stabbed with blood spurting as emphasis. This begins to indicate some merging of the victim and offender positions. The third frame includes two faceless figures in black and depicts the offender sodomizing the victim. The fact that the offender admitted to getting a knife from the kitchen to assault his friend indicates preplanning and fantasizing of the offense. The nature of the drawings suggest that, at some level, this is a re-enactment of abuse experienced by the youth.

This sequence of drawings indicates that the offender, through color, merged with the victim. Compared with other crime scene drawings, this youth has fewer gaps in the sequence of his acts and is willing to present important phases that express his confused identity both as a perpetrator and as a victim, and his identity as a male (sodomy). It is important for the staff nurse to be alert for suicide precautions because this youth is exposed in terms of his emotionality and his actions.

Figure 6. The juvenile in Case 6 drew three frames of the crime on the same piece of paper. These scenes show fewer sequence gaps than other crime scene drawings, indicating a willingness to present important phases that express the juvenile's confused identity as a perpetrator and a victim, and his identity as a male. The reversal of color between the victim and the offender in the first two frames and the similar color in the third frame suggests merging.

CASE 7: MERGING OF VICTIM AND OFFENDER

Another example of merging of victim and offender is noted in Case 7. A 15-year-old male (5'3" and 105 lbs) multiply stabbed a 27-year-old female neighbor (5'1" and 117 lbs) in her apartment while he was on probation for armed robbery of another neighbor. The juvenile made a telephone call to police after the murder stating that he had seen a man with blood on his shirt going upstairs towards the roof. He finally confessed to police that he helped the victim move a cabinet out of her apartment. She then offered him money or something to drink. He took her offer of orange juice and then claimed she made sexual advances towards him. When he declined her advances, she attacked him with a knife, at which point he threw his juice glass at her and attempted to flee, but she came at him with the knife. He said he screamed for help but the woman picked him up, threw him on the bed, and attempted to get on top of him and kiss him. He then pushed at the woman, gained control of the knife, and began stabbing.

This sexual murder was staged by the juvenile (telling police he saw another person fleeing the scene). The merging of the victim with the offender, as shown by the color black, the closeness of figures, and regression of line quality, suggests a pervasive deviant fantasy life focused on violent sexual acts that has not yet been revealed (Figure 7). The drawing

Figure 7. The sexual murder described in Case 7. The color black, the closeness of the figures, and the regression of the line quality suggest a pervasive deviant fantasy life focused on violent sexual acts; this fantasy has not yet been revealed. This juvenile has a dimension that is primitive and confused; he will say what he thinks the nurse wants to hear to consider him socially appropriate.

shows a primitive and confused dimension of this youth. The juvenile's major defense will be to accommodate the nurse and say what he thinks the nurse will want to hear for him to appear socially appropriate. He will adjust in the milieu. The danger is in accepting his adjustment and accommodation as a sign that he has dealt with the murder.

CASE 8: DISPLACEMENT OF RAGE

Unresolved childhood abuse in the lives of these juveniles often builds a state of rage and hatred that is either indiscriminately discharged, builds up over time and explodes, or is confirmed in a peer group that supports and reinforces explosive and aggressive behavior. This type of background can trigger the displacement of rage as noted in Case 8. A woman shopping for a neighbor returned to discover the body of her 74-year-old friend lying face down on her right side, suffering from stab wounds to the upper body. Investigation led to a 15-year-old youth who occasionally ran errands for the victim. These errands stopped a few weeks before the crime because the victim felt the juvenile had stolen money from her. When questioned, the youth confessed to the murder, saying he did not know why he killed her.

The youth is an only child whose mother had died when he was 2 years old. He was raised by his maternal grandmother, who was also 74 at the time of the killing. The youth was described as a good student, preparing to transfer from junior high to high school that fall. Treatment revealed severe neglect and physical abuse by the maternal grandmother, who repeatedly stated a wish to be rid of her grandson.

The drawing is after the murder (Figure 8). It does not match the description of the crime report (victim lying on side) and suggests that this is the vivid memory of the offender. The offender depicts himself with attribution (downcast mouth) and there is attention to extraneous details, such as the table flowers and television. In addition, the same color was used to draw the victim and the offender, suggesting a merging of the juvenile with the older woman. The perplexity on the part of the offender as

Figure 8. The drawing of the crime scene described in Case 8 does not match the crime report, suggesting this is a vivid memory of the offender. The juvenile drew himself with attribution (downcast mouth) and there is attention to extraneous details (the flower on the table and the television). The same color for the victim and the youth suggests merging, illustrating the perplexity of the juvenile as to why he committed the murder. This illustrates unconscious rage displacement from the juvenile's grandmother to the victim.

to why he stabbed this woman is explained in the merging of the drawing: the drawing reveals the unconscious rage displacement from the 74-year-old grandmother to the victim.

CASE 9: DRAWING DETAILS

The following questions help with the analysis of the drawing detail that lend understanding to the motivational dynamics.

- How complete a person does the youth draw?
- What does the drawing tell of developmental level?
- Does the youth use color?
- What type of details is in the drawing?
- Does the drawing show attribution (emotional expression)?

Juveniles may emphasize the crime details in terms of wounds, blood, the weapon, or the method of killing; or the drawing may indicate emotion, such as in Case 9. Two drawings of the crime scene suggest a promising prognosis for treatment. This 16-year-old Asian juvenile was charged with and convicted of manslaughter and attempted murder of his friend's stepfather and mother. The youth engaged in a $500 contract arrangement to murder the stepfather due to the stepfather's abusive treatment of his wife and stepson.

This murder is a criminal-enterprise, contract type. The effort to draw the crime scene reveals the anguish of the offender over the mistake that was made. He initially attempted to draw the couple in bed and then said "that's not right" (Figure 9). It was as if he could consider the male body but could not draw the body of the mother, whom he accidentally killed.

Figure 9. The illustration of the contract murder in Case 9. The first drawing is a mistake; apparently the juvenile could not draw the body of the woman he accidentally killed. The second drawing puts both victims in bed. Note the eyes with no pupils, which suggests an internal deadness and an abusive history. Because the drawing is before the murder, it suggests that the juvenile wishes to undo the crime; the fact that he corrected himself implies remorse.

The second drawing puts both victims in bed (Figure 9). The most important aspect of the drawings is the pupiless eyes, which suggest an internal deadness and a history of abuse in the juvenile's background. The drawing is before the murder, which suggests the juvenile's wish to undo the act; the fact that he corrected himself implies remorse and knowledge of how peer influence weighted his decisions.

Discussion

An important finding from this study was that juveniles were willing to commit to paper a series of drawings to assist in recalling memory and replicating images of themselves and of the murders they committed. This provides information for understanding aspects of the aggressive encounter that triggered the violent act, and presuppositions and beliefs of the offender that support continuation of such behavior. The assessment areas of phases of murder and motivational dynamics have the following implications for nursing intervention.

PHASES OF MURDER

The authors speculate that the phase of the murder drawn by the juvenile preoccupies his thinking as he reflects on the act. This may suggest distinct differences in terms of the triggering aspects of the violent act, ie, "the victim caused my rage" as opposed to "the victim was trying to overpower me." Such reference to the juvenile's thinking has valuable information regarding what needs to be changed in these offenders so they do not repeat these murderous acts. This analysis provides a starting point in working toward some cognitive and behavioral changes. In the first instance, therapeutic effort would be directed at separating the causal construct that another person is the cause from being responsible for one's rage and exposing the distortion. The juvenile has to address his own rage reaction patterns. In the second instance, offenders have to come to terms with their coercive, violent behavior and sense of seeking revenge on vulnerable people. In part, they have to address their capacity to victimize and they have to acknowledge their own prior experiences with victimization.

MOTIVATIONAL DYNAMICS

Insights gained from crime scene drawings will direct the nurses' attention to not only attending to the present ongoing thoughts, feelings, images, and behaviors of the adolescent and relationships with others, but also to assessing the origins and developments of the individual's capacity for self-regulation. This, in turn, will direct the nurse to assessing the value the youth places on rules, whether they are to be followed, and/or whether they are understood, eg, rules of conduct and relationships. It is not unusual for adolescents to clearly know the rules but to have little commitment to adhering to them. This lack of commitment will direct the nurse to assessing the nature of the adolescent's primary attachments and bonding with adults, siblings, and peers. The events of physical, psychological, and sexual abuse strike at core attachment issues. These events also challenge the individual's capacity to trust others, to relate with reciprocity and empathy, or to feel safe in the world; and to have an emergence of a meaning system that values the past, present, and future, assisting in the development, planning, and realization of personal goals.

Data from the crime scene drawing directs questions for intervention: is the intervention directed toward the set of values that justify killing? Is it around the acting out of a deviant fantasy? Is it a complex emotional issue being acted out and displaced onto another? Is the crime in any way reminiscent of victim experiences of the juvenile? These questions become particularly important in sexual crimes and crimes in which the juvenile kills an older person.

The observation of size distortion has important dynamic implications and suggests some juveniles are very much focused on the "power" aspect of the relationship with the victim, particularly evident graphically with depiction of the victim as much larger than the offender. The size distortion may imply boundary confusion and suggest that the murder may be linked with some covert re-enactment of a prior victimization; that is, something happens that recalls a memory of victimization (ie, the juvenile was rendered helpless or was vulnerable) and the aggressive act is discharged.

This is in contrast to drawings that focus on the "anger" aspect of the relationship and the difference between the victim and the victimizer. It may be that this kind of anger is a statement of power and/or displaced rage. Rage, control of anger, and its precipitants become an essential aspect of initial steps of intervention with this group. Rage and displacement themes identified in the present can then be associated to past threatening experiences that provoked defensive rage, as well as the heightened sense of injustice and being blamed.

References

Burgess, A.W., McCausland, M.P., Wolbert, W.A. Children's drawings as indicators of sexual trauma. *Perspect Psychiatr Care* 1981; 19(2):50-58.

Burgess, A.W., Hartman. C.R., McCormack, A. Abused to abuser: Antecedent behaviors of social deviancy. *Am J Psychiatry* 1987; 144(11):1431-1436.

Crowl, M. The basic process of art therapy as demonstrated by efforts to allay a child's fear of surgery. *American Journal of Art Therapy* 1980; 19.

Faulkner, M.E., McFarland, G.C. Juvenile offenders. Presented at the American Association of Criminology, Atlanta, GA, November 1, 1986.

Grant, C.A., Burgess, A.W., Hartman, C.R, et al. Juveniles who murder. *J Psychosoc Nurs Ment Health Serv* 1989; 27(12):4-11.

Hartman, C.R., Burgess, A.W. Child sexual abuse: Generic roots of the victim experience. *Journal of Psychotherapy and the Family* 1986; 2:77-87.

Hibbard, R.A., Roghmann, K., Hoekelman, R.A. Genitalia in children's drawings: An association with sexual abuse. *Pediatrics* 1987; 79(1):129-137.

Horowitz, M.J. *Stress response syndromes.* New York: Aronson, 1976.

Howe, J.W., Burgess, A.W., McCormack, A. Adolescent runaways and their drawings. *Art and Psychotherapy* 1987; 14:35-40.

Kelley, S.J. The use of art therapy for sexually abused children. *J Psychosoc Nurs Ment Health Serv* 1984; 22(12):12-18.

Raymer, M., McIntyre, B.B. An art support group for bereaved children and adolescents. *Art Therapy* 1987; 4(1).

Wohl, A., Kaufman, B. *Silent screams and hidden cries.* New York: Brunner/Mazel, 1985.

Reprinted with permission from the Journal of Psychosocial Nursing and Mental Health Services 1990; 28(1):26-34.

12 | Drawing a Connection from Victim to Victimizer

By Ann W. Burgess, RN, DNSc; Carol R. Hartman, RN, DNSc; Chris A. Grant, RN, PhD; Cathy L. Clover, MA; William Snyder; and Loretta A. King, BS

The mechanisms of transition from victim to victimizer are not yet well understood. Previous articles on juvenile offenders and their perception of the crime scene suggested using drawings as an associative tool to understand the subjective experience of the aggressive acts of the juvenile offender (Burgess, 1990). This chapter advances the use of the drawing technique to suggest that sexually aggressive behavior not only has its own history of development, but also that certain aspects of the behavior are repetitive fragments associated with earlier dissociated trauma.

Theoretical Framework

The information processing of trauma model developed by Hartman and Burgess (1988) explains how the abused child attempts to modify the sensory, perceptual, cognitive, and interpersonal alterations that occur during abuse. It hypothesizes how these behavioral alterations emerge in patterns specifically reflecting the abuse itself. This process is referred to as trauma learning and is characterized by actions that are a replay of the trauma itself. These actions can be direct re-enactments of the trauma in which the victim responds to others as if the trauma is ongoing, or they can be repetitions or displacements of the traumatic event, with the victim vacillating between behaviors of the victim and of the offender. Repetition is one step beyond reenactment in that the victim has a representation of the victim experience from the perspective of both the victim and the offender.

We believe that repetition characterizes early sexual offending behavior.

If the trauma learning process is not disrupted, it will be reinforced by the acting out behavior. The sexual offending behavior will become characterized by repetition; the ability to distinguish between victim and offender will become blurred until identification is almost entirely with the offender. Exploration of the response to childhood trauma reveals patterns of reenactment and repetition emerging as efforts to master disabling anxiety (Terr, 1991). This suggests that adherence to sexually aggressive acts originates in self-protective efforts.

The theoretical assumptions of the information processing of trauma model are derived from two broad areas of development in neuroscience. First, all stimuli, whether internal or external, are processed in primary brain structures before that information is responded to by higher cortical mappings (Giller, 1990). Of particular importance in the study of the evolutionary structures of the brain has been the limbic system and its identification as the primary system for the interpretation and regulation of emotional responses to stimuli. The limbic system is critical in terms of attachment, sleep-rest, and the mapping of sensory information, eg, olfactory, kinesthetic, visual, auditory. The key categorization and identification of stimuli is laid down in the neural mappings in these brain centers, which are related and innervated with the higher evolving cortical structures.

The second advance in neuroscience specific to understanding stress and its impact on memory, learning, and response has been the identification of subsystems in the limbic system. These subsystems are involved in the arousal and alerting behavior of the organism and influenced by various levels of stress. Intense and chronic levels of stress are responded to by neurohormonal subsystems aimed at controlling and regulating the degree of excitation of the organism. In the face of overwhelming stimuli, this arousal system is activated. If it fails to modulate the response to the stimuli, another system tranquilizes the organism. This has been referred to as the fight-flight system, eg, the arousal system of aggression or avoidance under threatening stimulation. The inability to fight or flee can trigger the opioid system, which preserves the organism from the toxic effects of excessively high levels of noradrenergic hormones. Learning under these conditions is either excessive or is blocked when the tranquilizing effects of the opioid system is activated (Giller, 1990).

Historically, the notion of trauma and its impact on basic neural systems was part of the theoretical and scientific work of Janet and Freud. Freud focused his attention on the meaning system influenced by language and symbolization. Janet focused on trauma disrupting the regulation of neural functioning in his concept of dissociation. Janet noted that traumatic events disrupted the protective mechanisms of the organism and understood trauma responses as being adaptive to the organism not only on the symbolic linguistic level of meaning, but also on the biological level of survival. Dissociation was the descriptive term to account for the disruption of memory at a sensory, perceptual, and cognitive level of memory (van der

Kolk, 1989). The dilemma of the persistent symptomatology after trauma has forced the reopening of the biological understanding of responses.

Treatment of Sex Offenders

Efforts to treat adult sex offenders have been less than optimal when the offending behavior is not addressed. Clinicians sometimes have focused on the origins of the behavior rather than on its self-sustaining characteristics. Investigation into the thoughts, feelings, and daydreams of rapists, pedophiles, and sexual murderers reveals an active fantasy life committed to the very crimes of these offenders (Ressler, 1988). Pleasure, excitement, and self-fulfillment are rooted in the offender's deviant fantasies (Burgess, 1986; Prentky, 1989).

The information processing model hypothesizes that the earlier the assessment and intervention into the trauma learning process, the more successful the interruption of sexually deviant interests. Juvenile offenders must address the reinforcing quality of their sex offense behavior (eg, the deviant fantasies) and the relationship of that behavior to prior abusive experiences. The linkage of sexually deviant behaviors to deal with the resonating consequences of the prior abuse cannot be ignored. Rather than placing singular emphasis on stopping the acting out behavior, nurses must make efforts to help the youth make a connection between the abuse, the deviant fantasies, and the offending behavior. From this connection, the offender then can begin to unlink and process the memory distortions that emerge to defend against the original abuse.

It would appear that intervention would be most successful if undertaken when the offender is a juvenile. However, the very factors of age and gender (most reported sexual offenders are male) act as impediments to that intervention. Fundamental to the problem of identifying antecedents to sexually abusive behavior is the reporting by investigators that those abused are not necessarily consciously aware of their own abuse history, and if they are, they will be likely to underreport sexual abuse if they are young males (Becker, 1986). Consequently, the very population that would benefit most from an intervention model is the one to which it is most difficult to apply.

We cite a drawing task used to focus on the juvenile's offense and his or her childhood trauma while the juvenile is in a residential detention center (Evans, 1988). The use of the offense drawing is a way of eliciting fragments to lift the denial. This allows the offender to be an observer of behavior rather than needing to defend the accusation. A case example follows with the offense and victimization drawing.

Figure 1.

Case Example

Tom, 17 years old, was charged with criminal contempt, burglary, terroristic threats, and aggravated assault. The victim, a 52-year-old woman, was the mother of a girl he had dated. At age 11, Tom was sexually abusing his 7-year-old half-sister. Tom had also witnessed this sister being abused by an 18-year-old uncle. When Tom was 8, he had been sexually abused by the 18-year-old daughter of his baby sitter. The abuse ended at age 11 when he went to live with his father. In the 2 years that he lived with his father, he suffered severe physical abuse from both his father and stepmother. He claims he had pressure from his peers to use drugs.

Offense and Victim Drawings

OFFENSE DRAWING

Tom's offense drawing is drawn in pencil, is detailed, and has considerable auditory and visual cues. In the first frame, there is the figure of Tom with his bag of troubles in front of two parallel buildings: a house of authority and a school. "Who needs it," the figure states. There is only a mouth talking (Figure 1).

The second frame is a back view of the offender still holding his bag and looking at a building with an open door. There is indication that a party is in progress.

In frame three, Tom is sitting on a bench with his bag of troubles. It appears he is outside the building and the door is closed. He says to himself, "Now what? I know!" Then he draws another picture of himself with his bag of troubles walking toward the victim's house.

In frame four, a square represents the victim's house and contains the words "fear," "anger," "frustration," and "all problems of past and present." Exiting from the house is the offender, again with no hands or feet and with the smallest indication of eyes and an exaggerated mouth stating, "I lost my bag. Oh well." An arrow indicates movement toward another building labeled YDC (Youth Detention Center). Another figure holds up a bag and says, "Hey, looking for this?"

The connection of the criminal act to troubles and problems is made by the offender in the drawing. There also is indication that the criminal act itself resulted in a momentary sense of loss of problems, only to have them return when Tom returns to the detention center. Although the details of the drawing begin to reveal conflicts, they avoid an explicit presentation of the criminal act itself. Tom at some level has consciously acknowledged and accepted his criminal behavior as an outlet for the emotional expression of his problems, both past and present.

Besides being a link to early trauma, criminal activity represents the juvenile's perpetuating behavior and has its own sensory reward system. The aim of the crime scene drawing is to decrease the crime pay off (eg, fantasy and arousal) by working to process the juvenile's childhood trauma that remains encapsulated. It is critical that the juvenile knows the nurse is cognizant of his or her crime behavior. Using the offense drawing, the following areas are explored with the youth.

- Review of crime details: How did the juvenile plan the crime? What did he or she bring along? What happened after the crime? What degrading acts occurred during the crime?

- Review of crime feelings: When did those acts happen to the juvenile and how did they make him or her feel? When were such feelings previously experienced?

- Review of the adolescent's own victimization: What were the types of abuse?

- Review of the adolescent's discipline and early sexual experiences: If not directly victimized, when was violence or sex witnessed? When was a sense of trust abused? (In witnessing, both the role of victim and victimizer are present; thus, the potential exists for both roles to be arousing to the witness. The excitation can lead to numbing.)

- Review of crime and victim linkages: How does the victimization connect to the crime?

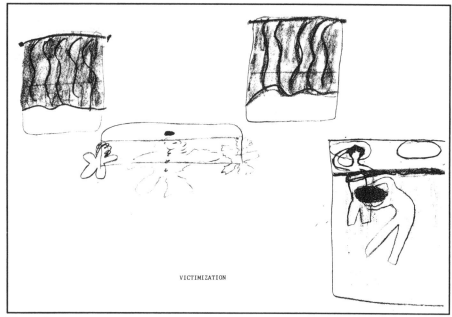

VICTIMIZATION

Figure 2.

The offense drawing involves memory work. The nurse examines all of the juvenile's sexually aggressive behaviors from planning to arousal and associates them to the youth's past. Such memory work will increase anxiety and will be upsetting. The nurse's aim is to desexualize and neutralize the aggression. The nurse can ask: Is there any point at which you would stop your crime? What would the victim have to do to stop it or to escalate it?

VICTIMIZATION DRAWING

After the offense memory work, the juvenile is asked to draw a memory of his or her victimizations. This task is usually several weeks later. The case example of Tom is discussed below.

Tom's victimization drawing reveals him in a passive situation in which a woman performs fellatio on him (Figure 2). This act takes place under the covers. This out-of-awareness presentation of victimization suggests that it is a surface representation of additional experiences of abuse. Details are included in the drawing: windows have curtains; a toy chest has stuffed animals set in front. Over time in discussing these drawings, Tom revealed that his stepmother, in the name of discipline, had tied him up in a bag.

Tom's offense was a rape of an older woman. In his offense drawing, one sees a representation of themes of his earlier victimization: the relentless bag of problems and the unseen, retaliative, vengeful act. The offense drawing is not fully detailed; this can be seen as a protective process.

Official records noted that Tom had sexually abused his stepsister. When confronted with this information, Tom did not respond but said he wanted to think about it and write in his journal. The following week he came to therapy with a journal entry of additional memory of the stepuncle abusing the sister. At that time, Tom's perception was that he was as much of a victim as the sister; he was forced to watch and then participate in the abuse.

The victimization drawing is processed via the crime details. To decrease the intensity and arousal of discussing both the crime and the victimization, the personal resources of the juvenile are emphasized. Intense feelings are dealt with in therapy. The repetition of crime behavior is difficult to unlink as it is the armor around the crime.

Processing Traumatic Memories

The nurse helps the youth process the crime, the victimization, and ongoing behavior. As daily thoughts and behaviors are changed, there will be an altering of the juvenile's response to trauma as it is stored at the sensory, perceptual, and cognitive/interpersonal levels of memory. The technique of pacing is used where memories are separated into manageable portions. The youth may become anxious and balk at anxiety-producing memories.

As the crime is processed, goals to alter and regulate behavior begin. It is critical to monitor the juvenile's behavior during such daily activities as eating and sleeping. As anxiety increases, negative behaviors will surface. Various questions need to be pursued: What has it meant to commit such a crime? What daily behaviors are stimulated by thinking of the crime and victimization?

Unlinking memories and behaviors comes through the adolescent being able to recognize that he or she has alternatives. The transfer of the processed information about the crime and victimization to past memory is the letting go of arousing material. Not to let go serves the purpose of not trusting and maintaining deviant fantasies. What will replace the void that remains after letting go? What does the youth want in relationships? How can the youth develop nondeviant relationships?

There is a need to deal with the antecedent sense of injustice that made the youth feel justified in committing the crime. The adolescent has to find alternatives to getting what he or she wants. Can the youth talk himself or herself down? Can aggressive impulses be held in check?

This phase works on building attachment. The nurse helps the adolescent retrieve and remember experiences in which he or she felt attached to other people. The adolescent needs time to realize this attachment. Many adolescents who act out sexually never had positive attachments to family or people.

Returning to the case of Tom, when discussing what he told himself that made it possible to commit the crime, he said he did not think or tell himself anything. He was then asked how he learned to block things out. He said, "I put myself in a bubble. . . . When I was living with my father, my mother used to hang me in the basement in a duffel bag and beat me with a stick. I would create a bubble so I didn't have to feel the pain." When the bubble did not work, he started using drugs and alcohol when he returned home. He was about 14 years old at the time.

Tom left the abusive home by running to his biological mother, but he found she had remarried and was pregnant. Until this time, Tom had been an only child. The father and stepmother had told him that his mother had not wanted him to live with her. His return to her home confirmed in his mind that his mother did not want him and triggered the criminal behavior. Tom joined a gang, began using drugs and alcohol, and became truant from school. He sought out films with violence and would go to the shopping mall and enjoy getting into fights.

He became involved with older teenagers. When talking of the offense, he said he had been trying to tell his mother that things were not right. He created situations where she would have to ask what was wrong. As he felt more rejected, he became sexually aggressive and committed the rape offense.

More details regarding the victimization were revealed. Tom's baby sitter's teenage daughter had access to the children in her mother's care. She let Tom play in her room as special recognition. She kept the door locked when she was away. She started to abuse him through this special relationship, eg, allowing him in her room to play with toys and dolls. Sometimes he would stay overnight and sleep on the couch in her room. One night she woke him up and said they were going to play a game and that they had to take their clothes off. She fondled and sucked Tom's penis. She said he could play in her room when she was away if he did not tell anyone about the game. The connection Tom made between his victimization and his crime was the bubble, ie, his dissociative state.

Tom was asked what he experienced seeing, hearing, and feeling during the offense. He said he heard screaming and the dog barking. Someone came downstairs, which is when he made his exit. He said he smelled alcohol on himself and visualized his tearing of the victim's nightgown. He said he could see the victim's mouth moving but he did not hear her. As he described this, he became nauseated and almost vomited.

Termination

Termination from therapy is a critical intervention. The nurse discusses the issue of positive attachment and loss and asks: "How do you communicate and maintain a sense of self?" This may be effected through emphasis on the positive relationships in the residential home itself. The regressive pull that will occur needs to be explicitly discussed as it is the fear of handling the future day by day. Any acting out needs to be interpreted as linked to early deprivation and abuse.

In this phase, the nurse helps the adolescent build a philosophy of life. This philosophy can be part of homework assignments and can include values clarification and the meaning of justice and of right and wrong. Debates can be held over these values. The adolescent must be able to transfer the internalized attachments learned in the milieu to the outside environment.

In the case example, Tom said he learned the cues that trigger him in stressful situations and he learned how to pay attention to the cues. He learned some ways to reduce stress and how to look into the future. He was released to the care of his mother. There had been family work done over his 2 years at the Youth Detention Center. He asked his mother if she knew about his victimization and why she did not know he was having problems when he was getting into trouble. He and his mother talked about the baby sitter situation, and there was agreement that the mother could not have known and it was not her fault.

Discussion

The unlinking of the criminal behavior emphasizes the importance of addressing the criminal act in detail and sequence from the period prior to the acts, through the acts, and the period prior to apprehension. This case demonstrated that focusing on the criminal act is less threatening for the youth than speculating about past abuse and victimization. It was in the context of detailing the crime itself that critical aspects of past abuse became apparent. As Tom became aware of his ideation during the criminal act and the perplexing and overwhelming physiological reactions, in particular nausea, terror, and revulsion, the link was made between the act and early traumatic experiences in which he was victimized and forced to victimize a younger half-sister. Also, the link was made to the location of his victimization and his offense.

Peculiarities of memory reconstruction of the crime scene included seeing but not hearing the woman scream. As the sensory information around the crime was tolerated, he was able to fill in and address the experience of the earlier abuse by his uncle. We see in the choice of the victim condensation of cues symbolic of the early abuse: helplessness and gender of the victim. There is a complex issue in the selection of the older victim. In some ways it addresses aspects of aggression toward the nonprotective mother and the sexually abusing baby sitter, but it also is a reversal of the assault on the helpless younger sister, which is the more emotionally fearful incident.

In his crime scene drawing, Tom carried a bag of troubles. This revealed an awareness of the interrelationship of his criminal actions with prior troubles. It is also interesting that after the rape is committed, he is able to, for a time, leave the bag of troubles.

Conclusion

The abuse of children is usually threefold: physical, sexual, and psychological (Burgess, 1990). The biological basis of the altered alarm/ dissociative process during and after sexual trauma impedes the development of information processing essential for the discerning of intention, personal responsibility (blame), sense of control over events, and trust in others. Once this imbalance occurs, the child is restricted in developing cognitive schema to deal with interpersonal intimacy. This, in turn, results in secondary patterns of aggression or avoidance. It is as if the child loses the capacity to develop the perceptual and cognitive schema to handle the nuances of interpersonal relationships. The necessary inhibition and discrimination is altered and there is a collapsing of categories that indicate danger.

The implication of this biological understanding of trauma and information processing for treatment underscores the necessity of reducing arousal, thus lessening the dissociative processes. Once this is done, primary learning can resume. The drawing experience of the criminal act and the victim experience, when brought into awareness, helps elicit cues connecting the two events, thus facilitating an increase in personal control over repeated aggressive acts.

References

Becker, J.V., Cunningham-Rathner, J., Kaplan, M.S. Adolescent sexual offenders: Demographics, criminal and sexual histories, and recommendations for reducing future offenses. *Journal of Interpersonal Violence* 1986; 1:431-445.

Burgess, A.W., Hartman, C.R., Ressler, R.K., Douglas, J.E., McCormack, A. Sexual homicide: A motivational model. *Journal of Interpersonal Violence* 1986; 1:251-272.

Burgess, A.W., Hartman, C.R., Howe, J.W., Shaw, E.R., McFarland, G.C. Juvenile murderers: Assessing memory through crime scene drawings. *J Psychosoc Nurs Ment Health Serv* 1990; 28(1):26-34.

Evans, E., Sunderman, J.P., Clover, C. *Victimization: Module I.* New Castle, PA: New Castle Youth Development Center; 1988.

Giller, E. *Biological assessment and treatment of post traumatic stress disorder.* Washington, DC: American Psychiatric Press; 1990.

Hartman, C.R., Burgess, A.W. Information processing of trauma: Case application of a model. *Journal of Interpersonal Violence* 1988; 3:343-457.

Prentky, R.A., Burgess, A.W., Rokous, F., Lee, A., Hartman, C.R., Ressler, R.K., et al.

The presumptive role of fantasy in serial sexual homicide. *Am J Psychiatry* 1989; 146:887-891.

Ressler, R.K., Burgess, A.W., Douglas, J.E. *Sexual homicide.* Lexington, MA: Lexington Books; 1988.

Terr, L.C. Childhood traumas: An outline and overview. *Am J Psychiatry* 1991; 148:10-21.

van der Kolk, B.A., van der Hart, O. Pierre Janet and the breakdown of adaptation in psychological trauma. *Am J Psychiatry* 1989; 146:1530-1540.

Reprinted with permission from the Journal of Psychosocial Nursing and Mental Health Services *1991; 29(12):9-14.*

Aggression originates from the Latin "aggressus," which means attack. Aggression refers to any malevolent act (physical or verbal) intended to hurt someone. Webster defines aggression as "an offensive action or procedure." Aggression is getting what is wanted at the expense of others. Aggressive behavior is seen as dominating, depreciating, humiliating, and embarrassing to others. Aggression is on a continuum with homicide at the extreme end and verbal abuse at the other. The resulting injury may be personal, property destruction, or psychological.

Assault is the "unlawful intentional inflicting injury, attempted, or threatened inflicted injury on another."

Battering syndrome is characterized by history of physical or sexual abuse, injury, general and often vague medical complaints, psychosocial problems, and unsuccessful help-seeking. Help-seeking by the victim results in neglect, increased abuse, or punitive responses by the abuser (Rosenberg, 1985).

Battery is the act of using physical contact in such a way as to cause physical harm or injury. The crucial element in battering is the use of aggressive behavior to gain power and control over a partner. Physical abuse is often used interchangeable with battery.

Emotional abuse is the use of threats, verbal assaults, or degradation that injure an individual's sense of self-worth. The intent of the verbal or nonverbal action is to provoke suffering. Emotional neglect is the lack of maintaining an interpersonal atmosphere conducive for psychosocial growth and development of a sense of personal worth and well-being (Drake, 1982). The result is emotional crippling and may end in failure to thrive (Quinn, 1990).

Expressive violence combines intense emotional upset and poor impulse control. The goal is to discharge the emotion and this is done through physical violence. The roles of the partners are not clearly defined, and each share responsibility for their responses. Mutual conflict, stress, and anger usually precede a violent incident. Genuine remorse and sorrow follow the incident as the violence is inconsistent with individual's values (Gage, 1991).

Financial abuse/material abuse is the misappropriation of finances as well as theft of property or possessions through theft, trickery, "conning," or extortion. Primarily in the case of the elderly, there is great potential for financial exploitation by caretakers. Violation of rights is demonstrated when an elder person is unnecessarily forced from living independently.

Incest is a specific form of sexual abuse. This is not limited to sexual intercourse, but includes any action performed to sexually stimulate the child or use the child to stimulate other person(s) as delineated by the National Center on Child Abuse and Neglect. In this offense, the perpetrator is a blood relative.

Instrumental violence is unilateral violence to exploit and control another. The role of the perpetrator and victim are fixed. Remorse is minimal, superficial, and manipulative as violence is integrated into the individual's value system. If the violence continues over time, the couple can move from expressive violence to instrumental violence (Gage, 1991).

Neglect denotes the failure to provide some degree of minimal care resulting in depriving a person of something needed to sustain daily living. This could include denial of medical care, withholding of food, or providing sanitary living situation (Phillips, 1983). In the case of the elderly, "self-neglect" becomes of great concern as the individual's ability to provide adequate self-care declines.

Psychological violence (abuse) is a nonphysical abuse. Forms include explicit threat of violence, implicit threats of violence, extreme controlling behavior, pathological jealousy, mental degradation, and isolating behavior. Occasional indulgences and enforcement of trivial demands are a part of the effectiveness of psychological abuse (Sonkin, 1985).

Physical abuse is intentional injury, harmful deed, or destructive act inflicted by a caregiver or person with whom an interpersonal, often intimate, relationship is shared (Drake, 1982). This form of abuse includes striking, shoving, shaking, or restraining (Breckman, 1968). This is synonymous with battering.

Sexual abuse refers to any form of sexual intimacy without consent or through force or threat of force. This abuse includes fondling, masturbation, unclothing, oral to genital contact, and the use of objects for the purpose of physical stimulation (Drake, 1982).

APPENDIX B
Instruments for Measurement

Beck Depression Inventory (BDI). Measures behavioral manifestations of depression consistent with both grief and learned helplessness. This is a 21-question 4-point Likert scale.

Beck Hopelessness Index (BHI). Measures behavioral and cognitive attitudes of hopelessness consistent with learned helplessness. This is a 20-question true-false questionnaire scale.

Blame Operationalized. Predictability of types of blame relationships to learned helplessness is measured on a 4-point scale. Interactive (self and partner) blame was found to be the least predictive of learned helplessness. External blame is second least predictive. Behavioral self-blame is the third least predictive. Negative characterological self-blame is the most predictive of learned helplessness (Miller, 1983).

Conflict Tactics Scale (CTS). This instrument has three versions, which are fundamentally the same, measuring the conflict within the role relationships. Questionnaire, in-person interview, and telephone interview formats have been developed (Straus, 1990). The score obtained on this scale is an "overall violence index." This scale considers annual incidences of violence and severity.

Deynes Self-Care Agency Instrument (DSCAI). The instrument measures perceived ability to care for self (learned helplessness). It is based on a grief model (Deynes, 1980; 1988).

Tennessee Self-Concept Scale (TSCS). This instrument measures both self-concept and body image (Fitts, 1972).

The Index of Spouse Abuse (ISA). This instrument measures the degree or severity of both physical (ISA-P) and nonphysical (ISA-NP) abuse inflicted on women by their spouses or partners. This is a 30-item self-report questionnaire with items representing forms of behaviors or interactions considered to be abusive (Hudson, 1981).